K2 : Lies and Treachery

K2 : Lies and Treachery

Robert Marshall

Carreg

First published in 2009 by
Carreg Limited
18 Parsons Croft
Hildersley
Ross-on-Wye
Herefordshire   HR9 5BN
United Kingdom

ISBN 978-0-9538631-7-4

Printed and bound in the UK.

Contents

Foreword

Who else but Robert Marshall has such vast and precise knowledge of the K2 affair? This has certainly earned him the right to prepare a book about such a sordid, painful matter as the much debated story of the conquest of this mountain. The fact is that Robert himself, in the 1980s, was the first person to shed light analytically on the 'mother of all lies' – that is, the scandalous business concerning the oxygen bottles used by Compagnoni and Lacedelli, which, according to them, became exhausted before they reached the summit. It was precisely from this original lie that over the years a squalid, complex plot developed, with false facts, false places, false times, false timetables, false pieces of equipment and their function.

I am very happy that my friend Robert Marshall has felt compelled to reveal the truth about this important Himalayan exploit. I am also most grateful for his initiative in making this testimony available to English-speaking readers.

Walter Bonatti
December 2008.

Introduction

Italy is possibly the most beautiful country on earth and can in many ways be regarded as the veritable cradle of civilisation. Since its leading role in the Renaissance, Italy has also been a world leader in the arts and can perhaps still be considered the true home of opera. Italians produce beautiful clothes, their famous fashion houses being world leaders. The sheer beauty of the countryside, the architecture of the cities and towns and the usually balmy weather make it the holiday centre of choice for many northern Europeans. There is a glowing ambience in Italian sunlight which is unforgettable, and the Italian Alps form an immense semicircle of snow-clad peaks, though shared in almost equal thirds with France, Switzerland and Austria: the Dolomites are even more spectacular – apart from their appeal to rock-climbers the fantastic limestone peaks present wonderful vistas as well as offering some of the best and most varied skiing in the world.

Italians themselves are justly regarded as a most courteous, urbane and affable people. Italy has produced scientists, writers, philosophers, engineers and all manner of artisans. Italian films are mostly excellent. The Italian language is melodious. Italian food is regarded by many gourmands as unparalleled in the world for variety and excellence, and Italy produces more wine, much of it superb, than anywhere else on earth. Italian motor vehicles are the quintessence of panache and elegance.

With all these marks of excellence it is perhaps surprising that in politics Italy is a byword for corruption and double-dealing, to the point where the country seems virtually ungovernable, and the frequent (often, seemingly, irrelevant) changes of power produced by ever-recurring elections are very difficult to follow. The Mafiosi and their methods are not only rife in Italy but have spread all over the world, and to the dismay of the citizens there are persistent rumours of Italian government links with the 'Honoured Society'.

In his superb book *The Italians*, Luigi Barzini presents an illuminating insight into the Italian psyche in order to explain how this strange combination of private virtue and public squalor has come about. He considers why so many Italian communal activities fail, relating this apparent paradox to the lack of any long historical background, Italy emerging as a unified country only in the latter part of the nineteenth century. He sees the Italian communal psyche as immensely suspicious of any sort of authority and as being concerned above all with the protection of family and self in an ever hostile world. This entrenched individualism is by no means confined to Italy, but somehow seems capable of rising there to great heights of heroism and selfless dedication on the one hand, but to great depths of corruption and villainy on the other – perhaps illustrated to perfection by the history of Fascism's rise and fall before and during the Second World War.

In the world of Italian mountaineering too we see at times the emergence of corruption, and exactly the same mixture of incompatible personalities. Although in most countries the motives of climbers are not always quite as pure and selfless as one might hope, every so often Italy in particular seems peculiarly capable of producing a mountaineering saga that, on close inspection, can seem a black joke – or perhaps more accurately a *storia all'italiana* – a Machiavellian tale which is dark and nasty, full of tragedy, betrayal and villainy as well as bravery, selflessness and dedication.

The first ascent in 1954 of K2, the second highest mountain in the world, produced just such a debacle. What could and should have been an uplifting, heartwarming story was converted to a seamy, disgraceful affair by the corrupt behaviour of some of the participants, aided by the later cover-up by officials who preferred to avert their eyes and pretend that all was well.

Italy produced two mountaineers in the latter half of the twentieth century, each of whom in his time was regarded as the greatest climber in the world – Walter Bonatti and Reinhold Messner. Sadly, both were victims of whispering programmes that could easily have ruined their lives. This book is concerned only with the former and with what happened to him on K2 and later.

Walter Bonatti was born in 1930 and his climbing career started after the war when he was still a teenager. He progressed with astonishing speed and was just 21 when in the summer of 1951 he achieved the then seemingly impossible feat of climbing the forbidding east face of the Grand Capucin, an extraordinary red granite pinnacle in the Mont Blanc massif. The climb coincided with the start of the decade that saw the first ascent of all the highest mountains in the world (apart from Shisha Pangma in Forbidden, Chinese-occupied Tibet) and Bonatti's emergence as a climbing prodigy providentially occurred just as Italy, desperately anxious to recoup its fortunes after the disasters of the Second World War, joined the international race for the eight-thousand-metre peaks of the Himalaya.

English climbers had been attacking Mount Everest since long before the war, and Germany had tried and failed on Nanga Parbat many times, but the French were the first to reach the summit of one of the giants in 1950, when Maurice Herzog and his team climbed Annapurna on their first attempt. The British at last succeeded on Everest in 1953, and the Germans finally conquered Nanga Parbat that same year. The Americans, after two unsuccessful pre-war expeditions, attempted K2 for the third time in 1953, and intended to return the following year, but were beaten to the punch by the Italians, who succeeded in climbing this 'Savage Mountain' in 1954.

This book is the story of the unhappy background, unhappy events and even unhappier consequences of that Italian K2 expedition. In particular, it follows the travails of Walter Bonatti for the next 50 years and his ceaseless efforts to correct the totally misleading official account of the final climb to the summit. In 1964 he was directly and quite specifically accused in the press of being a thief, a liar and a traitor, and although he mounted and won a successful libel case, his contribution to the success of the climb was unequivocally recognised in Italy only after many years of controversy.

Only recently has the Italian Alpine Club at last freely and officially admitted to the Italian public that the original report of the climb by the two summiteers was a deceitful pack of lies. The following account aims to set the record straight for the English-speaking mountaineering world.

The Ascent of K2

Though not as high as Everest, K2 is an even more formidable proposition because of its unrelenting steepness and the severity of the storms it attracts. Even now that the mountain has been climbed many times by most of its ridges, K2 is still a daunting challenge, as evidenced by the appalling tragedy in 1986 when thirteen climbers of many different nations perished miserably in one dreadful week. In 1939 the American Dudley Wolfe and three Sherpas died high on the mountain during an early attempt on the peak, and in 1953 another American, Art Gilkey, also died. Without the luck of a snagged rope, which allowed Pete Schoening to hold five men on a single rope as they slid towards a precipice and certain death during their retreat, disaster would have seen the entire expedition wiped out. That summer of 1953, after his winter ascents of the walls of the Lavaredo, Bonatti made many more climbs, including an unsuccessful attempt on the 'impossible' south-west pillar of the Dru in August with Carlo Mauri. His ambition for climbing at the limits of the possible was unbounded and by then he had established such a reputation that, despite his youth, his name was inevitably put forward as a possible candidate for the proposed 1954 Italian expedition to K2. He was just a lad and was still an amateur climber, working as an accountant in the city during the week and escaping to the mountains only at weekends. But so great was his reputation that he was considered on equal terms with the greatest professional guides of the day. He must have seemed to them a child prodigy, in a category of his own. Perhaps this very fact made it easier for him to be singled out later for antagonism by his climbing companions.

His inclusion in the K2 team was the prologue to a drama that was to change Bonatti's entire life: the arguments and upheavals that followed have continued ever since. But at the time Bonatti was overjoyed to be chosen. He had not the faintest idea when he reached the foot of K2 that his whole existence was to be irrevocably changed, with repercussions which would echo for the rest of his life. Perhaps the saddest aspect of the whole controversy is that Bonatti, who was later to be so vilified, was the man who made the conquest of K2 possible. Without him the expedition would have failed – no one else was capable of getting the oxygen to Camp 9, and without it the summit climbers, on their own admission, would not have been able to go any higher.

Bonatti was only 23 and, for such a youngster, K2 must have seemed the most marvellous and unattainable goal imaginable: it was known from the experiences of previous expeditions that for climbing performance at 8,000 metres the best physical attributes were to be found in men between 28 and 38. But despite his youth he was short-listed as a possible expedition member in December 1953. After an exhaustive series of extremely stringent medical and physiological tests, eleven climbers were chosen for the Italian K2 expedition: of them, Bonatti was by far the youngest. The others were Erich Abram, Ugo Angelino, Achille Compagnoni, Cirillo Floreanini, Pino Gallotti, Lino Lacedelli, Mario Puchoz, Ulbaldo Rey, Gino Soldá and Sergio Viotto. There were also four scientists and Mario Fantin, who was to make a film of the trip. Poor Puchoz was to be the only casualty: he died of pulmonary oedema during the climb at Camp 2 on 21 June. In Pakistan the expedition was joined by Colonel Ata Ullah of the Pakistan Army, who was to act as Liaison Officer.

The expedition leader was Professor Ardito Desio, who had visited Pakistan the previous year with Riccardo Cassin, the doyen of Italian mountaineers. After discussions with the Pakistani Government, Desio had succeeded in obtaining a permit for an attempt on K2 in 1954. His mission was helped by diplomatic pressure from the Italian Embassy in Pakistan: a large number of Italian tradesmen were working in Pakistan at the time, sent by the Italian Government to help restore the country after the disastrous, destructive war of partition between India and Pakistan, which had erupted after the Second World War when the British Raj was granted independence.

When Desio returned to Italy he discussed the make up of the expedition with the Committee of the Italian Alpine Club (CAI). It had originally been proposed that the expedition would have a dual purpose, not only climbing the mountain, but also carrying out scientific research on the glaciers of the Karakoram. Desio (a Professor of Geology) would lead the team of scientists and Riccardo Cassin would be the 'climbing leader'. But Cassin was quietly dropped from the team on the very dubious grounds of 'ill-health' relating to suspicions that he was suffering from 'heart trouble'. Cassin himself was bitterly disappointed to be excluded: he has insisted ever since that there was nothing wrong with his heart and that the whole affair was a plot by Desio to ensure the fame he (Desio) hoped to derive from the expedition would not be overshadowed by Cassin's reputation in the event that the attempt on K2 succeeded – it seems that Machiavellian scheming was rife even before the team left Italy. Interestingly, despite the concerns over his health, the CAI appointed Cassin leader of the 1958 expedition to Gasherbrum IV, an 'almost eight-thousander' in the Karakoram very close to K2. Then, in 1975 Cassin led an expedition which attempted the formidable south face of Lhotse, the world's fourth highest mountain.

The tone of the expedition was set very early by Desio who, in schoolmaster fashion, issued a plan which included the statement that all expedition members 'should conform to a diet and a hygiene regime calculated to maintain them in a state of maximum physical efficiency. This is an obligation on all … the indisposition of one or more members … due to over-eating or drinking may jeopardise the whole undertaking.' Desio's plan for the climb also indicated a lack of any real understanding of mountaineering, for although he noted the need for acclimatisation and the need to minimise the time spent above 7,500m, his four-phase plan amounted to little more than reach mountain, climb up, gain summit, go home. Exact timings were allocated to each phase: not surprisingly they turned out to be wrong.

The Italians chose the Abruzzi Ridge, which had been identified during early attempts as offering the most likely route to the summit. Their progress was aided by winches set up to aid the hauling of supplies from camp to camp, and by detailed information supplied by Charles Houston, who had led the 1953 American expedition. Progress was slowed after the death of Puchoz, but Desio, who had issued regular exhortations for greater effort couched in tones of nationalistic fervour, issued another noting that the team now had a 'moral responsibility' to succeed, and that success would mean their being hailed 'as champions of your race'. It went on to note that 'your fame will endure throughout your lives and long after you are dead … even if you never achieve anything else of note you will be able to say that you have not lived in vain.'

Not being a climber, Desio had devolved some responsibility for day to day decisions high on the mountain to Achille Compagnoni. Desio liked to get his own way and was intolerant of any dissent and seems to have found Compagnoni the most agreeable member of the team. At 40 Compagnoni was the second oldest member of the climbing team (Gino Soldá was 47) and probably realised that this was likely to be his only chance on an 8,000m peak. When, later, Desio put him in charge of the summit bid, Compagnoni must have become even more agreeable.

After initial steady progress, the expedition was hampered by bad weather. By late July Camp 8 had been established at the edge of the Shoulder (a shallower section of the peak below the summit pyramid) but, crucially, the oxygen required for the summit bid was in Camp 7 and there were only six climbers fit enough to help establish Camp 9 and make a summit bid. Compagnoni decided that he and Lacedelli would form the summit pair. The plan was that while the two of them climbed up to establish Camp 9, the others would go down to collect the oxygen and take it up to Camp 9 ready for a summit bid the following day. The oxygen was retrieved and carried towards Camp 9 in a superhuman effort by Walter Bonatti who, with the Hunza porter Mahdi, was forced to bivouac at 8,100m. The bivouac wrote another chapter in the saga of Himalayan climbing, fit to be compared with the epic feat in 1953 of the Austrian Herman Buhl, who survived a night in the open after reaching the summit of Nanga Parbat in an epic solo climb.

The consequences of his bivouac on the night of 30–31 July 1954 were to have a profound effect on Bonatti's later life, but he could have had no idea of the undercurrents at work as he struggled towards Camp 9 on K2. He described the climactic events of the first ascent of K2 in 1954 in his autobiography *Le Mie Montagne (My Mountains)*, published in 1960:

July 28th. Morning, Camp 7, 7,345 metres. I felt like a stranger as I helped with the departure of my companions who were preparing to make the final assault on K2. They were Erich Abram, Achille Compagnoni, Pino Gallotti, Lino Lacedelli and Ubaldo Rey.

Three days earlier, when we had first reached this altitude and established our seventh camp there, I too like the others had been sorely tried but was full of eagerness and hope. Then for the umpteenth time the weather broke and we were kept imprisoned in our tents for two days and three nights. The first evening I had eaten something which had disagreed with me, probably some tinned sardines, and from then on I could only manage to sip a little lemonade.

The moment had come to watch my companions leave for the heights, and everything seemed to have lost its meaning. I felt shaken, listless and useless. I cursed the

The upper section of the Abruzzi Ridge. The area which led to the protracted post-climb conflict is outlined. The Bonatti/Mahdi bivouac was near the top of the steep section below the overhanging ice cliff.

fate that stopped me from experiencing the moment I had awaited for so long. Twenty days had passed since I had left base camp for the last time, all of them passed in the best of health with the advance party, and now it seemed ironic I found myself in this state.

In fact I had already suffered a similar state of inefficiency and uselessness, which had happened right at the beginning of the expedition not long before we reached the base of K2. But the reason for that had been very different. We were still on the Baltoro glacier, at a place called Urdukas, where we had halted for a few days to become acclimatised to the altitude. It was just there I fell victim to a stupid accident which almost cost me my hide.

This is what happened: Lacedelli came into my tent one morning to wake me and jokingly picked me up in his arms – me and the sleeping bag in which I was wrapped fast asleep. The silly ass dragged me out of the tent and started to rock me to and fro in his arms till I suddenly slipped out of his grasp, out of the sleeping bag, and finished up rolling down the icy slope as naked as I had been under the eiderdown. It was what one might call an 'unfunny joke' from which I got such abrasions and bruises it left me on my back for more than ten days. When I came to my senses, stretched out in the big tent which functioned as a hospital, having obviously been carried inside by my friends, Lacedelli was standing nearby with all the demeanour of a whipped dog. However, to avoid problems from the very strict leader of the expedition I agreed with my companions to report my enforced convalescence as a 'stomach ache'. I must say just for the record that this 'illness' of mine, assumed out of kindness to protect my companion, was soon to become just one more negative attribute for myself, a diminishing note in the eyes of those who did not know the truth of the matter. And even worse was to happen when the story was repeated, because as a result of this episode people were to pin non-existent character defects on me. Yet again, as seems to be the rule, an altruistic gesture was followed by the ingratitude of those very people who not only knew the truth but also had been its direct beneficiaries.

However, let us go back to July 28th on K2.

Slowly and laboriously, step by step, my companions who had just left Camp 7 mounted the slope; the strain they were under was obviously exhausting. Their programme for the day was to establish Camp 8 in its pre-planned site at about 7,750 metres. It was to be just a single tent supplied with the bare necessities for the two men who were to stay up there. The two who were to occupy this advanced site would almost certainly be those who were destined to attempt the assault on the summit, always assuming their fitness lasted. I did not know then what I was to discover only on my return to Base camp – Desio had appointed Compagnoni leader of the final summit bid in an 'Order of Service' addressed to all the lead climbers, which I had somehow never received. By contrast, the others would concentrate on supporting these two, then go back down to Camp 7 for the night, and up again the next day with more provisions.

As the five companions went further and further up slopes made incandescent by the sun, I stayed in the tent, a prey to depression. I brooded so much on my misfortune that in the end a reaction welled up in me. I decided to eat at all costs, though the very thought made me feel sick; only in this way, I thought, would I be able to regain a little of my lost strength and resume my place up there. I often had to close my eyes and force myself to think of something else before I could manage to swallow even a single mouthful of the few provisions available; at times it seemed I would choke with nausea, but fortunately what I managed to swallow stayed down.

Little more than half an hour had passed since I had been left alone in camp, when suddenly Rey appeared in front of the tent, his face disfigured by fatigue and despondency. He told me briefly that, having gained little more than 50 metres in height, he had been stricken by illness which had forced him to leave his load on the snow and stop climbing. Never so much as then did I believe I could understand his state of mind without him needing to describe it to me. Such blows are always the hardest to endure for those who, like us, had been struggling for two months on a mountain of this sort.

The four men up there had become very small in the distance by now, and were about to be swallowed by the mist, which was becoming thicker. The fate of K2 now rested in their hands alone. A last silent look up towards our companions, then we closed the tent flap behind us. All that day an unhappy atmosphere reigned at Camp 7.

No one had come up from below all day. During our radio appointment with Base Camp at 5.30 pm we insisted the Hunzas must climb up with the previously arranged loads of equipment – provisions, fuel and cylinders of oxygen. We asked base camp, with which it was possible to communicate by radio relay, to transmit our message to Camp 5, from which the supplies we had asked for were to leave. Base Camp gave us the weather report, which was finally favourable: clear skies and a cold wind from the north promised a definite improvement. This was to be our last contact with base.

Towards evening two men could be seen coming down from the heights: Abram and Gallotti. So Compagnoni and Lacedelli were to be the lucky ones who would attack the summit. I was tremendously pleased Abram and Gallotti thought I seemed much better; in truth I myself felt I had almost completely recovered. It was like a miracle. They described briefly the layout of the new camp. They said that to get there one first climbed straight up the slope which rose above our tent, then traversed diagonally towards the right up a wide bowl. Finally, by now smack on the east wall, one took another slope less steep than the first, at the end of which the tent of Camp 8 had been placed in the shelter of a great wall of ice.

Contrary to what our original plan in Italy had envisaged, their companions had finished up making do with a lower altitude, so Camp 8 turned out to be at only 7,627 metres, and to get there fully laden took about four hours.

Gallotti then told of his adventure which had almost ended fatally. This is how he reported it later in his diary: 'We left Achille and Lino to pitch the tent, and I set off down with Erich. As usual, we were not roped. The descent turned out to be slower than foreseen. We half sank, even in the tracks we had just made, until suddenly during a traverse we went too fast and nearly had a disaster. Halfway down the last slope the snow must have balled up under my crampons, and suddenly I found myself going sideways before I had time to work out what was happening. I made several attempts to dig my axe in but without success. By now I had reached a terrifying velocity, when I unexpectedly found myself with my face to the slope. I gave a violent kick at the wall with my right foot – the two front teeth of my crampon got a purchase and a few metres further down I found I had stopped. Little by little I got my breath back and looked around. I had covered at least 50 to 70 metres in my slide, and the fact I had stopped gave me an indescribable sense of well-being. But my guardian angel must have got a devil of a fright and lost several feathers in the fall. I set off again to get closer to Erich, and I covered the final part of the slope between me and the tents mostly on my hands and knees ... .'

July 29th. The dawn was splendid and, considering the height we were at, I felt very well. My physical and moral well-being even made me feel I wanted some breakfast. Rey too seemed to have recovered; Gallotti and Abram, by contrast, still seemed worn out by the labours of the previous day.

The plans for the day were as follows: Lacedelli and Compagnoni would climb up from Camp 8 towards the wall of red rock which was crowned by the summit, and there, at an altitude of about 8,100 metres according to the initial plan, they would perhaps be able to pitch a camp, consisting of a little tent of the 'Super-K2' type furnished with the bare necessities. Then at the end of the day they would go back to Camp 8 where in the meantime our reinforcements were due to arrive. In fact from Camp 7, where we were situated, we were to commence a massive support operation – that is to say, during the day we were to carry to Camp 8 enough provisions to make it a large base for the assault on the summit. Naturally, our loads were also to include the two trestles of oxygen cylinders abandoned the previous day just above Camp 7. These cylinders were to serve Lacedelli and Compagnoni for their final thrust from Camp 9 to the top of K2. Meanwhile the Hunzas would arrive from below with the other provisions we had requested the day before over the radio.

Having made our preparations with enforced slowness, we got ready to leave; but all too soon, what we had always feared happened, and this compromised the situation not a little: Rey and Abram had to give up. No amount of encouragement could put fresh heart into them. They knew all too well the importance of their mission and the price of their refusal, but if they were now compelled to stop, it was solely because they had already given more than was humanly possible. Almost without uttering a word, they laid their loads down on the snow and started down, stumbling as they went. These were terrible moments not only for those who gave up, but also for those who persisted.

Abram was to spend the rest of the day at Camp 7 in the hope of being able to recover a little and rejoin us next day. Rey, on the other hand, had nothing in store for him but the journey back to Base Camp.

So only the two of us were left – Gallotti and myself. But Gallotti seemed so worn out I wondered if he could still go on. I did not have the heart to ask him to exchange his general load for the trestle of oxygen which Abram had just picked up but had immediately dropped again on the snow. Certainly Gallotti did not have the strength to carry it, otherwise I was sure he would have done so on his own initiative. These loads of oxygen were the two heaviest pieces of all the equipment we were carrying on our backs and they were of prime importance – I would even say indispensable – to our companions for their summit attempt. Despite this, I realised that to get only one oxygen pack up to Camp 8 of the two which were needed would not solve the problem into which we had been plunged and which had yet again upset our plans.

So there were only two of us, but there were four loads to carry up to Camp 8.

Furthermore, to continue we must also provide for our own requirements by carrying with us an irreducible minimum of provisions and fuel so as not to impinge on the already minimal reserves of Compagnoni and Lacedelli. Even more, we would need to set up at least one other tent up there. I therefore decided also to put down the pack of oxygen cylinders which I was still carrying on my shoulders, and replace it with enough things to set up a second tent at Camp 8 for Gallotti and myself. We would discuss with Compagnoni and Lacedelli later, and more in depth, the new problem which had just arisen and make a new plan of action for the morrow.

It was much harder to resume the climb after a prolonged stop, and we went on rather more slowly. Scarcely had we mastered the diagonal traverse to the right than mist enveloped us. Yesterday's tracks in the deep snow had been obliterated by the wind during the night, and we could therefore only tell where we were thanks to the infrequent coloured sticks providentially stuck in the snow by our companions the day before. Gallotti showed astonishing tenacity, and though he was almost at the end of his tether he continued to follow me.

It was late afternoon when we sighted the tent; the mist had hidden it from us until we were only 30 or 40 metres away. The voices of Compagnoni and Lacedelli answered our shouts. When we reached the tent and faced them they looked to be in a state of extreme fatigue. They told us they had taken hours and hours to overcome the wall of ice just above the tent. The effort was so sustained they had gained only a hundred or so metres in height all day, and they had then turned back exhausted after dropping their sacks for the next day on the snow. All in all, the situation yet again seemed somewhat compromised; but we put off talking about the problem until later, and before night fell, Gallotti and I hastened to dig out a small flat area on the snowy slope so we could put up our tent. We quickly got ourselves under shelter from the cold, which little by little was getting worse.

We had a bite to eat – we hadn't eaten since morning – and then all four of us curled ourselves up in our friends' tent to discuss what we ought to do next. Meanwhile the sky became studded with stars and it got colder and colder.

After a long discussion we came to this conclusion: if we were to have any hope of success in climbing K2 we would somehow have to manage, next day, to get the oxygen packs up to the now inevitable Camp 9, which had still not been established – at first we had optimistically thought we could do without it in an emergency like this. So the main problem was to recover the oxygen cylinders and then ensure they arrived at the new camp. It would be far too risky to attempt the final assault without the help of the precious gas, both for the outcome of the enterprise and for the safety of the climbers. We agreed we could not spread over two days the work of carrying up the cylinders left just above Camp 7 – if we did we would exhaust the fuel and our already very scarce provisions, including what should already be on its way up to us with the Hunzas. It would also mean our physical state would be completely run down, because when staying at such extreme altitudes one deteriorates rapidly even when completely at rest. Last but not least, the chances of a collapse in the weather would increase; it was uncertain even now, and a change would multiply the dangers which already existed. The use of oxygen would undoubtedly provide the best guarantee of success – the open circuit respirators would deliver oxygen for an average of ten to twelve hours with the benefit of being able to carry on at 8,000 metres as if one were at 6,000.

In the end, we agreed that next morning Gallotti and I would go down to the vicinity of Camp 7 to pick up the two oxygen packs and bring them up to Camp 9 in the course of the day. Meanwhile Lacedelli and Compagnoni would climb up to establish this blessed Camp 9. We agreed this shelter would be placed not where it had been theoretically proposed earlier in the general plan, that is, below and to the left of the great cliff of red rock, but on the contrary would be put much lower down, at least 100 or so metres lower than the planned site. The two of us would then be able to achieve our exhausting mission; more than 200 metres of descent towards Camp 7, then a climb of at least 500 metres (this is what was proposed, but in the event it turned out to be more than 700 metres) with a weight of nineteen kilograms on our backs, and what is more climbing at 8,000 metres. It was a very hard task, almost an act of madness, but as things stood the outcome on K2 depended on this very madness. If our plan succeeded, tomorrow night we would all four of us be up there in the tiny tent at Camp 9, just as we were now, and together we would await with impatience the longed-for dawn of victory.

That evening, though obviously tired, Lacedelli seemed in excellent shape, but by contrast, even though he did not admit it, obvious symptoms of exhaustion had emerged in Compagnoni. Doubting he was still capable of sustaining an extreme effort, I was more than once on the point of asking him to let me take his place. But in the end I didn't – a decision of this sort would be much better coming from Compagnoni himself. Instead, he evaded the issue of his physical state. However, perhaps it was better this way. Given the support team had an extremely hard task in store for it, and one full of unknowns, it would have been a worry if it had been allotted to Compagnoni. I was therefore torn between the thought I ought to replace my companion, the scruples which accompanied this idea and, without presumption, the fear that in my place Compagnoni would not be able to carry the oxygen up to Camp 9. It was almost a relief when, perhaps reading my thoughts and put to the test by the realities of the situation, he said precisely this: 'If tomorrow you are still in good shape up there at Camp 9, it might well be you will have to take the place of one of us'. Actually this was not a very probable outcome, given the exhausting day which still awaited me, and it all sounded at the time more like a bait astutely designed to get him out of an all too obvious problem. But his words served to convince me that for the present it wouldn't really be appropriate to change things. 'If tomorrow evening we need to reconsider these words of Compagnoni's,' I thought as I went back to my tent, 'it will mean all four of us have reached Camp 9, and those two terrible burdens of equipment will also have arrived up there. For the moment, that's all that matters.'

While we were settling down for the night, Gallotti complained of severe pain in his left foot because of the cold. We massaged it one after another until sensation returned to his toes, then turned in.

Next morning, July 30th, though all four of us had been making feverish preparations since 6.30, we were ready to leave only at 8 am. At that rarefied altitude, the mere putting on of boots, for example, takes about half an hour. Our surroundings were really inspiring, because apart from all else we could finally see our long-awaited peak from close at hand. The cliff which rose just above our camp concealed the middle section which preceded the final upthrust, and this was probably the reason the summit of K2 seemed so close one would say he could get there in a few steps. Off to the side, by now lower than we were, was enthroned Skyang-Kangri or Staircase Peak, a superb summit of 7,544 metres which had been denied to the expedition of the Duke of the Abruzzi in 1909 through sheer bad luck. Seen from up here, with its three huge steps delineating its hulking shape, it made one think of a huge staircase reaching to the sky. The horizon seemed infinite, composed entirely of peaks and glaciers, but towards the Kuen-Lun in particular it became a remarkable pale azure in which sky and mountain merged together.

We wished each other good luck and left our companions. Though unladen, we went down slowly. The snow dispersed by the breeze had once more obliterated the tracks of yesterday, so we tried to take very short paces to recreate the well-measured steps which would later make it easier for us to climb up again. Gallotti had not forgotten his slide of two days before, and when he reached the same place where the accident had happened he kept his eyes well and truly peeled. Meanwhile, looking down on Camp 7, we saw Abram coming towards us with the two Hunzas, Mahdi and Isakhan, who had arrived there the previous day. I felt great admiration for my friend Abram, who had managed to overcome his own crisis of the day before. All five of us arrived almost simultaneously at the place where the two oxygen kits had been abandoned two days ago, just above Camp 7. Among other things in our companions' packs were mattresses and reserve down-filled sleeping bags: and these looked most attractive to Gallotti and myself, because we had passed the previous night with rather scanty protection.

With a load of cylinders on my shoulders, but feeling perhaps less worn out than the others, I advanced at the head of a line of men up the snowy slope. Immediately behind me was Gallotti, with a gait so laboured his halts were longer than the time he spent climbing. At times he stopped with his face buried in the snow and seemed incapable of going on. Then, goodness knows how, he still found the will and the strength to resume climbing – only to fall again in the deep snow after no more than another metre. His face was ghastly, it was so swollen and disfigured by his efforts. When we got to Camp 8 I really thought he would not be able to take one more step. I realised I had been assisting at one of the most moving examples of tenacity and will-power a man could demonstrate in the conquest of a mountain. What Gallotti achieved on July 30th 1954 is extraordinary, and I think this in itself would have been enough to have made the ascent of K2 worthwhile.

Though a good step forward had been made, we were still a long way from Camp 9 and the situation seemed to be getting worse once again. Clearly one could no longer count on Gallotti. Abram said nothing, but it was obvious from his face there was little to hope for from him. Isakhan was shaking feverishly like a baby. Mahdi by contrast still seemed in great shape. This man was remarkable, and had always been the best of all the Hunzas. In my opinion he was the only one of these people who could stand comparison with the best Nepalese Sherpas. It would have to be Mahdi who would leave for Camp 9 with me, bearing the second load of oxygen which he himself had already carried this far. But how could I induce him to make such an effort without at least allowing him to hope it was possible for him too to reach the summit? This was the lever which would work better than anything else on the excellent and proud Mahdi.

But before broaching the subject we made some soup for us all with the few stock cubes and biscuits available; it undoubtedly makes for more optimism to discuss things with something in one's stomach. Then, starting with the promise of a reward in rupees when victory was ours, we laid out our proposal to Mahdi, giving him also the vague illusion that perhaps he would be able to climb to the summit together with me, Lacedelli and Compagnoni. This was a subtle but necessary deception which, however, did have a grain of truth in it. Mahdi accepted the proposal and got ready to resume the journey with me, adequately equipped with clothing from Gallotti and Abram, except for boots – we had no spare ones to give him.

Abram in the meantime was feeling a little better and declared himself ready to accompany us as high as he could, taking it in turns with us to carry the loads of oxygen. We put on our crampons and made a final check of our equipment. We had plenty of rope, a couple of karabiners and our ice-axes; we also took a little bag of extra tools, that is, a couple of monkey wrenches, some spare valves and other minor spare parts for the oxygen delivery system — Compagnoni and Lacedelli already had the face masks and connecting tubes in their rucksacks. There was finally an electric torch, and that was the lot. We were ready to leave.

Time had flown. It was half past three already, and we had only four hours of daylight left. Our companions up there would start to worry if they did not see us coming.

A deep groove towards the right showed us the route taken by Lacedelli and Compagnoni to attack the wall which crowned the edge of the camp site. We followed it. We were in shadow, and the temperature was noticeably more frigid. Our muscles were sluggish and, in contrast to a few hours ago, no longer answered our demands. It was the effect of the long halt, but even more it was the crippling weight of the packs of oxygen cylinders on our backs, magnified by the various accessories and made still worse by the inexorable effect of the rarefaction of the air. Consequently, we were compelled to stop after every three or four steps taken with extreme slowness, and every 20 or 30 metres we changed loads from one to another between the three of us.

At the foot of the wall, which was about 30 metres high, there was a wide and deep crevasse. The path crossed this crevasse at the only point where its two lips come close to each other. The upper lip was composed of a shelf of unsubstantial snow. This had been so damaged at its edges by the repeated passage of our companions these last two days that it made overcoming it very problematical with loads like these on our shoulders.

By about 4.30 we emerged on the slope above the ice wall, but we were anxious to know the path which still awaited us, and before even considering the spectacle of the summit which was by now close and visibly free from surprises, we called to our companions, shouting as loudly as we could. They heard us and answered. But where was their tent? A long line of footprints, interrupted here and there, rose in front of us up a long slope, becoming straighter and straighter until it reached the seracs which supported the summit. But just before the last feathery ridge the already tenuous tracks of our companions veered slowly to the left. Then they disappeared. It seemed they resumed much higher up, heading towards a steep zone of projecting rocks. We managed to follow them still a little further up to the foot of a huge boulder, then ... nothing more. Lacedelli and Compagnoni must certainly be there, in a tent hidden from our sight by the great rock. But why would they have gone right up there?

'Lino! Achille! Where are you? Where have you put the tent?'

'Follow the tracks!' a voice replied from above us.

The deep, relaxed tone of their answer reassured us and made us realise we were now within normal earshot: they heard us very well and then answered us in normal tones, without shouting. It was a comforting contact, but we were also somewhat taken aback by the near certainty the camp had been placed so high up. We resumed the climb in the tracks of our companions.

Now in my imagination I was up there where the tracks died out and I could already see myself in the tent of my friends. Indeed, I could see the place from where I was – not one problem raised itself against our ascent, though we thought it would be difficult to get there before it got dark. Moreover, we noted how the climb we had budgeted for the whole day had increased considerably and by now had reached 700 metres in height.

Step by step, halt by halt, our climb went on. We crossed a zone of great crevasses treacherously concealed by fragile snow bridges, and here I was happy to think K2 would have been conquered when we once more retraced our steps.

But this euphoria soon disappeared, yielding its place to cold logic. The higher we climbed the greater grew our suspicion the tent and our companions were not to be found beyond the large boulder. Actually, as it got closer to us, this rock really did not seem big enough to conceal any tent, no matter how small. On the other hand, there were no other sites in the vicinity more suitable for a camp. The slope was a succession of steep, iced-up slabs which continued right up to the great wall of red rock above. The best and safest place to put a tent would have been at about 7,900 to 7,950

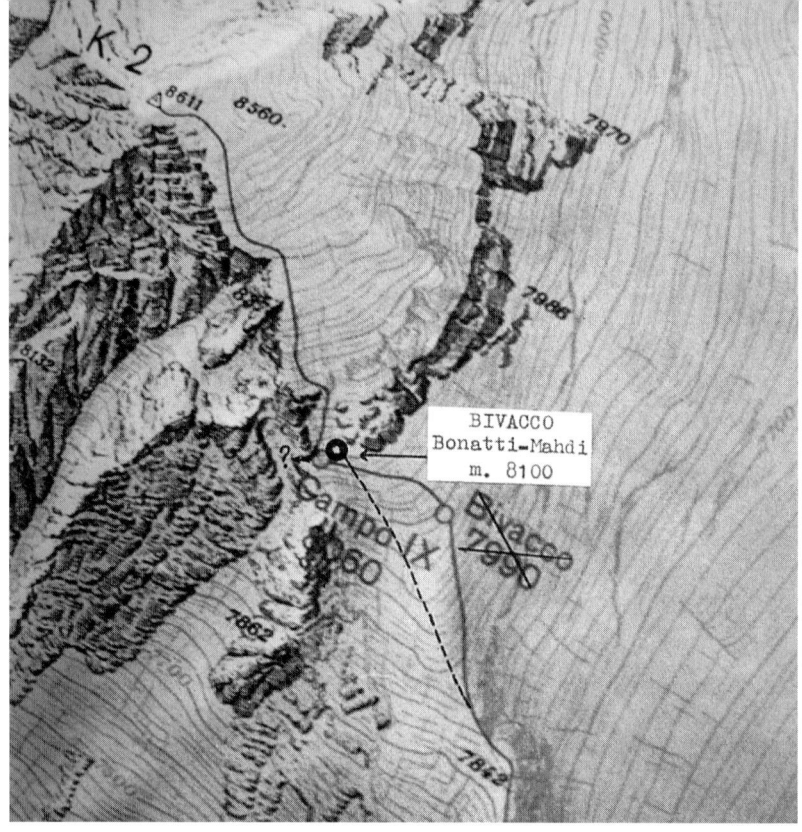

The dotted line in the photograph above indicates the route followed by Compagnoni and Lacedelli, as deduced from their tracks. The solid line is the route followed by Bonatti and Mahdi to their bivouac position (B) about 30 metres above the 'great boulder'.

metres, on the end of the snowy hogback which separates the two faces of K2 – the very place, indeed, on which we had already decided the previous evening. We became anxious again and formulated the wildest theories: could it be the indistinct tracks we were following up to the boulder were not footprints at all? Were they instead simply a track produced by a stone or by a block of ice rolling down the mountain? But in this case where could Lacedelli and Compagnoni be? Right over the right-hand side of the slope? No, that was illogical – the danger of icefall would be too great. But they might have found shelter, perhaps in some cavity – in a crevasse for example – which we couldn't see from where we were. What if they had decided on the place chosen in the original general plan formulated back in Italy? If this were the case, their orange tent would be seen on the crest of the snowy rib on our left, well outlined against the rock barrier above. But a solution of this sort did not form part of the programme we had decided on the previous evening. So they couldn't be on the left either! Besides, one would have seen the tracks of our companions leading towards the left of the boulder, since the snow was so deep. But the wind might have wiped them out. Most of all, a tent over there would be too far off the track ... . These doubts and conjectures are what occupied my mind, but I am sure Abram's too, because quite suddenly and with equal anxiety we both shouted simultaneously to our companions as loudly as we could. Their brief response had reached us from the boulder, or at least from that general direction. They must be there, we thought. We wanted to believe it so much we could do nothing else but delude ourselves.

Meanwhile, the sun had disappeared behind the crest of K2 and the air was suddenly biting. Everything around us had changed as if we found ourselves by magic in some other place. Until a short while ago, every fold of the mountain had been bright and sparkling in the sun; now it was dim, cold and gloomy. Everything had become mysterious, making me feel incredibly small and fragile. Never so much as then did I feel the power of K2 and the entire Himalaya which surrounded us. I had already lived for some twenty days in the 'death zone' but now I felt the spell of 8,000 metres taking possession of me. I think I was afraid.

From one sensation to another I had reached a sort of ecstasy, of rapture, which transported me far from reality and from all physical things – an experience I had never had before.

But the rationale yet again was there to shake me out of it. Abram complained that one of his feet had lost all feeling. Dear, good Erich, you had already decided to turn back once we had overcome the ice wall, but a couple of hours had passed since then and you were still there to share with us the heavy burden of the respirators in order to increase the possibility of success for our crazy mission.

I helped him to take off his great boot, and by turns, without losing a second, we rubbed his foot violently until it started to hurt, letting us know the danger had passed. We said our goodbyes, then for a few minutes I watched his slow descent towards Camp 8.

We were left alone, Mahdi and I. It was 6.30 and we went on in silence towards the great hogback which separated the eastern from the southern slope. We reached it, and in a little while, to the left, there opened beneath us a huge icy couloir which fell in a single bound right down to the Godwin-Austen glacier. This ridge was the obstacle which, seen from below, had interrupted the thin line of footprints, here and there obliterated by the wind. The tracks, now clearer, went on all the way up the long hogback. They then continued up the steep snowy couloir which followed and which in its turn widened out, flattened, and merged with the wall which dropped away under our feet. Continuing to follow the vague tracks with my eyes, they could be seen to turn abruptly left towards the centre of the steep couloir and from there to continue straight upwards towards a great boulder. Higher up nothing else could be seen.

After reaching the end of the snowy hogback, Mahdi started to shake with the cold and show signs of hysteria. I would have liked very much to know where those two up there were concealed. It would be dark in about half an hour and the situation was still not clear to me.

'Lino! Achille! Where are you? Answer me!'

Everything was silent.

'Perhaps they can't hear us inside their tent', I thought, 'But why aren't they keeping a look out, or just listening for us every so often? Wouldn't we all be a lot happier?'

Meanwhile we had reached the point where the traverse to the left towards the centre of the steep couloir started. Now, rather than follow the tracks of our companions, we headed directly toward the huge boulder.

The slope became more and more steep and treacherous, and at times it seemed our hearts would burst in our chests with the effort. We could not sit down on the snow any more to rest, it was too precipitous and we would have finished 3000 metres lower down. Ah, those cylinders! Those cursed oxygen cylinders! We felt crushed under their weight, our flanks had lost all feeling, and our backs could no longer stand the strain. Up to a short time before I had been able to alleviate the weight of the burden by going forward all crouched over, but now the slope had steepened I was forced to walk askew, all out of balance. Sometimes the physical pain was so acute we would hang onto an ice-axe planted in the snow and give vent to agonised panting in an attempt to get some relief.

What irony it was to think that what was oppressing us could at the same time be our best source of relief! It was pure oxygen we were carrying: 19 kilograms of precious gas which, mixed by the appropriate masks, could in an instant transport us to the atmosphere of 2,000 metres lower down, in the conditions prevailing at 6,000 metres. It would be so simple to turn a valve, and to the devil with the masks and regulators, which in any event we did not have because they were in the packs of Lacedelli and Compagnoni. Once the valve was turned, the thin air around us would be suddenly enriched by the precious gas, and for a few minutes (the time it would take for the cylinders to empty) it would be as if we were at home.

I was being ironic, needless to say, but I could not fail to note by what a fine thread the outcome of the expedition was suspended.

The sky began to grow darker and our repeated cries more anguished, but still there was no reply. Even though we feared it more and more, we could not believe we would not find the tent above the boulder. Why didn't Lacedelli and Compagnoni answer us? By now we were nearly there – within no more than 50 metres.

'Achille! Lino! Why don't you answer?'

Now we had both stopped, out of breath, in deep snow halfway up our thighs. In another few minutes the already faint twilight would give way to night. Like a madman, Mahdi started to shout feverishly. Naturally I could not understand him, but he was obviously very agitated.

This situation could not be permitted to go on. With a jerk, I freed myself from my load and, calling on all my remaining energy, laboured on all fours straight up the couloir until I was a little above the great boulder. Flat on the snow, with my vision clouded by the effort, I realised there was no tent behind the big rock: some tracks half obliterated by the wind rose obliquely towards the left, across the steep wall of rock and ice. For a moment I felt destroyed, as if everything had collapsed inside me. My thoughts raced wildly out of control. When I came to myself I had been in shock for some time. It was pitch dark. Mahdi was next to me, and I could see his eyes gleaming in the tenuous light of the stars.

I became aware my throat was tremendously dry, and instinctively carried a handful of snow to my mouth – indifferent to the cold, I had recovered a little and then, taking off my gloves, fumbled in my various pockets until I found the torch. I tried in vain to switch it on. Perhaps the extreme cold had stopped it working; in fact I recalled I had always kept it in one of my outside pockets in order to have it handy, consequently it was impossible to have any light.

By now there was no doubt about it: our companions were somewhere else, most probably beneath the great red barrier, but who knew in what angle they were hidden, since they could neither be seen nor heard. But why this change of programme? How were we now to tackle the steep and treacherous iced-up face in the dark to search for their tent? Seeing how things were, the most logical solution for Mahdi and myself was to return immediately to Camp 8, but next morning, those two over there – what would they do without oxygen? Certainly we could dig out a small shelf on the slope and leave the packs of cylinders there, but who could assure us they would not be lost in the night – perhaps covered by a storm, or buried by a snowslide, or dragged over the precipice by an avalanche, since we were right in the path of the great icefall?

'Lino! Achille! Answer me! Can you hear us?'

Silence still reigned, interrupted every so often by Mahdi's terrifying and ever more frantic shouts. I had an idea, and with great difficulty I managed to get it across to my companion. It was a case of making a final attempt to reach the presumed position of the tent. I thought to climb up the snow couloir in which we were standing and so get to the foot of the wall of red rocks. From there, a sort of snow ledge ran towards the left, and because I had seen it before it became dark, I thought it would not be excessively steep. In this way, besides avoiding the unsafe wall of snowy slabs, we would better be able to spot the tent and to reach it. Mahdi received my proposition almost with indifference and resumed his shouting.

I went down on all fours to recover the load of cylinders I had previously taken off my shoulders, then climbed back up again past the huge boulder to the place I had previously reached. When I rejoined Mahdi he was furiously brandishing his ice-axe at the heights – cursing everyone. Because it was dark I could not see the expression on his face, but I am sure it would have been fearsome. I realised his desperation was passing the bounds of reason. I felt dismayed and could foresee terrible consequences. Once more I lifted the burden on to my shoulders and again started to shout the names of my companions. Still silence. Mahdi was beside himself more than ever. Now he went up, now down, now sideways. He was no longer conscious of the burden he still carried on his back. He swayed in a terrifying way and every time he did so he was on the verge of rolling down. I could only keep him still by force, but in those moments of madness he was immensely stronger than I was. Finally he seemed to calm down a little and I, concealing my fears, managed to induce him to sit down next to me. If at that point he had not sunk so deeply in the snow, who knows how many times we would have finished at the bottom of the precipice?

By now the situation had deteriorated to the point where I could no longer think it possible even to attempt a return to Camp 8. The probability that Compagnoni and Lacedelli might find themselves without the oxygen next morning became a secondary consideration compared with the much more serious problems which almost certainly would befall Mahdi and myself if we tried to move in these conditions and in the dark. My companion, who was off his head, would undoubtedly slip and fall, while behind him I would neither be able to see what was happening nor withstand the tug on the rope caused by his sudden tumble.

Then I considered the terrible possibility of awaiting the dawn here in a bivouac: a desperate decision imposed by a crazy reality; not a deliberate one!

Instinctively I started to thrash about blindly with my ice-axe, with the intention of cutting a small platform on the slope, large enough for both of us to sit in side by side. While I was working on this project, I continued thinking and fretted myself with evil thoughts to the point of anguish, and suddenly surprised myself by shouting:

'No, I don't want to die! I mustn't die! Lino! Achille! Can't you hear us? Help us, curse you!'

Then I took to threatening them: 'Desio will hear about this when I get back!'

I lived through a crisis of rebellion and rage which it was difficult for me to allay. Apart from being treacherously abandoned I felt utterly betrayed. Finally it was as if I had woken from a nightmare. I realised I had excavated quite a large level space. Mahdi too seemed quieter now and resigned, since he responded to every proposal of mine with a mournful 'No Sahib!'

At intervals he trembled and shook with the cold.

At every blow, the pick of the ice-axe was now bouncing off the hard ice which it struck, and this compelled me to stop digging. But the shelf now seemed big enough to hold us both; in fact when I sat down to try it out for size, I found its lower border reached the point where my knees bent and the upper was the exact height of my head. It was about one metre wide and 60 centimetres deep. Mahdi, who until then had been sitting motionless a little way away watching me work, seemed to cheer up with an unexpected 'Yes, Sahib!'

Though we were resigned to our fate, before getting ourselves organised for the bivouac we called our companions one last time until we were out of breath. Our throats were so dry and hoarse we found it difficult even to pronounce their names.

Then, incredibly, in the profound silence, a light was kindled a little higher up than where we were – on the slope which led up to the rock barrier.

'Lino! Achille! Here we are! Why didn't you answer us before?'

In a very distinct and blunt voice Lacedelli justified his actions with these exact words: 'Do you want us to stay out all night to freeze for you?'

I was unwilling to take this rough outburst too seriously; one of the first effects produced by the rarefaction of the air is nerviness and irascibility. After all, I thought, I myself was hurling abuse at them just a little while ago, insulting them, cursing them and even threatening them.

'Have you got the oxygen?' the voice continued.

'Yes!' I replied.

'Good! Leave it there and go straight down!' *

'I can't!' I protested, 'Mahdi couldn't make it!'

'What?'

'I said Mahdi can't make it! I can look after myself, but Mahdi is off his head – he's crossing the face right now!'

In fact, while this dialogue was going on between us, Mahdi had jumped up again like lightning and, walking in the dark, groping for holds and raving, had gone straight onto the steep icy slope towards the light of the torch, quite unaware of the grave danger he was about to encounter. Not only was the light no help to him, but also he was dazzled by it.

---

*__Author's note:__ *In the original version of Bonatti's autobiography, published as* On the Heights *by Rupert Hart-Davis, the translator made a crucial mistake, rendering 'scendete' as 'come up', whereas in fact it means 'go down' – 'ascendete' means 'come up'. Lacedelli was* **not** *inviting Bonatti to join him at Camp 9, but brusquely telling him to go back down to Camp 8.*

'Mahdi! Turn back! No good!' I kept shouting.

But, driven by the survival instinct and by the hope of life which presented itself to him in the form of a ray of light, he went on his tightrope-walker's way. Suddenly the light disappeared. I thought the two of them were preparing to come to our aid. Mahdi on the jet-black slope had again begun to shout like a madman:

'No good, Compagnoni Sahib! No good, Lacedelli Sahib!' In short, another crisis had hit him.

Miraculously, he finally came to his senses and managed to turn back. We waited in vain for Lacedelli and Compagnoni to re-appear. We began to call again to ask for help, but no one answered us all night long. Just as if I had been burned by a fiery brand, I felt an incubus had entered my soul.

Between a promise and a prayer, I induced Mahdi to sit next to me. Realising the two over there had abandoned us, my companion now wanted to return to Camp 8 at all costs, and showed it by foolhardy attempts to leave. Twice I managed to restrain him as he was about to fall headlong.

I took the crampons off my feet to help the circulation, and did the same for Mahdi who, numbed by the cold, would have preferred to do nothing. Our throats and lips were parched and burning. Fumbling in various pockets I found three caramels, three and no more, as our only comfort and sustenance. We put one each in our mouths but immediately we were forced to spit them out again, because we had no saliva. The night was calm – only every so often could one hear the whistle of the wind, but the terrible cold started to become worse. I would have liked to know the time but it would have been too difficult to undo my buttoned-up cuffs, so I preferred not to look at my watch. It was some relief I could finally sit down: since eight in the morning we had not stopped, except for a couple of hours or a little more at Camp 8, mainly to get reorganised. In truth, the bivouac was still bearable at the moment, and because my muscles had just stopped working they were still warm, but what would happen later? I would have liked to be able to think of nothing, but found it impossible.

The sky was sprinkled with a myriad of stars so bright they cast their reflections on the snow. It seemed to me it had been much darker a few hours ago. There was no moon, but we could distinctly make out all the peaks which surrounded us. In the valley, by contrast, ever more compact mist collected and swallowed up the mountains to a height of over 7,500 metres. It was a wonderful spectacle. All the highest peaks of the Karakoram the eye could see seemed to arise by magic from a sea of milk. Look, there before us the peak of Falchan Kangri, and to the right, in contrast, the massive shape of Broad Peak, and further off the Gasherbrum summits. K2 dominated all these colossi and I ... I was right there amongst them. Instinctively I lifted my eyes to the mountain which still towered over me, and it seemed to challenge me, showing me the shadow of its horrific ice cascade clearly outlined against the sky. It evoked the mythical Sword of Damocles, a terrible menace suspended over us. If even the most minuscule fragment of that deadly overhanging structure were to detach itself, we would be swept away in an instant.

The terrible cold was paralysing us. We were shaken at intervals by prolonged shivers. We clung to each other, reducing as far as possible our contact with the ice on which we were crouched. Many times I realised I was on the verge of losing all sensation in a limb, and then I fought by every means I had to overcome the dangerous torpor. Often, movements of my arms and legs were not sufficient, nor was massage of the affected part, and I would then seize my ice-axe and repeatedly beat the place where the cold was attacking me. Apart from being effective in restoring my circulation, this method served also to avert the possibility of delirium caused by oxygen deficiency.

Suddenly, and as violently as a slap in the face, the first gust of driving snow hit us head-on; then another, and still another. In a short time a real blizzard had enveloped us, with whirls so violent our clothing was filled everywhere with icy powder, both over and under our garments. It was a torture, and only with difficulty could we manage to protect our noses and mouths with our hands so as not to suffocate; our eyes were almost blinded. Our struggle became more and more desperate. Soon we no longer knew whether we were fighting for our lives, nor why we were still alive.

Three times the swirling snow buried us after it had filled the space in which we sat, and three times we dug it out again, scraping at it all higgledy-piggledy with our hands and feet. By a stroke of bad luck we found ourselves in a bivouac right in the middle of the couloir where a great deal of snow stirred up by the wind accumulated during the storm. We stayed right on top of each other, each of us protecting the body of the other from the fury of the elements, now knowing each of us had to fight alone for his survival, with no hope for any assistance.

Then suddenly I heard a howl alongside me, a human howl and not one made by the wind, and instinctively I thrust out a hand towards a flying shadow, just in time to stop Mahdi making for the precipice. I will never know if this act of my companion was only a desperate impulse to flee back to Camp 8.

Still scraping with my hands I then dug a hole horizontally into the snow and immediately stuck my head in it, trying to find shelter in this way. The storm raged on.

Dawn. The wind fell. A sea of clouds swallowed up everything around us, up to a few hundred metres below. Then, little by little, the air became less hazy. A few stars emerged to shine in a sky which by now was almost clear. The wind ceased. The atmosphere was completely still; the cold was astral. I had no idea how long the inferno had lasted. I only knew my body felt as if it no longer belonged to me. I could not feel my feet or my hands; my legs were stiff and would not support me; my arms in particular were shaken by uncontrollable tremors. Fortunately, my thoughts were still lucid.

Impotently I watched the departure of Mahdi, who started the descent towards Camp 8 without waiting for the rays of the sun, which by now were close to us. I could do nothing to dissuade him from this rash decision. I had been able to do no more than help him put the crampons on his feet – nothing more. The awful cold of the night combined with the numerous anxieties he had suffered had disfigured my poor friend's face. He seemed confused, and when he started to reel downwards his movements combined stiffness with clumsiness. I wondered with anguish if he could manage not to fall. I did not know what to say. I confined myself to watching him, and thought how ironic it was that yesterday evening I had feared so much for his life, while now I sat there helpless and looked at him going down alone. Luckily his feet sank well into the deep snow which had accumulated during the night, but this new factor also redoubled the danger of avalanches. Suddenly, some 40 metres below me, he stopped dead on the dangerous slope and stood facing the snow. He stayed there for a long time without moving. Finally he started down again, and with my heart in my mouth I followed his precarious descent, interrupted every few steps by a painful halt. It was with great relief I saw him get to the end of the tremendous, very steep first 200 metres of the couloir. Now he could trip over and roll down as far as he liked; the risk of a precipitous fall down the mountain was over.

I wondered where Mahdi had got to in assessing and understanding the experience we were undergoing. That night, before the blizzard began, in order to curb his desperate wish to go back and to convince him to stay, I had even reached the point of promising him (assuming he understood me) a large sum in rupees which he had seemed to accept willingly enough. Would he curse me now for doing this? The unwise, desperate retreat he was now making – though extremely human – posed several questions. Who knows, I wondered, whether his agreement to stay up here in our bivouac depended more on a mercenary attitude than on the logic of survival? If the former were the main reason, perhaps he would now think he had been unwise, not understanding our night in the open without the least shelter had been unavoidable. I asked myself if it had been a mistake to make him this particular sort of promise. But what else could I have done to make possible the impossible?

Like a sublime vision, the sun suddenly burst forth from the sea of cloud, giving rise to countless bands of light and shadow. Soon its warm rays put new life into me and immediately reduced the violent tremors which had spread through my whole body. I took off my gloves, which were frozen solid. My hands were unrecognisable, they were so stiffened and wrinkled; but they began to regain sensation and to hurt me.

At last I could look at my watch, which until now had been imprisoned by cuffs and gloves cemented together by ice. It was a few minutes to six. And those two on the far side of the couloir? It was broad daylight and still they hadn't shown themselves – even now the site of their tent remained a mystery. I went on massaging myself, removing the snow blown in by the blizzard from every nook and cranny of my clothes. The freezing powder encrusting my beard had produced on my face a veritable carapace of ice which was hard to get off. I re-exposed to the light the two trestles of oxygen cylinders which had been buried by the storm. Then I put on my crampons and I too started down towards Camp 8. It was incredible how insecure I felt, even though I was completely unladen.

At every step I had to plant my ice-axe and hang on to it so as not to fall. In my turn I too left behind me the 200 metres of steep slope and now, even though my steps were still uncertain, I felt my stability improving. Soon the cold completely disappeared.

I advanced cautiously into the labyrinth of crevasses and negotiated them. Then a cry reached me from above. I peered up intently, but could not make out anyone. I could still see nothing except the multicoloured oxygen packs, exactly as I had left them. However, I lifted my ice-axe and shook it in the air in answer; then resumed my descent.

Here was the embankment above Camp 8. Before lowering myself behind this obstacle, I turned again to look at my bivouac site and its surroundings, hoping to discover a human presence up there, but in vain. It was exactly seven o'clock. Then I concentrated on my goal, which by now was close, and said to myself: 'Keep it up! One more effort and you'll be with your friends, in a tent, under shelter!'

Now it was much easier to cross the crevasse, I had to do no more than let myself slide on my back. No sooner said than done! A swoop into space and I found myself four metres lower down, plunged in the snow up to my waist. With some emotion I saw the two tents of Camp 8 just below me. It seemed to be a mirage – the tents were just there, a few steps away, but I seemed unable to reach them; it was the effect of the relaxation which often comes at the end of any undertaking when morally it is all but over.

On my arrival in Camp 8 I found myself face to face with the Hunza Isakhan, who had come out of his tent to get himself some more snow to melt. To my questions about Mahdi he reassured me, giving me to understand he had just arrived and was in the tent with him. I took the crampons off my feet and went into the tent occupied by Abram and Gallotti. The latter was to write in his diary concerning this episode:

'A little before seven we were awakened by the tent flaps being thrown back. It was Mahdi who faced us. He was distracted, and showed us his hands and feet, which were martyred by the cold. His feet in particular had toes which were blackened and distorted in a most distressing way. His explanations, given in a laboured voice, were not at all clear and left us in a state of profound apprehension. Erich and I looked at each other without the courage to make any guesses.'

A little later I arrived.

Poor Mahdi, my generous, unfortunate companion. Strong as you were, you were not new to extreme conditions in the Himalaya, though never before did you suffer such a harsh fate. My thoughts, full of emotion and admiration, picture you, still there on the rarefied heights of your mountains. I see you on a great icy wall, and strapped to your shoulders is a man with frozen feet whom you are carrying step by step down to the valley. It is Hermann Buhl, the lone conqueror of Nanga Parbat.*

I recounted the drama of the night briefly to my friends, and even then I could not fully understand the significance of all the aspects of the experience I had been through. What still astonishes me to this day is that I was unscathed.

At 5.30 pm, Isakhan appeared at our tent and said this, in English:

'A Sahib is about to climb K2!'

We rushed outside. I had a lump in my throat from emotion: two tiny dots were slowly and steadily advancing, climbing up the slope of the summit, which was blue as the sky in that hour of sunset.

At 11 pm, five hearts were exulting over the same victory in the same tent at Camp 8. They belonged to Abram, Gallotti, Compagnoni, Lacedelli and myself. At that moment, and only for that moment, I forced myself to forget all other reality. But to erase an experience like this from the mind forever would be unjust, if not sheer wishful thinking. Indeed, things like this leave indelible scars on a youngster's mind, and unfortunately play havoc with his still unformed spiritual values.

---

*__Author's note:__ In the Skardu hospital he was to undergo various amputations of his fingers and toes.

Bonatti's Troubles

When the lead climbers arrived back at Base Camp after the successful ascent of K2, Bonatti was unscathed, Compagnoni had frost-bitten fingers, Lacedelli was similarly affected, but poor Mahdi had very extensive frostbite of all his toes and most of his fingers – though in his book on the expedition Desio makes no mention of this and, with what seems remarkable *sang-froid*, says only that Madhi and the other Hunzas had arrived at Base Camp later than the Italian climbers, having 'lingered in the camps on the Abruzzi Ridge'. Later, as the expedition prepared to leave Base Camp, Desio comments that 'Mahdi was apparently no longer in a fit state to walk and would have to be carried on a stretcher'. It is somewhat surprising that the Expedition Leader was only 'apparently' aware of the condition of the porter who had contributed so much to the success of his expedition.

A couple of weeks later, as the expedition was making its way back to Karachi, the Pakistan press erupted with an extraordinary accusation. It was alleged that Compagnoni, the climbing leader, had forced Mahdi to wait a few metres below the summit rather than allow him to share in the glory of climbing K2, and this was why Mahdi had been so badly frost-bitten. The Italians were vilified and condemned out of hand in the newspapers, and accused of providing ' ... a most flagrant example of unpleasant, cunning and selfish human nature'. When Desio and his team finally reached Karachi, reporters deluged them with questions about Mahdi and his frostbite, to the exclusion of all else.

In response to an open letter of complaint, and in order to refute the allegations, the Italian ambassador to Pakistan, Dr. Benedetto d'Acunzo, held an inquiry. He interviewed Bonatti,

Compagnoni and Lacedelli at the Embassy in the presence of Colonel Ata Ullah (Liaison Officer), Doctor Guido Pagani (the Expedition's Medical Officer) and Amedeo Costa (Vice President of the Italian Alpine Club). Pakistani officials were there as well. It seems most significant – and highly irregular in the legal sense – that, although Mahdi was the injured party, he was not called as a witness. He was, at the time, in hospital undergoing treatment for his frost-bitten hands and feet, but it seems strange that no effort was made to obtain a declaration from him concerning whether he had indeed been 'forced to wait near the summit' and, if so, who had given him this order. With hindsight it would seem that the Italians perhaps did not wish to hear what Mahdi had to say.

After the enquiry, the Embassy issued a long report describing in some detail the crucial events and the movements of all the climbers at the end of July near the summit of K2. At the end of the report the following conclusions were set down:

1. Camp 9, situated at an altitude of more than 8,000 metres, was established by Compagnoni and Lacedelli, without the help of any porters;
2. Bonatti and Mahdi did not reach Camp 9, but stopped at a lower altitude;
3. The porter Mahdi caused Bonatti great concern by his wild behaviour and his unwise and undisciplined attempts to get out of their predicament;
4. Bonatti decided to spend the night where he was partly through fear that Mahdi's agitation would cause an accident while descending in the dark, and partly in the hope of being able to reach Camp 9 next morning with the two respirators;
5. He managed to restrain Mahdi during the night, but not after dawn;
6. He then followed Mahdi down to Camp 8, leaving the respirators at the bivouac site (as Lacedelli had advised him to do the previous evening, shouting this to him across the space that separated them);

7. Compagnoni and Lacedelli on the 31st had to descend from Camp 9 to fetch the two respirators before starting their climb towards the summit.

The Pakistan government and the press accepted this as a satisfactory explanation. Everyone concluded that the newspaper accusations were completely unfounded, and Compagnoni was exonerated. Bonatti naively supposed at the time that the inquiry was precisely what it appeared to be – it was not until accusations were made against him in the Italian press ten years later that he realised Desio, the Italian Alpine Club and Compagnoni must have had a hidden agenda from the very beginning.

Soon after the expedition arrived back in Italy, relations between Bonatti and the K2 team became progressively strained, for reasons that he did not even suspect at the time. He became more and more estranged from his fellow climbers, and later events make it clear a whispering campaign was going on behind his back. Bonatti could not understand why the official version of the climb in Ardito Desio's official book *The Conquest of K2* paid almost no attention to his bivouac, which was dismissed in no more than one somewhat inaccurate paragraph.

Desio's Version of the Climb
(from *La Conquista del K2* – Garzanti 1954)

July 30th was a beautiful day – the sky was clear, there was no wind. Compagnoni and Lacedelli left Camp 8 and again climbed the ice wall. They recovered their loads (the contents of their rucksacks left the day before) and headed towards the steep gully which cuts through the rocky wall beneath the icy coverlet covering the summit. The snow was deep and floury, and they sank to their waists. Higher up, the going became even more tiring. They reached the foot of the gully menaced by the seracs of the overhanging ice roof, then turned to the left and went on under a wall of rock encrusted in clear ice. They overcame a series of difficult slabs and managed to erect their tiny high-altitude tent on a narrow little terrace at an altitude of about 8,050 metres. That same morning, Bonatti and Gallotti had descended towards Camp 7 to recover the two respirators left on the track by their companions, and they managed to carry them up to Camp 8 by midday. Meanwhile, two Hunzas, Mahdi and Isakhan, had arrived at Camp 7 the previous evening, and the next morning they climbed with Abram towards Camp 8, carrying provisions, fuel and camping equipment. At 3.30 pm Abram, Bonatti and Mahdi took the respirators and other equipment and climbed the ice wall above the camp, following the tracks of Compagnoni and Lacedelli. But Abram eventually had to return to the camp, which he reached at seven in the evening. The other two carried on laboriously through the fresh and floury snow. The sun sank towards the horizon, but Camp 9 was still a long way off. Their march continued with painful slowness into the twilight. Night was by now close at hand. The two of them shouted to make themselves heard by Compagnoni and Lacedelli, but the wind which blew from the north face drowned their voices for some time. Finally they heard the calls of their companions, who suggested that they should go down at once. Below Camp 9 there were very steep slabs covered with ice, and it would have been extremely dangerous to try to cross them in the dark. The two, realising the impossibility of descending without grave risk to life, excavated a cave in the snow. There they dug themselves in, preparing to pass the night – a night assuredly terrible at that altitude ...

The events of the actual summit attack were described in Desio's book in a chapter written by Compagnoni, in which his description of the summit eve and the events leading up to Bonatti and Mahdi's bivouac was quite different from Bonatti's account. He glossed over completely his lack of communication with the oxygen bearers and made no mention whatever of why he had placed Camp 9 so much higher than had been arranged the previous night at Camp 8. Nor did he mention why Camp 9 had been set up on the far side of a dangerous traverse which made it impossible for Bonatti and Mahdi to reach. He also wrote that Bonatti's shouts were heard 'at dusk' rather than at 10 pm, although he also said that by then it was dark. Further on in his account he described in graphic detail how he and Lacedelli had carried their heavy, empty oxygen cylinders for another two hours to the summit after the cylinders had become exhausted at 4 pm. This epic story was taken up by the Italian public with enormous enthusiasm and Compagnoni and Lacedelli were feted as national heroes – and indeed almost as supermen, because in those days it was universally accepted that Everest and K2, the two highest mountains in the world, were just too high to be climbed without the use of bottled oxygen.

Compagnoni's version of the assault on the summit
(from *La Conquista del K2*)

On July 30th we left Camp 8 at about 7,740 metres and the two of us climbed up and established the so-called Camp 9 – in reality merely one very light tent. It was a hard nut to crack, because of a wall of ice which took us several attempts, followed by a traverse over a series of very tricky slabs. In addition, above this traverse, a terrifying collection of seracs thrust out for several metres. They looked as if they were likely to collapse on top of us at any moment.

We tried to get up as high as possible under the barrier of rocks which interrupted the last stretch of the east face and represented the last serious unknown.

The weather was calm. Towards 3 pm we emerged onto a small secondary ridge which seemed suitable. We erected the tiny high-altitude tent. We were at about 8,100 metres.

It had been agreed that before evening Abram, Bonatti and one of the Hunzas would join us, bringing us the cylinders of oxygen for the decisive attack. As the sun descended, we never tired of studying the rampart above us, trying to unravel its secrets. Meanwhile we started to become anxious for our companions, who should be arriving with the oxygen. What if they didn't make it? The two of us did not have even one cylinder. 'At the worst we'll do without!' we thought. Unless fate had some diabolical trick in store for us, we were sure to reach the summit.

But lo and behold, towards 4 pm, three tiny black dots appeared on the edge of the plateau. As we were to discover later, they were Bonatti, Abram and the Hunza Mahdi, who were slowly trudging up the steep slope. Would they reach us before it got dark? Unfortunately no. The sun fell below the ridge of K2 and our three comrades were still a long way off. A little later, Abram was to descend to Camp 8, but Bonatti and Mahdi should be able to reach us and spend the night with us.

However, when darkness fell, Bonatti and the Hunza Mahdi had still not reached the beginning of the dangerous traverse of the slabs. And in the dark, to venture onto those cursed rocks would be suicidal. At dusk we heard some shouts. We immediately came out of the tent. Bonatti and Mahdi could not be seen because the sky was already dark. But their voices reached us. Unfortunately our conversation was extremely uncertain because the wind blew our words away. Lacedelli finally believed he understood: he had the impression that the caller was Bonatti, who said that he could manage by himself, but Mahdi wanted to go down.

'Go back!' we shouted to him. 'Go back! Leave the respirators! Don't come any further!' It never crossed our minds that the two of them would consider spending the night at that altitude with neither a tent nor a bivouac sack. But Bonatti's voice was now silent; evidently, we thought, he has already left and gone down. It would be disastrous if he were to attempt to reach us in the dark. On those slabs he would only come to grief.

So we re-entered our tent and prepared to fight against the cold. Then started the long anxious vigil with our thoughts of the great struggle of the morrow. Freezing cold!

Dry throats which were starting to ulcerate! Thirst which could not be relieved! We made ourselves some soup and then, later, some camomile tea – this was the drink which gave us most relief ...

Back in Italy, Bonatti became more and more unhappy with the wall of silence that surrounded him in relation to K2 and the way in which his contribution to the success of the climb was never even discussed. Even the official K2 film, released to celebrate this marvellous achievement of an Italian nation bent on recovering international prestige after the disasters of the war, at first made no mention whatever of his epic bivouac, nor even of his role in carrying up the vital oxygen for the summit bid. Finally he protested, and the film was changed. Two blurred figures were portrayed trudging through a storm while the voice-over of a commentator had just enough time to mention their bivouac after failing to reach Camp 9. The change seemed merely to make matters worse and Bonatti became more and more disillusioned and depressed. His whole career as a climber seemed to have lost its meaning and, although he continued to climb, the joy had gone out of it.

Furthermore, Compagnoni recounted in Desio's official book in great detail how he and Lacedelli were forced to carry their empty oxygen cylinders to the summit after they had run out two hours early. This completely mystified Bonatti, because it could not possibly be true – the arithmetic simply did not add up. However, by far the worst outrage was that he and Mahdi had been abandoned the night before the summit day and left for dead – and no one was willing even to discuss the matter.

At the time Bonatti had no idea why he was being treated this way, or why no one had ever so much as thanked him for the crucial part he had played in the conquest of K2. Neither Compagnoni nor Lacedelli ever made the least apology for what had happened that night. They never made the slightest reference to his forced bivouac, nor did Professor Desio.

Bonatti's depression deepened and finally, in 1955, in a desperate attempt to restore impetus to his life and prove to himself that he was not finished, he set out alone in an attempt on the west face of the Petit Dru, near Chamonix. This vertical, at times overhanging, face had been described by many climbing authorities as 'the very essence of the unclimbable'. For five days Bonatti struggled upwards, overcoming seemingly insuperable difficulties, his only companion a heavy sack full of bivouac gear. When he finally reached the summit he felt re-born. The 'Bonatti Pillar' of the Dru has become one of the essential test pieces for aspiring alpinists and a classic route *par excellence* in the Alps.

Later that same year Bonatti conceived the idea of returning to Pakistan to make an attempt on K2 solo without oxygen, but was unable to obtain any of the financial support required to enable a penniless climber to make such a climb. Bonatti had very carefully worked out the logistics of the attempt and, based on his experience in 1954, thought he had a good chance of succeeding. But everyone he approached simply laughed at the idea: the proposal must have seemed utterly absurd, so far beyond the bounds of common sense that Bonatti was regarded as a crank who was merely trying to find a particularly elaborate way to commit suicide. It was to be another 30 years before Reinhold Messner succeeded in climbing Everest without oxygen.

With the idea of the solo expedition abandoned, Bonatti continued his career as an Alpine guide in Courmayeur, climbing with clients but also between times as an amateur. At Christmas 1956 he made an attempt on the Brenva face of Mont Blanc with a client – Sylvano Gheser. The two men met two others, Jean Vincendon and François Henry, who were attempting the Brenva Spur, at the Fourche hut. The following day the two pairs separated at the Col Moore, but Bonatti and Gheser soon realised that an ascent of the Pear was out of the question as it was too dangerous. They therefore transferred to the classic Brenva Spur route and the two ropes combined forces. Then, close to the top of the spur the weather, until then glorious, suddenly changed, a storm forcing all four men to bivouac. The weather made retreat impossible, so Bonatti led the group through the storm to the top of the climb. Then, continuing as two pairs again, and making trail alternatively, they climbed to the summit of Mont Blanc. Now Bonatti and Gheser were leading as they set off for the Vallot hut. They arrived, Gheser with frostbite to both hands and feet. But Vincendon and Henry did not appear. In fact they had decided (most unwisely) to attempt a direct descent to Chamonix. After spending a freezing night in the Vallot hut, Bonatti and Gheser descended, heading for the Gonella hut via the Dome du Gouter and the Bionassay Ridge. They reached the hut after a difficult day, battling through very deep snow, but could go no further because of Gheser's frostbite. A rescue party reached them two days later. Bonatti was told that Vincendon and Henry had been spotted alive on the Grand Plateau by a helicopter. Later, he was to learn that the rescue helicopter had crashed, the pilot surviving but suffering frostbite before he was rescued: Vincendon and Henry died of exposure.

There was a great deal of unfavourable publicity after this disaster, and in some quarters Bonatti was unjustly blamed for the tragedy, with some suggesting he had abandoned the less experienced pair at the summit even though he had done his best to ensure their safety, and had rescued his own, frost-bitten, companion.

In 1958 Bonatti was a member of the Italian expedition to Gasherbrum IV, the 'almost 8,000er' near K2 in the Karakoram. Bonatti reached the summit with Carlo Mauri. From it could see K2 on the other side of the Godwin Austen Glacier. But although the expedition had been successful, Bonatti became somewhat disillusioned with large expeditions, which seemed to him too politically oriented, and from then on he confined his overseas climbing to much smaller groups. With these he climbed peaks in Peru and Patagonia, while at home he continued to set new standards in the Alps.

Tragedy struck again in 1961 when he was involved in a terrible disaster on Mont Blanc. Bonatti had been drawn to the Central Pillar of Freney because it was the highest Grade VI climb in Europe, leading straight towards the summit of Mont Blanc. He had been waiting for nine years for the right moment to make this climb, and the week after arriving back in Courmayeur from Peru he set out with two friends. The three Italians took the teleferique to the Torino hut and immediately headed for the Fourche hut on the frontier ridge. There they encountered four French climbers bound for the same objective. The two groups joined forces, crossed the Brenva glacier and climbed to the Col de Peuterey, an ice-shelf perched on the ridge between the Brenva and the Freney glacial basins. From the col they started up the Pillar. The climb went smoothly for the seven climbers until they reached a point only 80 metres from the summit of Mont Blanc de Courmayeur. There they were forced to halt when a fierce blizzard made it impossible to go on. The climbers crawled into their bivouac tents, forced to endure a storm which continued without ceasing for the next four days and nights. Then, unable to climb up, the men were compelled to retreat in appalling conditions. Under Bonatti's leadership the team made for the Gamba hut, but three of the Frenchmen and one of his Italian companions died on the way from exhaustion, exposure and dehydration.

The aftermath of the disaster was an absolute public frenzy, which saw Bonatti criticised mercilessly for his role in the tragedy. He was also most unhappy with the behaviour of his fellow guides, who were less than enthusiastic in their rescue attempts. His feelings of disaffection toward official Italian mountaineering circles, which had their roots in the K2 affair, finally came to a head during the tragedy of 1961, and soon after with the publication of his autobiography *Le Mie Montagne* (*My Mountains*). This included his description of the bivouac on K2 (reproduced in Chapter 1), which was clearly at odds with the official account in Desio's book. Although this did not endear him either to Desio or to the Italian Alpine Club, the real cause of the final rift between Bonatti and the Italian Establishment emerged only three years later.

At the end of July 1964, on the tenth anniversary of the first ascent of K2, two articles appeared in the *People's New Sunday Gazette* in successive weeks: in them, Bonatti was accused of treachery on K2 towards all three of his companions – Compagnoni, Lacedelli and Mahdi. The stories had been written by a specialist mountaineering journalist, Nino Giglio, who alleged in the bluntest terms imaginable that Bonatti had deliberately plotted against the summit team, and then actually attempted to get to the summit before them. He also said Bonatti had partially used the oxygen bottles during his bivouac to avoid frost-bite, which had caused Compagnoni and Lacedelli to run out of supplementary gas two hours before they should have next day. Even worse, the articles directly accused him of deserting Mahdi and consequently of being responsible for his severe frostbite. These accusations were a complete bombshell to Bonatti; but at least the cause of the rift between the K2 team and himself was now out in the open. He decided he had endured more than enough and that tolerance could go only so far, and therefore issued a libel writ against Giglio and the newspaper. He sought only to clear his name, specifying that any damages awarded were to be donated to an orphanage.

Giglio's Articles

From the *People's New Sunday Gazette* , 26 July 1964.

After ten years the truth about K2.
How Bonatti tried to precede Compagnoni and Lino Lacedelli.

'… The highest camp was established at an altitude of 8,100 metres amongst the rocks alongside the tricky central couloir which descended from the summit. The two climbers (Compagnoni and Lacedelli) on the afternoon of July 30th were waiting for the respirators – those pieces of equipment which would allow them to climb at 8,000 metres as if they were at 6,000. But the respirators had not arrived. In the late afternoon Compagnoni and Lacedelli had made out three small black dots which were climbing slowly up towards them: one of those dots had then disappeared. At the outset, with the heavy respirators on their shoulders, Abram, Bonatti and the Hunza Madhi had left their Camp at 7,500 metres. These three were excellent climbers who were to play a prominent part in the events which followed … Of the three, Abram, exhausted, had soon returned to Camp 8 – hence the disappearance of one of the three black dots. Bonatti, in his account, even went so far as to admit he had induced Mahdi to follow him by giving him a spark of hope they would reach the summit together. The respirators, in this case, were to be used by those who already had them, that is by Bonatti and Mahdi.

Compagnoni and Lacedelli would have waited in vain. Hence, ten years later, the accusation which Lacedelli and Compagnoni advance against Bonatti of playing a dirty trick on them.

The two conquerors of K2 justify the very understandable aspiration of a strong young climber like Bonatti to climb the second highest peak in the world. 'He didn't need to do that,' they say in short – 'up there, there were sacrifices and fame enough for everyone. Bonatti still says he didn't see us or hear us. We were 100 metres above him as the crow flies, out of our tent among the rocks. We shouted and asked him if he needed our help. He answered, and told us not to worry ourselves about him. We didn't abandon him. It was he who disappeared from our sight when night fell. **Such deceptions are degrading. Because of this slap in the face by Bonatti we risked the loss of K2.'**

At dawn the next morning Compagnoni and Lacedelli left their tent and saw a man going down towards Camp 8. It was the Hunza Madhi, who brandished an ice axe in a way which seemed almost menacing. 'We couldn't see Bonatti' – this was their conclusion – 'even though in his account he wrote later he had gone down after Mahdi'.

Where was Bonatti? Why had he deserted the Hunza who had suffered frostbite to his feet? Had the terrible night in the open demoralised him and the instinct of self-preservation forced him to leave his comrade? …

The accusation thrown at Bonatti in Pakistan was that he had betrayed the duty he had undertaken with the Hunza to help achieve a complete Italian victory. Interrogated later by our ambassador, Bonatti had to tell the truth – a truth, observe Compagnoni and Lacedelli, which has not been included in the account written about the events of K2 by Bonatti. In the witness box Bonatti admitted he had in fact tried to precede Compagnoni and Lacedelli on K2. He even had the respirators with him. These respirators, as is well known, once recovered by Compagnoni and Lacedelli, ran out before the expected time. Had someone already made use of them for at least an hour? Remember, Bonatti and Mahdi had no tent for their bivouac. It was therefore Bonatti, at first unable to resist the cold and the rarefaction of the air at 8,000 metres, who was responsible. The cave scooped out in the snow could in no way have protected them adequately at that altitude.

At first light Bonatti started to descend towards Camp 8. This explains why Compagnoni and Lacedelli did not see him. Mahdi, who was slower, stayed put. The Hunza perhaps was hoping he would be able to join Compagnoni and Lacedelli. Severely injured by frostbite to his feet he too then desisted from this crazy plan. Hence his angry gesture with the ice axe at the two climbers who had directed shouts of greeting at him when they saw him descending!

In the next issue of *People's New Sunday Gazette* on 1 August 1964 was a second article by Nino Giglio.

The tenth anniversary of K2 celebrated at the home of Compagnoni.

The Karachi envoy confirms the Hunza Mahdi attempted an attack on the summit with Bonatti. "… Ata Ullah arrived with his wife and the Pakistani pilot who had carried equipment and provisions for the expedition. The Colonel, if he chose, could write about 'the Italians on K2' in a way which could finally bring justice to the truth and make the controversies which have divided the group of climbers for the past ten years seem ridiculous. 'If I have the time I'll do it' he permitted himself to say.

He confirmed verbally what we had learned only recently: the Hunza Mahdi, victim of the night in the open spent with Bonatti at 8,000 metres between July 30th and 31st 1954, and then hospitalised in Karachi and dragging himself painfully along with orthopaedic boots because of emergency amputations of the toes of both feet – '**over the years in Pakistan this same Mahdi has continued to confirm Bonatti proposed to him they should attack the summit together, without the knowledge of Compagnoni and Lacedelli, who had been chosen for the final assault'.**

The accusation which the two victors of K2 have levelled before against Bonatti has now flared up again. However, Compagnoni does not make a great issue out of all this. He thinks it understandable that Bonatti, a youthful mountaineer and one of the boldest, had also wanted to try for the summit himself. He regrets only a certain lack of loyalty and wishes, ten years after the prestigious victory, there could be a general burying of the hatchet – based, however, on a frank and honest explanation.

Giglio was later to testify he was merely quoting from Compagnoni and Colonel Ata Ullah. One can almost sympathise with him: he obviously saw no reason to doubt a story not merely told to him by Achille Compagnoni, the famous conqueror of K2 and now doyen of Italian mountain guides, but also independently confirmed by Ata Ullah, the universally respected and presumably quite impartial Pakistani liaison officer who had been on K2 in 1953 with the Americans, and in 1954 with the Italians.

Nevertheless, both the journalist and his editor surely should have thought more deeply before rushing into print with these allegations. Giglio should have realised there was something very odd about Compagnoni's statements, which were not only libellous but contrary to common sense. In particular, as he had a background in mountaineering it should have been clear to him that no one but a madman could have contemplated a bivouac in the open at 8,100 metres as preparation for an attempt next day on the second highest mountain in the world. But the articles said Bonatti had done just that.

Bonatti's story of the ascent of K2 makes it abundantly clear the official account of the climb published by Desio and Compagnoni in 1955 was inaccurate to say the least: but this new attack by Giglio, quoting the apparently reliable sources of both Compagnoni and Ata Ullah, went much further than a fanciful tale of oxygen cylinders running out early. It was no longer just a matter of Bonatti's contribution to the conquest of K2 being ignored; he had now been quite specifically accused of disloyalty, treachery and much worse.

The effect of the articles on the Italian public may well be imagined. By the 1960s, the conquest of K2 was a well-established part of Italian folklore. Compagnoni and Lacedelli were firmly entrenched as national heroes – almost single-handed, these two famous mountaineers had restored Italy to its rightful place of honour in the world after the disasters of the Second World War. They were regarded with much the same sort of national pride and reverence accorded the RAF fighter pilots of the Battle of Britain by the British public. As for Bonatti – he was of course a famous climber who had also been part of the K2 team, but he had become notorious in the eyes of the Italian public because of his unfortunate habit of being virtually the sole survivor of mountaineering disasters such as those on Mont Blanc in 1956 and in 1961. On both those occasions it had been intimated that he was guilty of all sorts of nameless crimes against his companions – not that many people would have been able to recall the precise details. It is all too easy to imagine where public sympathy would have lain on the tenth K2 anniversary – Giglio's articles must have found a most receptive audience.

The legal process ground on – slowly, as always: it was to be another two years before the case was heard by the Tribunal of Turin.

But before it was heard Bonatti had decided he was through with extreme climbing. In April 1965 he was to leave for Alaska on the first of a series of adventurous odysseys as a photo-journalist for the Italian magazine *Epoca*. This was to be his profession for the next fifteen years, and during that time he produced a beautiful series of illustrated articles about the wildest areas of the Earth, as well as a series of travel books which were to make him even better known throughout Italy than he had been as a climber. However, even after his extraordinary mountaineering feats of the past he still felt he had one more climbing bridge to cross and, as a postscript to a remarkable career, before leaving for Alaska he made one last solo climb in mid-winter on the north face of the Matterhorn as a celebration of the centenary of Edward Whymper's first ascent. The route set new standards, so far beyond anything any other climber had done it was almost unbelievable, and was described in the press as the summation of the three 'impossibles' – the most direct route, in mid-winter, and alone. He was awarded the Gold Medal for Valour by the President of Italy, an award that gave rise to many furiously angry letters to the press from those who thought mountaineering a useless pastime – the same sort of people who had attacked him after his Christmas on Mont Blanc, and again after the tragedy on the Central Pillar of Freney. But there were also many who defended him just as strongly, his climbing career remaining controversial to the very end.

The Libel Suit

Bonatti's defamation action against Nino Giglio and his newspaper was heard in 1966. The matter to be decided was whether or not he had been libelled by being wrongly accused of trying to get to the summit before Compagnoni and Lacedelli, of using some of their oxygen during the night of his bivouac, and of deserting Mahdi the following morning and so contributing to his frost-bite. Bonatti's attorney put forward his case as follows:

TO THE MOST ILLUSTRIOUS ATTORNEY OF THE REPUBLIC, TURIN

The undersigned, Advocate Roberto Ferrari, of 40 Corso Venezia, Milan, as council for the defence, in order to start proceedings on behalf of Signor Walter Bonatti (Aosta) effectively domiciled for the purpose of the present proceedings at 15 Via Assarotti, Turin, care of Advocate Caesare Amerio, submits that:

1. In the journal *People's New Sunday Gazette* published in Turin on 26 July 1964 appeared an article signed 'Nino Giglio', dated 'Cervinia 25 July 1964' and bearing the title:

'After ten years the truth about K2'
and the subtitle
'How Bonatti tried to precede Compagnoni and Lino Lacedelli'.

(Here followed the text of Giglio's first article – see Chapter 2)

2. In the journal *People's New Sunday Gazette* published in Turin on 1 August 1964 appeared another article signed 'N.G.', that is Nino Giglio, dated Cervinia 31 July 1964, and bearing the title:

'The tenth anniversary of K2 celebrated at the home of Compagnoni'
and the subtitle:
'The Karachi liaison officer confirms that the Hunza Mahdi attempted an attack on the summit with Bonatti'.

(*Here followed the text of Giglio's second article – see Chapter 2*)

3. In the articles cited above, from which the passages which concern the present controversy are quoted, three specific accusations are, in substance, made against Walter Bonatti:

1. To have planned and attempted to reach the summit of K2 with the Hunza Madhi, without the knowledge and against the wishes of Compagnoni and Lacedelli, depriving the latter two of the respiratory apparatus intended for them, and continuing with the same respirators towards the summit rather than leaving them for their two comrades who had been chosen for the attempt.

2. To have abandoned the Hunza Madhi who was suffering from frostbitten feet on the morning of 31 July 1954 at the site of the unforeseen bivouac at 8,000 metres, where he had spent the night with him, and descended to Camp 8 before his companion, who was in difficulties.

3. To have put at risk the outcome of the final assault of their two comrades Compagnoni and Lacedelli, by making use of the respirators destined for them for about an hour, and subtracting in this way the availability of an equivalent amount of oxygen.

We will take these accusations one at a time, examining the elements on which they are based.

1. The accusation of having tried to precede Compagnoni and Lacedelli to the summit of K2.

The account by Professor Ardito Desio, the leader of the expedition, in the volume *La Conquista del K2* (Garzanti), relies completely on the report by Compagnoni and Lacedelli. In the section referring to the events which concern this controversy (we quote only the relevant passages from Chapter VII 'The assault on the summit', they state:

'On July 30th we left Camp 8 at about 7,740 metres. The two of us climbed up and established the so-called Camp 9 … It had been agreed that before evening Abram, Bonatti and one of the Hunzas would join us, bringing us the cylinders of oxygen for the decisive attack … Towards 4 pm, three tiny black dots appeared on the edge of the plateau. As we were to discover later, they were Bonatti, Abram and the Hunza Mahdi who were slowly trudging up the steep slope. Would they reach us before it got dark? Unfortunately no! The sun fell behind the ridge of K2 and our three comrades were still a long away off. A little later, Abram was to descend himself to Camp 8, but Bonatti and Mahdi should be able to reach us and spend the night with us. However, when darkness fell, Bonatti and the Hunza Mahdi had still not reached the beginning of the dangerous traverse of the slabs. And in the dark, to venture onto those cursed rocks would be suicidal. At dusk we heard some shouts. We immediately came out of our tent. Bonatti and Mahdi could not be seen because the sky was already dark. But their voices reached us. Unfortunately our conversation was extremely uncertain because the wind blew our words away. Lacedelli finally believed that he understood: he had the impression that the caller was Bonatti, who said that he could manage by himself, but Mahdi wanted to go down. 'Go back' we shouted to him then. 'Go back! Leave the respirators! Don't come any further!' It never crossed our minds that the two of them would consider spending the night at that altitude with neither a tent nor a bivouac sack. But Bonatti's voice was now silent: evidently, we thought, he has already left and gone down. It would be disastrous if he were to attempt to reach us in the dark. On those slabs he would only succeed in having an accident. So we re-entered the tent and prepared ourselves to fight against the cold …

A hard and interminable night. As soon as the sky in the east got lighter, we burst out of the tent. Delusion! Though the sky above us was clear, below us extended a solid sea of cloud which boded no good. Then we tried to spot the oxygen apparatus which Bonatti and Mahdi should have left on the snowslope beneath us. 'Look, there's someone going down!' Stupified, we saw a figure which receded from us with uncertain gait. Who was it? Bonatti or Mahdi? At that distance one could not tell. We called to him in a loud voice. He stopped and turned, but without answering. Then he again started to stumble down the steep incline. This sight left us bewildered. What had happened? Had Bonatti or Mahdi perhaps come up that morning from Camp 8? No, it was not possible. In that case, we thought, we would have seen him climbing, not descending. All in all, it was an inexplicable mystery. We thought of all possible explanations except the correct one. What had really happened did not seem likely: that two men had resisted the cold and the wind for an entire night without shelter at over 8,000 metres.'

Finally the account refers thus to the arrival of Compagnoni and Lacedelli on their return from the summit to Camp 8:

'We shouted, hoping that our friends would hear us, but the only response was the whistle of the wind. Perhaps they had not heard because between us and the Camp there was a small hump of snow. We went on a little further until we could see the Camp.

One of the tents was lit up. Then moving shadows, cheers, familiar voices. Arms which grasped us, questions, thumps on the back. Abram, Bonatti and Gallotti literally made great leaps of joy. Mahdi and Isakhan, the two Hunzas, also seemed extremely gratified.'

In the light of all the versions of the enterprise and of a critical (or even only cursory) examination of the circumstances, the accusation, levelled at Bonatti in the articles quoted, of planning and trying to reach the summit of K2 all unbeknown to Compagnoni and Lacedelli, helping himself to the respirators reserved for them, appears absurd and contradictory to the most elementary good sense. The matters of fact on which the article writer bases his accusation are as follows:

that Bonatti and Mahdi did not reach Compagnoni and Lacedelli at Camp 9, as planned, but bivouaced in the open on the night between July 30th and 31st 1954

that Bonatti, questioned by the Italian ambassador to Pakistan, had confessed that he had tried to get to the summit before Compagnoni and Lacedelli

that Bonatti wrote in his book that he had proposed to Mahdi the possibility of taking part in the final assault in order to induce Mahdi to help him carry the respirators up to Camp 9.

The columnist deduces inevitably from these facts the conclusion that Bonatti planned and then attempted to get to the summit before Compagnoni and Lacedelli, but had to desist because he was exhausted by the night passed in the open.

It must be said first of all that the supposed confession of Bonatti to the Italian ambassador in Pakistan is a flight of fancy by the journalist. Bonatti denies most absolutely that he has ever declared to anyone that he had tried to precede Compagnoni and

Lacedelli to the summit, and furthermore that anything else was done unbeknown to them.

As to the 'admission' of Bonatti in his book that he had proposed to Mahdi the possibility of participating in the final assault, it suffices to read the complete text of Bonatti's narrative (we submit to the court the volume *Le Mie Montagne*) to realise that he, together with Gallotti and Abram, used that argument only to give Mahdi a motive to carry the respirators up to Compagnoni and Lacedelli. This was done precisely as had been planned by consensus with Compagnoni and Lacedelli, with whom he and Mahdi were to have passed the night in the small tent at Camp 9. Any other interpretation of Bonatti's account is completely unjustified.

Finally, as to the fact that Bonatti and Mahdi did not reach Camp 9, but spent the night in the open, it is enough to consider a few very simple facts to demonstrate that not even the most vivid fantasy could in good faith have interpreted this fact as proof of the supposed plot. In fact:

a) The alleged plan to make the final assault on the peak of K2 unbeknown to Compagnoni and Lacedelli would have had to contemplate a bivouac in the open at 8,000 metres (Bonatti and Mahdi had neither any bivouac equipment whatever nor any provisions). Everyone in the expedition considered such a bivouac impossible.

In all the accounts the greatest surprise is expressed that Bonatti and Mahdi survived the ordeal. Mahdi in fact suffered very severe and incurable frostbite which cost him the amputation of all his toes. Compagnoni and Lacedelli say in the book *Uomini sul K2* (Veronelli) [Author's note – translated as *Men on K2*] on page 57, 'According to all the laws which govern the life of the human body Bonatti and Mahdi ought to have frozen to death'.

It is therefore absurd to think that Bonatti, an expert mountaineer, could have intended a bivouac in the open at 8,000 metres without equipment and without food, a bivouac in which mere survival would be uncertain, as a vigil in preparation for the final assault on the summit of K2.

b) The insinuation that Bonatti and Mahdi had deliberately avoided reaching Compagnoni and Lacedelli's tent is contradicted in the same account of these latter two, who refer to having followed the last part of the ascent of the two climbers laden with the oxygen cylinders and to having seen that at sunset they were still a long way off, so that at nightfall they still had not reached the start of the dangerous traverse of the slabs. They conclude 'and in the dark, to venture onto those cursed rocks would be suicidal' and further on 'it would be disastrous if he were to attempt to reach us in the dark. On those slabs he would only come to grief'. Thus Compagnoni and Lacedelli are the first to recognise that, because night had fallen, Bonatti and Mahdi would not have been able to reach them in the tent from where they were.

c) The insinuation that Bonatti and Mahdi would have tried to prepare themselves for the final assault on the summit by avoiding joining Compagnoni and Lacedelli is also contradicted by the unquestionable fact that, having reached the start of the dangerous traverse of the slabs, Bonatti and Mahdi repeatedly called Compagnoni and Lacedelli until they received an answer. It is clear that if they had planned to attempt the final assault unbeknown to and against the wishes of the two occupants of Camp 9, Bonatti and Mahdi would best have avoided making themselves heard.

d) Lastly, Bonatti and Mahdi would not in any case have been able to plan an ascent to the summit of K2 helping themselves to the oxygen cylinders without the knowledge of Compagnoni and Lacedelli, because the oxygen masks with their regulators, essential for the use of the respirators, were in the possession of Compagnoni and Lacedelli. Consequently, Bonatti and Mahdi, who had none, would not have been able to help themselves to oxygen from the cylinders even had they wished to do so.

These four obvious and elementary reasons are enough to demonstrate how gratuitous, preposterous and unsustainable is the accusation levelled at Bonatti that he had cultivated and tried to implement a plan to substitute himself by fraud for Compagnoni and Lacedelli.

2. The accusation of having abandoned the Hunza Mahdi on the morning of July 31st 1954, when he was in difficulties because of frostbite.

This accusation is founded on the impression attributed to Compagnoni and Lacedelli that they had seen Bonatti descending ahead of Mahdi.

In the official account of Compagnoni and Lacedelli just quoted, it states: 'Stupified, we saw a figure which receded from us with uncertain gait. Who was it? Bonatti or Mahdi? At that distance one could not tell.' Compagnoni, in his book already cited, says: 'And next morning, emerging from the tent for the final assault, Lacedelli and I saw a man moving in the snow. At first we thought he was climbing, that he was coming to bring us the respirators, but then we suddenly realised that he was going down. We shouted, and he responded by waving his ice axe in salute. We were later to know that it was Mahdi, who was returning to Camp 8. Bonatti must already have left.'

It is therefore unquestionable that neither Compagnoni nor Lacedelli recognised the men whom they saw descending. Compagnoni asserts that he realised later that it was Mahdi, and he surmised that Bonatti had already gone down.

Since neither Compagnoni nor Lacedelli could say, through having recognised him, who it was that they saw descending, the direct testimony of those waiting at Camp 8 is decisive on this point.

Engineer Gallotti, who with Erich Abram and the Hunza Isakhan was awaiting the return of the four in the summit team in the tent at Camp 8, states in his diary: 'Saturday 31st. A day of drama from the start: a little before 7 we were wakened by the tent flaps being thrown back. It was Mahdi who faced us. He was distracted, and showed us his hands and feet which were martyred by the cold. His feet in particular had toes which were blackened and distorted in a most distressing way. His explanations, given in a laboured voice, were not at all clear and left us in a state of profound apprehension. Erich and I looked at each other without the courage to make any guesses. Not much later, however, Walter arrived …'

3. The accusation of having used, for about an hour, the respirators intended for Compagnoni and Lacedelli, putting the result of the final assault at risk.

The journalist states that the oxygen in the cylinders carried by Bonatti and Mahdi gave out earlier than expected, and from this arises immediately the question, clearly hinted at, that someone had already made use of them. From the tone of the article, this someone could be no one else except Bonatti and Madhi.

But it follows from the account of Compagnoni and Lacedelli already quoted that they started to use the respirators at about a quarter past six. 'Up then! It was a quarter past six. With the oxygen entering our lungs, breathing was easier'. (*La Conquista del K2*, by Ardito Desio, page 180).

It is stated later in the same account that they arrived on the summit at six in the evening – that is, eleven and three quarter hours later.

The cylinders ran out about four in the afternoon (*Men on K2*, Veronelli, page 63). Therefore they lasted for ten hours.

These bottles were predicted to last, at maximum output, for 10–12 hours. Therefore they did not run out earlier than they should have done.

Furthermore, as has been stated above, Bonatti and Mahdi would not have been able to make use of them because they had no masks and regulators.

From this summary examination one concludes that not only is there not one single fact to confirm what the journalist Nino Giglio has written, but that his affirmations cannot withstand even the most elementary criticism and are refuted by the most ordinary common sense.

In this, one recognises not only the existence of defamation but also the specific intent to defame. In fact, the columnist, merely referring any accusers to the affirmations of Compagnoni, Lacedelli and Colonel Ata Ullah, sets out these statements without subjecting them to any criticism whatever and without showing the least personal reservation. He has in fact called his article **'After ten years the truth about K2'** so affirming his personal conviction that the revelations contained in the articles constitute not merely one version, but the truth.

The subtitle also, in absolutely affirmative vein, enunciates **'How Bonatti tried to precede Compagnoni and Lacedelli'** without resorting to the least appearance of debate, which any objective or even prudent journalist should have adopted.

The whole text of the article is contrived to give the precise conviction to the public that the accusations against Bonatti are not a one-sided and disputable version but are the revelation of a long concealed truth, documented by a confession and by eye-witnesses.

The columnist is a specialist in the presentation of mountaineering topics and is aware (or anyway dealing with such a delicate topic should have been aware) of the accounts published about this exploit. He had all the elements necessary to submit the accusations which were made to the criticism which we have set out and perceive that they are not only unfounded but absurd. Not to have done so is proof that the precise wish to defame Bonatti and to diminish his stature as a mountaineer and as a man has prevailed over the duty of objectivity.

With all this as premise, Walter Bonatti with the present action, puts forward this formal ...

COMPLAINT

Against Signor Nino Giglio of Turin and the responsible editor of the *People's New Sunday Gazette*, Signor Giorgio Vecchiato of 2 Corso Valdocco, Turin, for the crime of defamation, by publishing all this in the guise of established facts possessing the widest faculty of proof.

The complainant specifically reserves and establishes himself as plaintiff to obtain just apportionment of the onus of responsibility and also financial compensation for moral and material damage, which will be donated to the Orphanage of Mamma Isa at Volta Mantovane.

Designated as witnesses are:
Engineer Pino Gallotti
Signor Erich Abram

The following documents are produced:
1) *People's Gazette*, 117th year, No 196, 26 July 1964.
2) *People's Gazette*, 117th year, No 202, 1 August 1964.
3) *The Conquest of K2* by Prof Ardito Desio, Garzanti, 1954.
4) *On the Heights* by Walter Bonatti, Zanichelli, 1961.

with all due obsequies

Roberto Ferrari, Turin, 9 October 1964.

In the course of the trial, the court requested a deposition from Mahdi in Pakistan, which was taken by the District Magistrate in Gilgit. The document turned out to be rather strange, to say the least, and neither Bonatti, nor his attorney, nor the Turin Court could make any sense of what seemed for the most part to be nonsense. Bonatti later published the report verbatim in his book *Processo sul K2* (Trial on K2) Massimo Baldini Editore 1985 and said: *'in any event, I wish to reproduce Mahdi's deposition here, complete, with all its positives and negatives, so readers can form their own opinions. I have added some personal comments in brackets.'*

Tribunal of Turin

Deposition by the Hunza Mahdi, son of Ghulan Ali, Casta Mughul, aged about 50 years, resident in Hassan Abad, Hunza (Gilgit Agency) who makes this solemn affirmation:

Question 1: What do you know about the final ascent of K2 as far as Compagnoni, Lacedelli and Bonatti are concerned?

Answer: I took service as a high altitude porter to the Italian expedition to K2 of 1954, led by Professor Desio. **After establishing the last camp (that is Camp 8), Sahib Compagnoni decided to attempt the ascent of the summit and he asked me to accompany him.** *(This is nonsense. When Mahdi arrived at Camp 8 with me, Compagnoni and Lacedelli had already left to set up Camp 9. WB)*

Later he left me and took Lacedelli with him on the summit attempt. Then Sahib E Abram asked Sahib Bonatti and myself to follow them with the respirators and we did so. **After climbing for about 400 feet (130 metres) Sahib Bonatti decided to precede the Sahibs Compagnoni and Lacedelli and asked me to follow him towards the summit.** *(Not true. WB)* **He also decided to use the respirators destined for**

Compagnoni and Lacedelli if the need arose. *(Not true, nor in any way could it be true, since the only two masks with oxygen regulators which arrived at the high camps were in the possession of Compagnoni and Lacedelli. It would have been impossible to use the cylinders in any other way. WB)* I accepted his proposal and **he started the climb following a different route from that taken by the Sahibs Compagnoni and Lacedelli.** *(Not true. WB)* **By late evening we found we had climbed about 200 metres more than Compagnoni and Lacedelli had been able to manage.** *(Absurd. WB)* They had a tent with them and we did not. Besides, they were equipped for sleeping while we had nothing. Consequently we had to spend the night without a tent, sleeping bags, and all the other equipment necessary. Unfortunately my feet became frozen and there was no other alternative than descending to the camp lower down.

In the early morning **we** started the descent and **we reached …** *(clarification – Mahdi should have said 'I' started the descent and 'I' reached ... WB)* **… Camp 8 about 5.30 am, where also were Sahib Abram and Isakhan, the high altitude porter.** *(Not true. In fact, one reads in the diary of Gallotti: 'A little before 7 am we were awakened by the tent flaps being thrown open. It was Mahdi' WB)* **We saw Compagnoni and Lacedelli leave their tent and start the climb towards the summit.** *(Abram and Gallotti, who were also at Camp 8, did not see Compagnoni and Lacedelli leave their tent, nor could they have because it was physically impossible to do so. Neither did I see them, despite my being in a place which offered the maximum field of vision, where I stayed until 7 am. WB)* Finally **we saw Compagnoni reach the peak and Lacedelli about half an hour later.** *(Not true. Lacedelli and Compagnoni arrived on the summit almost simultaneously. The final slope of K2 was the only part of the mountain visible from Camp 8. All of us could follow their arrival at 6 pm. WB)* They took some summit photos and then turned back towards Camp 8. At one place **they**

encountered some difficulties and they asked me to help them *(Not true. WB)* but Sahib Abram told them my feet were frozen and it was impossible for me to help. In fact they got to Camp 8 at about 11 pm one after the other. **Sahib Compagnoni arrived a little in front and Sahib Lacedelli after about another fifteen minutes.** *(Not true. WB)* I noticed then they were not on speaking terms with each other when both of them were talking to Bonatti and me. I did not notice Compagnoni and Lacedelli were on bad terms with Bonatti. The next day we all went down to base camp.

Question 2: Is it true Bonatti tried to precede the others and asked you to follow him towards the summit, and to use the respirators which were intended for Compagnoni and Lacedelli?

Answer: Yes! He did so with the statement that if we were to reach the summit before Compagnoni and Lacedelli, he would bring honour to his country, Italy, and I to mine, Pakistan. *(Not true. But in what language did I say all this? Anyhow, concerning the respirators, see my note in answer number 1: the rest is pure fantasy. WB)*

Question 3: What use did Bonatti make of the aforesaid respirators?

Answer: We made no use of them because there was no need to use them.

Question 4: Is it true Bonatti told you the respirators should be used by those who already had them in their possession – that is, by the Hunza Madhi and Bonatti?

Answer: Since I do not understand Italian, I am unable to say exactly if he said precisely that to me. **However it was his**

intention to use them if necessary. *(Not true. See again my third note in answer number 1. Apart from that, how could Mahdi know my intentions, or even only interpret them, since we were speaking two very different languages? WB)*

Question 5: What language was Bonatti speaking and how did the two of you communicate?

Answer: Bonatti spoke only Italian and I Urdu, so we could not understand each other; but we managed to express ourselves with signs and gestures.

Question 6: Is it true that on the morning of 31 July 1954 you were abandoned by Bonatti at the 8,000-metre bivouac even though you had frost-bitten feet?

Answer: No, on the contrary, he helped me to go down towards Camp 8.

Question 7: Going back to Camp 8 that morning, when you saw Compagnoni and Lacedelli, did you wave an ice-axe at them?

Answer: No, at that time it was dark and the question of waving the ice-axe on seeing them did not arise. *(In answer to number 1 Mahdi had already affirmed he had seen Compagnoni and Lacedelli leave their tent, now in contrast he refutes this(?). Anyway, in homage to the truth, I must point out it was not dark at that hour but broad daylight. However, Mahdi nevertheless could not see anything because there was nothing to see: Lacedelli and Compagnoni had still not moved from their tent. WB)*

Question 8: What significance did that gesture have? Did you intend to salute the two climbers, or to express your dismay you had been abandoned by Bonatti?

Answer: Since I didn't wave the ice-axe the question does not apply.

Question 9: What was your state of health immediately after the climb?

Answer: My feet didn't feel too bad until Base Camp, where Dr Pagani started to treat me. After the medications, I was in intolerable pain.

Question 10: Is it true that in the following years you declared publicly Bonatti had asked you to precede Compagnoni and Lacedelli, who had been chosen for the final ascent.

Answer: No.

Re-read and certified accurate.

Signed by the Hunza Mahdi.

During the hearing, the logic of Roberto Ferrari's submission proved irrefutable. The ambassador's report of 1954 was produced; Gallotti, Abram and Compagnoni were called to give evidence. Mahdi's evidence was considered, but judged to be incomprehensible. In the end, Bonatti was completely exonerated by the Tribunal – the charges made by Giglio at Compagnoni's instigation were found to be false. The journalist and his newspaper were ordered to pay damages, which were donated to an orphanage.

Bonatti assumed the matter was now closed, but this proved to be very far from the case. The Tribunal had been asked only to decide whether Bonatti had been libelled or not: the judgement was not concerned with the origin of the accusations, but only with whether they were true. And the court decided they were untrue, but no more than that. Apart from paying damages, the

People's New Sunday Gazette was ordered to print a retraction, and in 1967 this finally appeared. The new article written by Nino Giglio repeated in large measure exactly what had been said in the Ambassador's report of 1954, and concluded with this summary:

> The most important conclusions of Minister d'Acunzo's inquiry and of the more recent investigations definitively rule out the suggestion the Hunza Mahdi was in any way duped by the Italians: or that Bonatti had tried or even only planned to get to the summit ahead of Compagnoni and Lacedelli; and they have confirmed Bonatti gave Mahdi all possible help during and after the terrible night in the open. (Nino Giglio)

One might have expected this would be the end of the matter, but Bonatti was to find himself as unpopular as ever with the mountaineering establishment, which behaved as if the libel action had never happened. One can only wonder how many of those who had read Giglio's original articles (and no doubt nodded wisely over them) even knew there had been a court case. It is a commonplace that if mud is thrown, it tends to stick, and events over the next three decades were to show this was certainly so in this case.

The success of Bonatti's libel action made not the slightest difference to the establishment. On 28 September 1969, the Italian Alpine Club Central Committee for Publications sent Bonatti a letter to tell him it was preparing an anthology, *Italian Alpinism of the World*, which was to comprise '800 pages'. This book was to bring together the principal extra-European exploits of Italian mountaineers through the personal accounts of the climbers themselves. Bonatti was asked to supply three passages contained in *Le Mie Montagne* relating to his climbs in Peru, in Patagonia and on Gasherbrum IV, that is, all his extra-European alpine climbs with the exception of K2. He agreed, but with one proviso, that together with these three accounts they must also publish the one which concerned K2 *in its entirety and to the letter*, because not to include that particular chapter would be quite unjustifiable. Those responsible for the anthology responded (in December 1969): 'The book has already been set up and cannot support any alteration in the number of pages' – and therefore they told him they could not include more than part of the K2 chapter, which had to be reduced to what the anthology could receive. Bonatti would not accept this, and wrote to the President of CAI Publications – 'I understand the technical problems which the compilation of the work makes inevitable, but I also know that what I ask is not basically impracticable. I am therefore sure that your Excellency will be able to provide the anthology with the space and balance needed to make room for my chapter on K2 in its entirety'. The reply was: 'We had intended to publish as much as we could of your original story of K2, in *Italian Alpinism of the World*. We are however constrained to abandon this intention and to substitute a simple chronicle compiled by us. Naturally, we will explain the reason for this to the readers'.

The first volume of the anthology was finally published three years later, in October 1972. It stated, 'Bivouac at 8,000 metres by Walter Bonatti, K2 – The High Camps. We have been unable to include the chosen text indicated above, which was already prepared and set out, because of the author's lack of assent to its publication'. With this underhand trick the Italian Alpine Club duly launched 'this monumental work' about mountaineers. It consisted of two volumes and a total of 1,300 pages of text (compared to the 800 pages Bonatti was originally told). It was put forward as 'the most complete work which has ever been published … a milestone in the history and documentation of extra-European Italian mountaineering from its origins until the present'. The CAI had deliberately silenced Bonatti's account of the events on K2 in its important official monograph.

For the next decade, Bonatti roamed the world as a photo-journalist, producing a formidable series of books about his

The IGM map of K2 (scale 1:12,500), which incorrectly locates the site of the Bonatti/Mahdi bivouac. Bonatti has corrected the bivouac site and indicated the route he and Mahdi followed. The corrections are consistent with the direction of the light beam from Camp 9 on the evening of the bivouac, as indicated in the photograph opposite.

travels as well as regular articles for *Epoca*, but at the end of the 1970s his association with the magazine ended and he came back to live in Italy for much of the time. He continued to write books, but had more time for contemplation. In 1981 he became increasingly frustrated at symptomatic inaccuracies in all manner of publications relating to the site of his bivouac on K2, which had been at about 8,100 metres but was persistently referred to as being lower down the mountain at about 7,990 metres (as Compagnoni's 'official' version has it).

In particular he was incensed that the Military Geographic Institute of Florence still published contour maps showing the completely inaccurate location. So he wrote the following letter to the Institute (with a copy for the Italian Alpine Club, Central Section) in an attempt to clarify the matter:

Dear Sirs,
I should have written this letter 27 years ago, the day after the publication of the official book of the conquest of K2 by Ardito Desio. I did not do so both because I was optimistic and also because a few years later my autobiography was to be published. In it I clarified facts and events as they

appeared to me, including those which relate to the subject of this letter.

A later corollary was a court case about the events on K2 instigated by myself because of a grave defamation against my character: this lawsuit confirmed and authenticated the contents of my book and its chapter 'K2, the High Camps' which was tabled in court. After that, I believed that things had been settled once and for all. But the emergence of a new generation of Italian climbers has resulted in new exploits which, when they appear in books, repeat the inaccuracies set down in official books. In particular these official sources give inaccurate details on the location and altitude of my bivouac on K2 the night before the conquest. They draw (with subsequent inaccuracy) on the inexact 'official accounts'. In particular those documents which carry the stamp of officialdom give, amongst other things, the location and altitude of my bivouac on K2 the night before the conquest.

Among these authoritative sources of the history of K2 is regrettably the Military Geographic Institute (IGM), to which I now turn my attention. I presume that in compiling the cartographic documents relating to that enterprise, the IGM trusted, in good faith, the technical expert Captain Lombardi and Professor Desio. However, as is well known, neither of them was a direct witness of events near the summit of K2. These two spokesmen had to rely on what was reported by others, amongst whom, strangely and unjustly, I did not figure. I was never interviewed by any reporter genuinely intent on recording positions and altitudes relating to the final phase of the conquest of K2.

From the contour lines and from the particulars and the positions of the camps marked on your map (scale 1:12,500) it follows that I spent the night at an altitude of 7990 metres, and that Camp 9 was in the great gully – the feature which has today come to be known as the 'Bottleneck' at an altitude of 8,060 metres (since 'Camp 9' appears on the chart immediately below the thick 8,100 metre contour line). On the enclosed photograph, which shows the same area, I have marked the actual position of my bivouac with a small red circle. To substantiate this there are four other photographs, also enclosed: they portray the real route in this zone of K2: in them can also be seen the big rock where, 20 metres higher up, I spent my night in the open with the Hunza Mahdi. I also include some separate photocopies of the pages of my book *Le Mie Montagne* in which emerge other details relating to the position of my bivouac during that unforeseen adventure.

By analysing these documents I am sure that your experts will be able to clarify the position and actual altitude, not only of my bivouac but also of Camp 9, which I was unable to discover during my movements. The position of this camp, deduced by myself from the torch which appeared late in the evening, was in the direction and at the angle of inclination I have indicated in green on one of the enclosed photographs. I can however certify that it was not in the line of sight of anyone climbing the steep gully which leads to the so-called 'Bottleneck'. This is so at least up to the altitude I reached, which I have good reason to believe was a little more than 8,100 metres. The historic fact to which these inaccuracies refer is important, and the self-styled 'official accounts' continue to do me an injustice. It therefore seems to me just and fair that you should correct your plate, since yours is the sole publication now in print and available to the public.

Yours faithfully,

Walter Bonatti.

Enclosed   4 photocopied pages
6 photographs

Perhaps unsurprisingly, there was never the slightest sign of any response, neither from the Military Institute nor the Italian Alpine Club.

Processo al K2

At the end of July 1984, as part of the celebrations for the 30th anniversary of K2, Compagnoni and Lacedelli were interviewed on a television talk-show, and Bonatti was exasperated beyond endurance by their repetition of the same old story of the oxygen running out at 8,400 metres, 200 metres below the summit. They also continued to insist that they had left Camp 9 at about 4 am, whereas Bonatti knew perfectly well that there had been no sign of them at 6.30, when he had started his descent to Camp 8. It was only half an hour later that he had heard their shouts from above and even then they were nowhere near the oxygen bottles, which he could see quite clearly. There was no longer any mention of his alleged use of the oxygen during the bivouac, which had been revealed as nonsense during the libel case in 1966, but what he had come to think of as the 'mother lie' of the ascent was still blithely accepted by the TV interviewer – and no doubt the national audience.

This exchange occupied the central seven minutes of the TV programme 'Special TGI' broadcast from Milan on 30 July 1984 at 10.30 pm.

Commentator – Alberto La Volpe
Guests – Ardito Desio, Achille Compagnoni, Lino Lacedelli, Francesco Santon, Gianfranco Balbo (President of the Bormio Section of the CAI), Eugenio Marcucci (journalist – *Radio News*).

La Volpe: Listen Compagnoni, and Lacedelli, you must tell us – what about this vigil of yours? In fact, we are going on air at the exact time that corresponds to that wonderful evening before the

climb. They were in a tiny little tent which was – think about it
– only 70 centimetres high, where they couldn't even stretch
themselves out but had to lie on their sides. So – what did you
eat that evening? What did you do all night? Did you sleep?

Compagnoni: No, it was impossible to sleep. It was such a
business to cope with being in this little tent; so much so that …

La Volpe: The temperature?

Compagnoni: Oh, the temperature was about 40 degrees, that
night.

Lacedelli: Below zero.

La Volpe: Forty degrees below zero.

Compagnoni: Yes.

La Volpe: The weather?

Compagnoni: The weather wasn't too …

Lacedelli: It wasn't too good – all overcast.

La Volpe: Was it misty?

Lacedelli: The mist had started to come up by then.

La Volpe: Is it very dangerous – mist?

Compagnoni: At that height, yes.

La Volpe: So if the mist had stayed like that, you wouldn't have
been able to climb?

Compagnoni: Well it would have been difficult, very difficult.

La Volpe: In that case you would have turned back?

Compagnoni: Yes.

La Volpe. But the cloud was coming and going?

Compagnoni: The cloud hadn't all gone in the morning, but it
was as we (muffled words follow) … we'd noticed before, that
during the climb it had always been a bit overcast, and we had
the luck to get to the summit just in a few minutes …

La Volpe: But we're talking about the night.

Compagnoni: Oh, the night – it was long and hard – it seemed as
if day would never come.

La Volpe: I mean – could you talk?

Compagnoni: Well, only a bit because at that height you haven't
– you haven't enough breath to talk; and when we had to turn

ourselves around in the tent because we couldn't be all the time on our sides, we'd touch each other's backs, and that was the signal that we had to start our – our change – our changing of position.

Lacedelli: We had to help each other to turn because the place was so narrow.

La Volpe: **And when did you suddenly decide to leave the tent and attempt the climb?**

Compagnoni: In the morning, in the morning …

La Volpe: Listen, did you have a watch? Or is this just a rough estimate?

Compagnoni: An estimate – oh no – a watch – on the contrary – I tell you that this is the watch that was on the summit of K2.

Lacedelli: We had a watch, up … (a few muffled words follow).

La Volpe: So this, this is the wa … ?

Compagnoni: Yes, yes.

La Volpe: As well as an ice-axe, this is the watch?

Compagnoni: **Yes. It was. It would have been four in the morning, maybe even earlier.**

La Volpe: And which one of you said: 'Right, let's go'?

Compagnoni: Oh no, both of us together. That decision was taken – taken together.

La Volpe: **So then you left the tent at about four in the morning?**

Compagnoni: **Well, four, half past four.**

Lacedelli: **About four, half past four.** But the big difficulty was to get out of the tent, first of all because it was so small, and then the problem was to put on our crampons. Now in turn (some muffled words follow) we had to help each other, first one, then in turn he helped the other.

La Volpe: How long did it take you to … ?

Lacedelli: To put them on? My hands started to freeze and stick to them.

La Volpe: You had frost-bitten hands as well?

Lacedelli: Yes, nine of my fingers froze.

La Volpe: And Compagnoni too?

Lacedelli: And Compagnoni too …

La Volpe: Was this on the summit?

Compagnoni: Yes, on the summit.

La Volpe: You lost practically … ?

Compagnoni: Two and a bit fingers, and also a little bit of this one.

La Volpe: This happened more than anything else through taking photographs. Have a look at this, cameraman …

Compagnoni: It was, it would have been because on the summit, really even the position of orientation was the position to the north; indeed it was very cold, let us say we had a moment of – when it was necessary …

La Volpe: **Well, at four you decided to get going, practically?**

Compagnoni: **Yes.**

La Volpe: So, at what time did you get up to the peak?

Lacedelli: At six, about six in the evening.

La Volpe: Six in the evening. To go how many metres?

Compagnoni: Six hundred.

La Volpe: Six hundred metres?

Desio: Difference in elevation!

La Volpe: Difference in elevation. **So you took about fourteen hours?**

Lacedelli: **Yes,** because we had to cross some very dangerous slabs, because the previous evening, when we had reached Camp 9, we knew that, after us, some other climbers should arrive carrying the oxygen, and we were worried that we had seen no one. Then suddenly we saw three dots in the distance; we knew that they must be coming but we didn't know who they were … Oh, I got worried every so often and I went out, Compagnoni went out to see if they were coming, to see if he could see them. Finally and suddenly, when it was already dark, we heard a voice shouting: 'Lino! Lino! Answer me!' It seemed to me that I heard this but … what with the atmosphere, the distance, I went out – we went out with a torch. 'Give me a light! Give me a light!' But it was rather a long way off …

La Volpe: Now this is the problem, which posed itself then and also arose more recently, with Bonatti – and there he was. But there were other men – well, there they were too! To be precise, Professor Desio, from what we have read, had in practice authorised them, you see, to…

Desio: It was Compagnoni who had the responsibility for directing the final assault.

La Volpe: So.

Desio: And also the choice of the men.

La Volpe: Sure. Well, what happened then? So, Bonatti was climbing from the other side …

Marcucci: Compagnoni chose Lacedelli and they climbed together to set up Camp 9, from which they were to leave for the summit. The others had to climb from Camp 8 at about 7,700 metres to carry the cylinders of oxygen …

La Volpe: Why didn't you stay together?

Lacedelli: Well, the problem was a bit … a bit tricky because … on the 28th of July, at Camp 7 from where we started, Compagnoni was roped to Rey, and I was roped up with Abram, and we had to carry up the oxygen for the two who were to be the summit pair. Suddenly, after a bit, Rey couldn't continue, and with great sorrow we saw him sit down on the ground, put his head on the snow, and almost cry with frustration that he couldn't go on. Then … he said, tie on with me, up we go. Well … we all went up – all three of us; Abram said, 'I've had it, you go'. So we left the pack saddles of cylinders on the snow and I tied on with Compagnoni. And so we went on and set up Camp 8. Consequently, those few who were left were all limping, because Gallotti too was in a very bad way – he was walking two or three steps, two or three paces on his knees, really! He had made a wonderful effort to carry some mattresses and other things to Camp 8, and without this effort of his I don't know what sort of night we would have had at Camp 8. But the cylinders were left behind on the track. Then, on the 29th, we went on up and we had had a very tough day. We had covered only 350 metres and suddenly it was late afternoon we were only just up on the Abruzzi spur, on terrain ... let us say less challenging, however ... it was too late to go on and establish Camp 9. So we returned to Camp 8 where we found [*They found nothing whatever, because when Gallotti and I reached Camp 8, Compagnoni and Lacedelli were shut up in their tent resting. WB*] ... there was Bonatti, there was, there was...Gallotti and Abram [*Abram was not at Camp 8 but at Camp 7. WB*] and there we decided that next day they ... at first we had said 'Let's go and pick up the cylinders!' 'No, no,' we thought, 'let's go up and try again!' All right! Then in the morning we left, determined to get up as high as possible, because seeing the condition our comrades were in, we were afraid that our strength would suddenly go like theirs had, since we were stretched to the limit. Also, we thought that as they had already given everything they had, we would also try to give it our best shot, and who knows where we would get to?

La Volpe: So that's how things went?

Lacedelli: That's how it was!

La Volpe: Good. Now, following this sequential story of ours, as far as things on K2 were concerned, let's go back. Let's go to 1929. Well, let us see a most interesting short film which dates back to that era ... (He drops the subject).

Compagnoni was interviewed a little later by the press, and was reported in the weekly magazine *Oggi* (*Today*) on 8 August 1984 as saying: 'Bonatti was the youngest of the group. The only thing that counts is what he testified in Pakistan in the official report – and that is still on file. In that report he didn't accuse anybody. I could go into details. But that would be very unpleasant ...'.

Compagnoni seems to be hinting here that Bonatti made some sort of damaging admission during the Ambassador's enquiry in Pakistan, but in fact there was no controversial matter raised at any time during the hearing, as can readily be seen from the full report of that enquiry, included here in Appendix 1.

The events of this thirtieth anniversary made it clear to Bonatti that his successful court action in 1966 had changed nothing and that he must write a book about the whole affair, and he did so. *Processo al K2* (*Trial on K2*) was published the following year. In this book Bonatti amplified the account of *K2 the High Camps* he had already produced in *Le Mie Montagne* and made it clear that the story of the oxygen running out two hours below the summit was absolutely impossible to believe.

Bonatti's Analysis in *Processo al K2* (*Trial on K2*)

The Conquest of K2 by Ardito Desio, and *Men on K2* by Achille Compagnoni were published in 1955 and 1958, respectively. In them, my story of 30 July 1954 was dismissed in an off-hand, peremptory manner.

Compagnoni's account of the summit day in his book *Men on K2* was as follows:

Dawn on the great day (July 31st 1954) found us on our feet ... In the still uncertain light we made out below us a figure which seemed to be approaching ... We decided to try without respirators. We threw ourselves down on the ground to strap on our crampons ... We started to move, traversing to the right, retracing backwards the route of the evening before to get ourselves back on to the direct line of ascent which passed, without alternative, up the huge ice gully ... After twenty steps, perhaps rather more than fewer, we realised that without oxygen we would not be able to go on: our lungs heaved uselessly like the gills of a fish out of water; our heads buzzed, our legs buckled ... A snowslide started under our feet ... Head down I kept descending until finally, in a swirl of snow, I found myself standing next to the respirators ... Just an hour had passed since we had set out ... We regained our breath and took a quick inventory ... We decided to leave the rucksacks where the respirators had been. We tried to load the cylinders and the corresponding packsaddles on our shoulders, after we had verified they were working. The one which I took contained 78 atmospheres, the one Lacedelli took, 83 ... Up then! It was about a quarter past six. We climbed slowly towards the rock barrier. The effect of the oxygen was an advantage much greater than the disadvantage of the 18 kilograms ... It took us three hours to reach a point below the great ice gully, which represented the key to overcoming the wall of rock and ice, from the crest of which rose the terminal dome. We were at about the same altitude reached the previous evening ...

And again, further on in the account:

Now victory seemed assured, the summit was near at hand. It was about 4 pm, and we still had a few hours of light. Suddenly I experienced an anguished sensation of suffocation ... The oxygen was finished. Ten minutes later it was to be Lacedelli's turn. We were at an altitude of about 8,400 metres. Perhaps more ... We resumed the climb, with eighteen useless kilograms on our backs. Why didn't we take off the respirators? It was simple – to lift off the packsaddles we would have had to sit down on the snow, with the risk we would not be able to move again. Besides, I had tied onto the pack the camera which I was determined to carry with me to the summit. To take off the packsaddles and untie the camera would only have involved a considerable loss of time ... The summit: we reached it at 6 pm.

Official meteorological tables relating to K2 make it clear that dawn on 31 July 1954 was at 4.54 am. The 'figure' which according to Compagnoni 'seemed to be approaching' was myself, descending after the night's bivouac – and not indeed 'in still uncertain light' as he says, but on the contrary in the blazing reverberation of full day: it was actually after 6.30 am.

Let us consider the question of the oxygen cylinders. The values 78 and 83 atmospheres, as set out by Compagnoni, can have no meaning whatever other than to be tendentious. Presumably the coefficients 78 and 83 refer to the average pressure in the two trestles, each of three oxygen cylinders. In a single pack of three 2.6 litre cylinders at an average pressure of 80 atmospheres the total volume of oxygen available would be 3 x 2.6 x 80 = 624 litres. Delivered at the normal rate of three litres per minute, this would last for only about three and a half hours!

The steel 'Dräger' cylinders were in fact filled at a pressure of 220 atmospheres: each complete respirator contained 1,700 litres of pure oxygen. However, when we checked them with the heavy, independent manometer at base camp a few weeks earlier, most of the cylinders registered a pressure of no more than 200 atmospheres, and at normal delivery rates would have lasted for about ten hours. Naturally, only the fuller bottles were chosen for the summit attempt.

Compagnoni writes: *It took us three hours to reach a point below the great gully. We were at about the same altitude we had reached the previous evening.* But which precise part of the climb does he mean by ... *a point below the great gully*? To which place does he attribute the beginning of the *three hours* of climbing? Was it from their tent, or from my bivouac where the oxygen cylinders lay? Finally, what was the true altitude they reached on the evening of 30 July?

And there is another question. Just when did they start to use the oxygen cylinders Mahdi and I left up there at about 8,100 metres? I can guarantee our bivouac site was deserted until 7 am on 31 July, because I had it and the surrounding area constantly under view until then. I repeat – until 7 am no one moved in that high zone of K2 apart from Mahdi and myself!

As already noted, according to official meteorological tables the sun rose on K2 that day at 4.54 am (though Compagnoni, referring to his departure that morning, speaks of *still uncertain light*). I know for sure, because I was there (as I testified in court in 1966), that Compagnoni and Lacedelli started to use the oxygen no earlier than 8.30 am. Let us suppose in fact they got moving from their tent at 7 am – that is, scarcely an instant after they were out of my field of view, just at the time I was reaching the lower camp. Let us accept what Compagnoni himself says, and agree they took an hour to reach the oxygen cylinders. At the very best, they could only have reached the site of my bivouac at eight in the morning and absolutely no earlier. But at that altitude it would take at least another half hour for all the various little tasks needed to get ready for the final thrust. The two could not possibly have been able to leave for the heights, using the oxygen, any earlier than 8.30 am. The precious gas would last for some nine and three-quarter hours – that is, until about 6.15 pm. The summit of K2 notoriously was reached at about six.

According to Compagnoni's book, the flow of oxygen ceased at about 4 pm, at an altitude of 8,400 metres. This poses yet another conundrum. How would it have been possible for the summit pair to cover, in only a couple of hours, a good 200 metres from 8,400 metres to the peak of K2 without the benefit of oxygen – and even more carrying, who knows why, the heavy containers which by then were an empty, useless and exhausting burden? Carrying those contraptions right to the bitter end would have been agonising and almost impossible, and they were perfectly easy to take off. The previous evening, while nearing the site of my bivouac, I took mine off and put it on my back again many times without any particular difficulty.

And the astonishment increases if one compares this exploit with a part of the same account which is a little more accurate, at least as far as that era was concerned. To climb the initial 300 metres from my bivouac to 8,400 metres took a good nine and three-quarter hours (according to Compagnoni). Certainly the first part of the climb presented some pitches of greater difficulty compared with the following section. However, this first portion of the ascent had the advantage of taking place at a lower altitude, when they were not so tired. Also, they were both breathing oxygen.

From this it follows inevitably – the sites, altitudes, timetables and oxygen usage set out by the summit pair (and transcribed by the official spokesman Desio with neither criticism nor verification) are not truthful.

But beyond these purely technical facts, let us also consider some human aspects of the affair. Compagnoni and Lacedelli found it quite acceptable that Mahdi and I were to descend in the dark, on that dramatic evening of 30 July, from the highest slope of K2. We had arrived there *in extremis* after we had spent all day carrying the oxygen packs. According to the programme established by common accord the previous evening we were to have used the same tent they did. By then the tent was quite close, but it turned out to have been pitched across the slope from where we found ourselves, though at about the same altitude. A tent like the one at Camp 9, though small, would quite certainly have held all four of us, even though it would have been a little cramped. Indeed, 24 hours later at Camp 8, after the return of Compagnoni and Lacedelli from the summit, five of us spent the night in a tent only a little larger. The one at Camp 9 would not have been a comfortable solution, nevertheless it was the solution foreseen.

As it was, Mahdi and I were left marooned on a steep icy wall, about 100 metres from those two companions of ours, who could not be discovered, and who could do no better than shout at us: 'Leave the cylinders there and go down!'

And they both stayed right where they were, hiding under their shelter, heedless of our cries and of our entreaties throughout the long, long night.

For Mahdi and myself it was a terrifying bivouac at an altitude of more than 8,100 metres. We were destitute of every least thing essential for survival and in danger both from the altitude itself – at that time unknown and lethal – and from the storm which soon hit us.

'It was a misunderstanding, the north wind blew away their words,' Compagnoni and Lacedelli wrote in their own justification: and in this way the thing was dismissed in two lines in the official book by Ardito Desio. But if one were to accept it was indeed just 'a misunderstanding', after this offhand explanation no one would ever feel the need to shed light on what provoked and accompanied it, but tend instead to keep quiet about it all so as to avoid the predictable effects on public opinion, and never say a word on the subject – as if this would suffice to cancel it from memory and even from reality – all this is known psychiatrically as 'denial'.

The journalist Nino Giglio, whom I sued after his libellous articles appeared in 1964, was backed into a corner when his evidence was refuted in court. He defended himself by testifying that what he had written had been told to him by Achille Compagnoni. And Compagnoni surely can't have forgotten how he was called as a witness by the Tribunal for that very reason in November 1966.

This anniversary is a good time to review these bitter words and events, this irresolvable mish-mash of silence, falsehoods and travesties.

K2 has been a source of humiliation and suffering for me, but sooner or later, if it takes a hundred years, the truth will have to be recognised by those to whom the verdict of history belongs. However, history must have 'sources', and it is for this reason I am writing – for those who one day will decide to get to the bottom of things responsibly, not with prejudice and cowardice as has been the case in the past, but by intelligently analysing and putting the now completely established evidence to the test.

What happened after the libel case? The whole squalid affair produced no reaction whatever from the mountaineering world. The Italian Alpine Club, for example, evaded the issue, quite indifferent to what was going on and, at the end of the day, hushed up the whole sordid business of what had happened on K2. It really behaved as if the whole affair was not to be re-examined, and my ten companions from the expedition took exactly the same attitude, despite the fact I had called two of them to give evidence as eyewitnesses. Incredibly, I found myself isolated and was left to fight alone against public defamation. And this had arisen from an expedition organised and sponsored by the CAI, for the success of which I had given my best and had risked my very life.

No one takes from Compagnoni and Lacedelli the credit of having been the first to reach the summit of K2. As far as I am concerned, I am proud to have contributed to the success of the expedition. I voluntarily took on the extreme, though limited, role of carrying the indispensable cylinders of oxygen up to the heights. And I must add: in those days it would have been impossible to conquer K2 without oxygen. But the pride I took in doing my duty did not abolish the bitterness it brought me – and not because I was not to reach the summit, as some people still insinuate. On the contrary, my intense bitterness lies in having discovered, especially after the event, how men can be so unpleasant that they can even lie to themselves.

Up there I was just reaching 24 and was incredibly ingenuous – a youthful idealist whose crime was to believe in 'utopian' values such as loyalty, selflessness and friendship. On K2 I saved myself – and I owe my survival to myself alone – after a desperate bivouac at over 8,100 metres with the Hunza Mahdi. We curled up on a little ledge of ice no more than 70 centimetres wide. We were destitute of everything – in danger not only from the altitude (then mortally new and unknown), but even more from the storm which hit us. But the official account of the K2 expedition barely mentioned either my bivouac or what happened in the last hours before the conquest. Instead it was inaccurate, incomplete, contradictory, and full of lies. I have repeatedly contested these ridiculous accounts with precise evidence in my books and articles, but it seems a certain circle of the mountain world cannot face and recognise the errors committed in the past (and perhaps at first even innocently) precisely by those who represented authority. This particular circle still remains deaf and blind to the facts.

The Italian Alpine Club was, and still is, the worst offender. Naturally I refer to its prime authority, the Central Committee, which promoted and sponsored the K2 expedition – it was in charge of the whole affair and therefore was obliged to run it properly. The President General of the CAI, on 25 December 1953, assured us the society had 'assumed moral responsibility' for the mountaineering aspects of K2. The CAI should therefore be duty-bound to shed light on the controversy. Today, after so much controversy (even including a court case) one certainly cannot say we lack the elements of justice to accomplish a peaceful work of repair. Ample proof is now freely available to everybody. The truth about the last hours before the conquest of K2 has been established over and over again, completely contradicting the official story. But the CAI remains in limbo, completely immobile, ignoring the problem and all the evidence. It is as if the ascent of K2 – which it initiated and organised – is now sacrosanct. Time will bring justice, I am sure, but it is incredible that even after 30 years I still find only myself defending the truth about the affair.

I insist my bivouac on K2 happened in a place different from, and at odds with, what was described in the official accounts, despite Desio's unsustainable statements to the contrary. The bivouac site corresponds neither to the position nor the elevation officially described, but was at a different and easily identifiable point above 8,100 metres. What I say is not mere nit picking, but is above all necessary to restore sense and logic to the decision which I made that night in 1954. Yet again I insist that if on that far-off night I had found myself on an easy slope on the snowy ridgeline (as the official map of the IGM wrongly has it), instead of on a steep exposed incline at 8,100 metres, I clearly would have been able to avoid that terrible bivouac. Mahdi and I could have descended with all tranquillity back to Camp 8, even in the dark, and then our experience on K2 would have been very different.

Let us once more look at the linchpin of the story of the conquest of K2, the key point which illuminates the entire story.

It is a matter of establishing once and for all when Compagnoni and Lacedelli started their assault on the summit on 31 July 1954. In a recent television programme, the two of them confirmed yet again they left between 4.00 and 4.30 am. But for my part, and I know for sure because I was there in person, I can testify they started to use the oxygen cylinders no earlier than 8.30. The climb did not last fourteen hours as they claim, but only for some ten hours. The oxygen in the bottles lasted about ten hours (according to their own story). They arrived at the summit of K2 at 6 pm, ten hours after they began their climb, and there must still have been some oxygen left in the cylinders. This is a logical, guaranteed fact, and only this can explain their arrival on the summit with the heavy, useless cylinders still on their shoulders. The official story is mere words and humbug, which has been palmed off on the public for the past 30 years. And what is more, if Mahdi and I had not carried the oxygen cylinders up there, K2 would have remained only a dream for Compagnoni and Lacedelli, not to mention my country.

When interviewed on television in 1984, the official historian of the expedition, Ardito Desio, insisted he had related everything in his book 'very faithfully'. 'I accurately interrogated all the participants', he said, and concluded arrogantly, 'Those are the facts!' I am sorry to have to contradict, but this simply isn't true. If he questioned 'everyone', why didn't he question me as well? Indeed, to do so was his specific duty, and I could have asked for nothing better. If Desio really had interrogated me while writing his story, wouldn't it have been in my own best interests to provide him with a detailed account of my experiences? At least this would have established the exact site of my bivouac and its precise altitude, as well as what happened to me and the precise timetable of events I saw up there with my own eyes. Everything, I repeat, which is missing, merely inaccurate, or even completely wrong in Desio's book.

Reporters, interviewers and officials have always ignored the precise questions which hold the key to the truth. At best they are skated over; the same old attitude which has been assumed by the Italian Alpine Club from the very beginning. The CAI was the sponsor of the expedition and should have been the moral guarantor – I repeat this for the hundredth time.

Here then are three questions which I put forward once again for critical analysis by the reader. The people involved have still not supplied clear and definitive responses:

A) At what time did Compagnoni and Lacedelli commence the assault on the summit? When did they start to use the cylinders of oxygen Mahdi and I carried up to the place where we spent the night?

B) Since, according to Compagnoni, the cylinders became exhausted at 8,400 metres at about 4 pm, how was it possible for them to climb a good 200 metres in a mere couple of hours from 4 pm to 6 pm, without the help of oxygen, and indeed carrying the heavy containers which were by then an empty, useless, exhausting burden? It had taken them nearly ten hours to climb the first 300 metres from my bivouac to 8,400 metres, despite the fact they were at a lower altitude, were less tired and, what is more, were constantly breathing oxygen from the respirators!

C) How and from whom was the place and altitude of my bivouac on K2 established for the official account of the expedition? Mysteriously, not only was I neither interrogated nor even consulted about it, I was not even so much as listened to after the event.

Like it or not, we have reached the day of reckoning, and this book is the proof of it. The time for post-mortems is now past. There have been far too many of them, and those who still debate the issue are by now merely grasping at straws. Concerning this episode there remains nothing to dispute, nothing to discover that has not already been completely exposed to the light; nothing to prove that has not already long since been proved. It is justly said that each of us has his own truth, but facts are facts and always stay the same. My accusations, repeated *ad nauseam* in my articles and books and now set out here, are neither interpretations nor hypotheses but precise facts, concrete data, well-authenticated evidence. But for 30 years I have been attacked, accused, provoked and slandered: and all this because I had voluntarily offered my life – I repeat my very life – in the service of my people and my country.

Commentary

The author's involvement in this unhappy saga began only after reading Bonatti's story in *Processo al K2* in 1986 and learning for the first time about the libel suit 20 years earlier. It seemed clear immediately that neither Bonatti nor his attorney had really understood the implications of Mahdi's deposition to the court, so I wrote a commentary setting out my analysis of what had really happened on K2 and, with some trepidation, sent it to Bonatti to see what he thought of the idea. He immediately agreed there could be no other explanation. This analysis was written in 1986, but first published in Italy in 1994.

Commentary on K2 – 'Mere lies and humbug'

What is one to make of Bonatti's final questions? Did Compagnoni and Lacedelli really leave Camp 9 at 4.15 am, climb slowly for ten hours or so on oxygen and then take off like rockets for the summit after the cylinders were exhausted? Or did the oxygen last right to the top, as Bonatti has always insisted? In the absence of direct evidence, one can only rely on arithmetic, and Bonatti's calculations are certainly very persuasive. But why was it necessary for Compagnoni to invent the fairy-tale about the oxygen? Surely his climb was quite dramatic and heroic enough already? And what are we to make of the other half of the story – the preposterous accusations Bonatti had tried to get to the summit first, used some of the oxygen, and then deserted Mahdi? Who started all that, and why?

The whole complicated farrago of lies and half-truths seems inexplicable at first sight and, when he wrote *Processo al K2*

(*Trial on K2*) in 1984, Bonatti himself was still, after 30 years, obviously mystified as well as angry. He was perfectly clear on what did and did not happen on K2, but had no explanation at all for the sordid aftermath, and in particular confessed himself baffled by Mahdi's evidence. The Tribunal accepted the logic of Roberto Ferrari's submission about the climb. It decided Bonatti was telling the truth and the accusations against him were a pack of lies, but did not even try to explain how the whole affair had started. That was not the issue before the court. Consequently, there are still some questions that have never been answered.

First, should Bonatti's story be accepted in its entirety? Is he hiding something? Is he a fraud and a liar? Impossible! His career speaks for itself: his whole life has been dedicated to uncompromising struggle, striving to explore his own physical and moral limits. No man of this stamp could lie and go on lying more and more stridently for years if he were guilty. His outrage is too obviously genuine: every word spells it out. We must accept, as the court did, that Bonatti's version is the truth. But then:

Why did not only Compagnoni but also Colonel Ata Ullah (of all people) falsely accuse Bonatti of trying to get to the summit first? Surely there could not be a conspiracy between the Italian guide and the Pakistani liaison officer? What possible motive could this highly respected soldier have for telling lies about Bonatti to a journalist in Italy in 1964?

Why did Mahdi's evidence, garbled or not, specifically and quite independently accuse Bonatti of exactly the same thing? Where did *he* get the idea?

Why did Desio not confront Bonatti if he had been accused of treachery and worse? Why did he never ask Bonatti for his version of what happened? Why was Bonatti's role in the first ascent of K2 played down, misrepresented and all but completely ignored for years? In particular, why on earth did the official film make no reference to his bivouac? Why would no one even answer his letters? Why the wall of silence from the Italian Alpine Club?

To understand what went on near the summit of K2 in 1954, one must re-consider the testimony of the one neutral participant, Mahdi. His evidence was dismissed by Bonatti, his lawyers and the Tribunal as self-evidently confused and completely unreliable. But was it?

What sort of man was Mahdi? He is strangely neglected in the accounts of Bonatti, Desio and Compagnoni, which all present him merely as the classical 'faithful servant' of European tradition. Bonatti praised and admired him, but thought of him only as a 'porter' – yet, like Tensing on Everest, Mahdi was proud and ambitious as well as brave, and had his own private dreams of reaching the summit of K2. That much is obvious from his deposition. But he did not realise the Italians' agenda was quite different from his own.

Let us try to see things from his viewpoint; was he really 'crazy' in 1965? After all, the Hunzas are an extremely healthy race, and often live very long lives. Their country has become famous for that very reason. Mahdi was a very fit high-altitude porter. He would be less likely than most to have lost his mental faculties by 1965, when he was still only 50 years old – so there is good reason to start any discussion of the events on K2 in 1954 with the proposition that, however mistaken he might have been, Mahdi was quite sane and was telling the truth (as he saw it) when he gave evidence ten years later.

However, he did make some extraordinary statements. In particular and quite spontaneously he said Bonatti had tried to race Compagnoni and Lacedelli to the summit and had intended to use their oxygen – exactly the same story Compagnoni told Nino Giglio. Wherever did Mahdi get this idea? Certainly not from Compagnoni or Lacedelli – he could neither speak nor understand their language – and even more obviously not from Bonatti. But no one else was there. The conclusion is inescapable – it was Mahdi himself who invented this story and somehow it was taken up later by both Compagnoni and Ata-Ullah. Although at first sight this might seem absurd, there is simply no other possibility. But how could Mahdi have come to believe such a thing? On reflection, and whatever one might make of his other apparently nonsensical allegations, the answer (to this question at least) seems clear enough.

When Bonatti and Abram tried to motivate Mahdi they spoke to him not as a fellow climber but as their paid servant. They did not ask his opinion; they merely wanted him to act as a porter, but unfortunately chose to dangle the summit in front of him as a prize. And the stratagem was all too successful: Mahdi became convinced he and Bonatti were to attack the summit '... for the honour of Italy and Pakistan'. But he had no way of knowing about the prior agreement on the proposed site of Camp 9, and when they climbed up laden with the oxygen but did not meet Compagnoni and Lacedelli he must have concluded Bonatti was indeed leading him to the summit by a different route. Moreover, since Mahdi had been told repeatedly how essential oxygen was for any such attempt (which was why he was being asked to carry it up), it is scarcely surprising he thought Bonatti intended to use it.

Nevertheless, the proposition that everything in Mahdi's evidence is the plain truth (as he saw it) can be accepted only if all the apparent absurdities can be explained as honest mistakes. And he made no fewer than fifteen separate statements that Bonatti labelled 'untrue' or even 'crazy'. At first sight they certainly seem so – but let us look at them through Mahdi's eyes.

1. '... *after establishing the last camp (that is, Camp 8) Compagnoni decided to attempt the ascent of the summit and asked me to accompany him.*'
Mahdi had in fact been told by Compagnoni some days earlier that he might join the Italians in a summit attempt once the high camps had been established. Compagnoni himself in *Men on K2* admits to having spurred on both Mahdi and Isakhan in this way – and he later did the same to Bonatti at Camp 8. But if this

simple explanation seems inadequate there is an even more obvious possibility.

Abram told Mahdi in so many words before they set off from Camp 8 that he '... might be able to go on up to the summit with Bonatti, Lacedelli and Compagnoni'. Mahdi probably assumed quite reasonably that Abram was speaking on behalf of Compagnoni, the climbing leader. Or maybe, to convince Mahdi the invitation was genuine, Abram actually told him he was relaying his leader's direct orders.

2. '... *Abram asked Bonatti and me to follow them with the* respirators.'

True, as far as Mahdi was concerned. It was Abram who was speaking, not Bonatti. Mahdi could not understand what Abram and Bonatti were discussing in Italian. However, if Mahdi did think it was Abram's idea, the situation takes on a different aspect from the Hunza porter's perspective. The stage was then set for Bonatti to change 'Abram's' plan and decide to use the oxygen himself.

3. '... *after climbing 130 metres, Bonatti decided to precede Compagnoni and Lacedelli and asked me to follow him towards the summit.'*

This accusation is not nearly as crazy as it seems. Mahdi and Bonatti climbed together towards Camp 9 after Abram had left them and gone back. Mahdi already 'knew' he and Bonatti were to attempt the summit – Abram had told him so. Bonatti was in front and Mahdi was following. Mahdi could not see the summit pair's tracks, since Bonatti himself was having great difficulty in doing so and was himself making the only tracks Mahdi could see. Mahdi only knew that when night fell, he and Bonatti were far across to the right from where Camp 9 was pitched and in a direct line under the 'Bottleneck' which led up to the summit.

He would naturally assume this was deliberate on Bonatti's part. Why should he think otherwise? Bonatti had certainly 'asked' Mahdi to follow him, and urged him to greater efforts, by using signs and gestures. So Mahdi concluded Bonatti was trying to get ahead of Compagnoni and Lacedelli. He must have wondered, as they climbed, where Bonatti proposed to spend the night. Perhaps he thought another tent was already set up and waiting for them – he had never been above Camp 7 before that day. It is easy to understand why he became hysterical when he saw Bonatti chopping out a seat for a night in the open.

4. '… (Bonatti) also decided to use the respirators…'
This accusation follows inevitably. Mahdi could scarcely have reached any other conclusion. He 'knew' he and Bonatti were going for the summit. He knew oxygen was necessary for a summit attempt. He also knew he and Bonatti had the oxygen. He did *not* know Compagnoni and Lacedelli had the only available masks and regulators. Mahdi knew nothing about oxygen apparatus and had never had anything to do with it before – he had been on Nanga Parbat with the Germans the previous year, but they had no oxygen equipment. He would naturally have assumed Bonatti had everything they needed. But he added quite truthfully that they did not use the oxygen 'because there was no need to do so', which incidentally also confirms he believed they *could* have used it if necessary.

5. '… He started the climb following a different route from that taken by Compagnoni and Lacedelli.'
This too is a perfectly reasonable conclusion for Mahdi to have reached. He is obviously referring to the last steep slope up to the bivouac site which they took after Abram had left to go back. Bonatti did, in fact, take a 'different route' at that stage: he and Mahdi climbed on into the dusk, but did not reach Camp 9 which, as Mahdi was to see, was beyond the couloir and the steep slabs. So he thought Bonatti had deliberately chosen a more direct path to the summit.

6. '… By late evening, we found we had climbed about 200 metres more than Compagnoni and Lacedelli had been able to manage.'

Far from being 'absurd', this is the most significant and interesting statement in the whole of Mahdi's evidence. At first sight, he certainly seems to be saying he and Bonatti had climbed 200 metres higher than the other two, which is patently ridiculous; but this obvious interpretation is not necessarily correct. The court record says 'climbed' (*salire*), not 'climbed up' (*scalare*) ; and 'more in amount' (*in piu di quanto*), not 'higher' (*piu in alto*). 'Climb' and 'salire' can certainly mean 'climb up', but can just as easily mean 'climb along' or 'climb across', both in English and in Italian.

With this in mind, a new perspective emerges when seen from Mahdi's point of view. From where he then found himself, below the only possible route to the summit via the 'Bottleneck' which splits the rock and ice barrier, it must have seemed to him that Compagnoni and Lacedelli had climbed up the left flank of the great couloir and established Camp 9 there at about the same altitude as the bivouac site. So they still had some 200 metres of horizontal traverse to cover before getting to the place that Mahdi and Bonatti had already reached, and from which they could then climb up to the summit. Next morning, in fact, this was precisely what they did. Mahdi therefore concluded he and Bonatti had taken a more direct line and were '200 metres further on' along the route to the summit than the other two. This must have completely clinched his belief Bonatti was trying to get to the top first.*

---

*The Italian text of the court proceedings says 'about 200 metres', but Mahdi would **not** have used the word 'metres'. If he was speaking English he might well have said 'about 200 yards' (and if Urdu, who knows what?), and 'yards' in English would imply a measurement on the same level rather than a vertical height. Unfortunately, the Magistrates Office at Gilgit has not responded to requests for a copy of Mahdi's original deposition.

Incidentally, it also confirms the bivouac site must have been just where Bonatti says it was – almost at the same altitude as Camp 9. If it had been lower, Mahdi could not possibly have concluded they were 'further on' than Compagnoni and Lacedelli and were 'racing them to the summit'.

7. '… we started the descent and we reached Camp 8 …'
The substitution of 'we' for 'I' is a trivial grammatical error and could easily be the result of multiple translation. But it need imply no more than a descent more or less at the same time. Considering Mahdi's state that morning, he was in no condition to know or care how far behind him Bonatti was as he went down. Perhaps he thought his companion was following him quite closely. He would scarcely have expected Bonatti to stay where he was. At least this comment gives the direct lie to the allegation Bonatti deserted him, though in fact Mahdi specifically denied this elsewhere.

8. '… we reached Camp 8 about 5.30 am.'
This is the first and only statement in Mahdi's deposition which is quite clearly wrong. It is contradicted not only by Bonatti but also by Gallotti and Abram, who were at Camp 8 and saw Mahdi arrive 'just before 7 am'. The most obvious explanation is that Mahdi's watch had simply stopped during the night – which would not be surprising considering how cold it was. But perhaps he had no watch and had to guess the time. If so, he was surely in no frame of mind that morning to be precise and one can only wonder how he could be so definite ten years later. Was this '5.30' suggested by someone else? It all fits in rather too neatly with Compagnoni's contentious statement that he and Lacedelli left Camp 9 at '4.15 or thereabouts' – which is not possible to reconcile with the fact that Mahdi undoubtedly reached Camp 8 at 7 am, and Bonatti a little later.

Actually, the internal contradictions of Compagnoni's account are self-evident on the evidence of Gallotti's diary alone because, in Desio's book *The Conquest of K2,* Compagnoni describes how they *'saw a figure which receded from us with uncertain gait ... We called to him in a loud voice'* and in *Men on K2* he relates how *'next morning, emerging from the tent for the final assault, Lacedelli and I saw a man ... waving his ice-axe in salute'*. Since it is quite certain the man they saw was Bonatti and it was then after 7 am, this confirms the summit pair got moving from Camp 9 much later than they say they did.

9. '... We saw Compagnoni and Lacedelli leave their tent and start the climb towards the summit.'

This seems nonsense at first sight because Camp 9 could not be seen from Camp 8. But it also seems a strange thing for Mahdi to have invented – it is such a matter-of-fact comment. On reflection, it makes perfect sense if Mahdi's 'we' refers *not* to the entire group who spent the summit day at Camp 8 but merely to himself and Bonatti. Did he see Compagnoni and Lacedelli sitting outside their tent at Camp 9 putting on their crampons as he staggered down the slope that morning? Bonatti could not see them from the bivouac site, but Mahdi went down first and knew exactly in which direction Camp 9 lay; he had seen Lacedelli's light the night before. Bonatti says Mahdi 'stopped dead on the dangerous slope some 40 metres below me and stayed there for a long time immobile'. So Mahdi had plenty of time to look around. Perhaps he could see Camp 9 from his changed viewpoint, past the rocks which had previously blocked his view. If so, it neatly confirms Bonatti's estimate of the time Compagnoni and Lacedelli first got moving.

10. '... We saw Compagnoni reach the peak at about 6 pm and Lacedelli about half an hour later.'

This is certainly inaccurate – as confirmed by everyone at Camp 8. However, Mahdi had been lying frost-bitten in Isakhan's tent all day. No doubt he came out to see the last few steps that Compagnoni and Lacedelli took, but perhaps he saw only the second man moving. Conversely, half an hour before that he had heard Isakhan say to the Italians (in English) 'A Sahib is about to climb K2!' Isakhan was only a few feet from him, standing by the other tent. His belief the two reached the summit 30 minutes apart would then be quite understandable.

11. '… Compagnoni and Lacedelli reached Camp 8 … fifteen minutes apart.'
Compagnoni and Lacedelli reached Camp 8 at 11 pm, long after dark. It is inconceivable Mahdi was waiting for them outside his tent. His feet were terribly frost-bitten. No doubt he would have heard excited voices in Italian, but he would not have been able to recognise who was speaking. Surely his comment indicates merely that the two men looked into Mahdi's tent to see how he was (as they must have done) 'fifteen minutes apart'. Nothing could be more natural.

12. '… At one place Compagnoni and Lacedelli encountered some difficulties and they asked me to help them, but Abram told them…'.
This cannot be true if Mahdi was referring to their descent from the summit to Camp 8. He must have been speaking of the next day, when all the climbers were descending from Camp 8 to base, because Abram was present. If this is so, the statement makes perfect sense; though it does not say much for the sensitivity of Compagnoni and Lacedelli.

13. '… (Bonatti's) statement that if we were to reach the summit _before_ Compagnoni and Lacedelli, he would bring honour to his country, Italy, and I to mine, Pakistan.'
Apart from the single word 'before' this is a completely accurate report of what Abram (not Bonatti) said to Mahdi in English: Bonatti spoke neither English nor Urdu, and Mahdi no Italian. Obviously Abram would not have said 'before'. He presumably said something like 'also' or 'too' or 'with'. Mahdi's use of the

word 'before' is no doubt merely an embellishment to make his story consistent. Witnesses often do this. After all, Mahdi 'knew' Bonatti meant 'before' rather than 'with' because of what happened during the climb, and he would naturally transpose Abram's words in just this way when asked about it ten years later.

14. '… However, it was his intention to use them (the oxygen cylinders) if necessary.'
One can almost hear Mahdi adding in frustration, under his breath 'how else do you think the two of us were going to reach the summit?' This was a completely natural assumption on Mahdi's part once he believed he was to attempt the summit with Bonatti. Although he could not have been told this by Bonatti, and certainly was not told it by Abram, he would take it for granted this was Bonatti's intention. What other conclusion could he have reached?

But just before this, Mahdi had said 'Since I do not understand Italian, I am unable to say exactly if he said precisely that to me'. This cautious, precise and perfectly sensible statement proves Bonatti's 'intention to use the oxygen' was merely a logical assumption on Mahdi's part and not what Bonatti actually said. And in his next comment, Mahdi again said he and Bonatti could communicate only by signs and gestures.

15. '… Going back to Camp 8 that morning, when you saw Compagnoni and Lacedelli, did you wave an ice-axe at them? No, at that time it was dark …'
This answer does seem utterly confused at first sight. It was not dark when Mahdi was going down, it was broad daylight (Gallotti, Abram, Bonatti, Compagnoni) and in any event the summit pair had not yet left their tent (Bonatti, Mahdi). However, this was quite certainly the very first time Mahdi had ever heard of anyone waving an ice-axe. The incident was never mentioned until *Men on K2* was published in Italy in 1958. He

could not have had the faintest idea what the question was about, nor when the incident was supposed to have happened.

His answer suggests a simple rift in communication. The Tribunal of Turin prepared the questions in Italian: they were then translated into English: put to Mahdi in English (or perhaps in Urdu and then into English?): back into Italian for the court hearing: and now into English again. The quoted form of the question is a literal translation from the Italian of the court transcript. The hanging adverbial phrase '*going back to Camp 8 that morning*', though very common in literary Italian, is not often used in English. But this was the original form of the question in Italian sent by the Tribunal to the Italian embassy in Pakistan. The most appropriate idiomatic English translation would be '*Did you wave an ice-axe at Compagnoni and Lacedelli while you were going back to Camp 8 that morning?*' But if the English translation prepared by the embassy was literal rather than idiomatic, the question was put to Mahdi in the quoted (Italianate) form 'Going back to Camp 8, did you wave an ice-axe at Compagnoni and Lacedelli?' Mahdi's answer would depend on how he interpreted the question. If he assumed 'going back' referred to Compagnoni and Lacedelli rather than to himself, then his answer makes perfect sense. It was indeed 'dark at the time' – it was almost 11 pm! The point of all this is to clarify how easy it is for shades of meaning to become confused when multiple translations are necessary. Nevertheless, Mahdi also answered 'No!' which confirms it was Bonatti whom Compagnoni saw brandishing the ice-axe. It seems likely enough it was shaken 'in a way that seemed almost menacing' (to quote Compagnoni). Although Bonatti says merely he 'shook his axe in the air in answer', he certainly had plenty to be angry about that morning.

So Mahdi's evidence is by no means 'crazy'. His answers, nonsense though they might seem at first sight, are on reflection completely consistent with Bonatti's story. In other words, **Mahdi was perfectly sane and his deposition was what he believed to be the precise truth.**

The whole thrust of this analysis is that Bonatti has been unjustly accused and pilloried for years simply because Mahdi did not understand what was happening, and no one explained it to him later. It is sad to reflect that, even so, a little goodwill, honesty and common humanity could still have defused the situation and cleared Bonatti's name. But as we shall see, none of these qualities seems to have been much in evidence on K2. Or back in Italy later.

After the Climb

Mahdi came down to the K2 Base Camp convinced Bonatti had tried to race Compagnoni and Lacedelli to the summit. But how did his story come to be taken up by both Compagnoni and Ata-Ullah? It was they, not Mahdi, who talked to the journalist in Italy ten years later.

Ata Ullah undoubtedly questioned the unfortunate Mahdi in the normal course of his duties as liaison officer, soon after the return of the summit party to Base Camp. Mahdi must have told him Bonatti had unsuccessfully tried to get to the summit first and this had led to their night in the open. Perhaps Mahdi blamed Compagnoni as well as Bonatti. He surely must have told Ata Ullah how he had yelled in vain for help and tried desperately to cross the couloir. In fact the newspaper controversy which erupted in Karachi a few weeks later alleged Compagnoni (not Bonatti) was responsible for Mahdi's injuries – perhaps the other porters started some such story as a garbled version of what Mahdi told them. The inescapable fact was that the three Italians had all returned from the heights practically unscathed while their Pakistani companion had lost his fingers and toes – and almost his life. No one cared to ask whether Bonatti had almost lost his as well.

Ata Ullah did not broadcast Mahdi's accusations, but he obviously knew all about them because he was directly quoted in 1964 by Nino Giglio as saying 'Mahdi in Pakistan had continued to confirm publicly over the next ten years that Bonatti had planned to precede the chosen summit pair' (though Mahdi himself later denied he had done so 'publicly'). The liaison officer must have confronted Desio at once with the story Mahdi had just told him – to do otherwise would have been gross dereliction of duty. He was surely outraged poor Mahdi had come back from the summit with terrible frostbite of his hands and feet, and would have demanded to know how a porter had suffered such horrendous injuries while the Italians were relatively unharmed, how it was Mahdi had climbed to Camp 9 without proper footgear, why he had been forced to bivouac in the open at 8,000 metres and how he came to arrive alone at Camp 8 next morning.

Ata Ullah did not talk to Bonatti, and could not have known the true facts of that terrible night, but one thing seems certain. He talked to Mahdi in his native language, Urdu, and with no chance of misunderstanding heard the whole story that Mahdi told the magistrate ten years later. Ata Ullah in his turn surely must then have told Desio how Bonatti had induced Mahdi to go with him on an independent and unauthorised summit attempt, had then actually tried to get to the top before Compagnoni and Lacedelli and had intended to use the oxygen himself instead of giving it to the summit pair, but something had gone wrong and he and Mahdi had been forced to spend the night in the open

It is easy to picture the irate Pakistani officer storming into Desio's tent with these allegations, and one can readily imagine the state of mind this would produce in Desio. He would see his precious expedition being vilified and himself being publicly disgraced – despite the success of the climb. He must have been beside himself with rage that this young fool Bonatti had disobeyed orders, nearly killed himself, gravely injured Mahdi and almost ruined the entire expedition just as the summit was within reach! How would Desio have reacted? What sort of man was he?

Professor Ardito Desio was 57 years old when he led the K2 expedition. He was an aristocrat, as well as an autocrat – a professor of geology and a member of the Italian elite, with attitudes towards underlings similar to those of aristocrats everywhere. Desio was absolutely intent on his expedition succeeding. He had decided the mountain was to be overcome by a massive assault. He studied old weather reports in great detail, planned a winch for load-hauling between the seven lower camps, established radio communications up the Abruzzi ridge, and even chartered an aeroplane to make a close-up inspection of the summit cone.

His book *The Conquest of K2* clearly demonstrates his authoritarian attitude towards his team. He regarded conquest of the mountain as his personal responsibility. There was to be no acceptable excuse for failure. He emerges as a single-minded man, a martinet who would brook no disagreement with his decisions. If Desio were given reason to believe Bonatti or anyone else was contemplating actions not ordered by himself or his deputy, he would be extremely angry. If he thought Bonatti had not only defied his orders but might also bring the whole expedition into disrepute in the eyes of the Pakistan Government, he would regard it as outright mutiny. He would be concerned first and last with the honour of Italy and the expedition, and not at all with the feelings of his underlings.

His attitude is well illustrated by an 'Order of Service' he issued on K2, which dealt with the precise issues raised by the bivouac. Desio said he would tolerate no dissent from his orders, and threatened he would *not hesitate to derogate anyone who even retards the success* of his expedition. In Bonatti's case, he has kept this exact promise for more than 30 years. He emerges as a stickler for discipline with rigid views that would be very difficult to change.

His response in this matter was all too predictable – he threw Bonatti to the wolves. With a stroke of masterly diplomacy he blamed the whole affair on one irresponsible 24-year-old climber

– but since no indictable crime had been committed, he could insist the whole business be hushed up in the interests of amicable Italo-Pakistan international relations. No doubt he promised Ata Ullah he would deal with the miscreant Bonatti personally, as he later did!

When the newspaper controversy erupted in Karachi, Minister d'Acunzo and Amedeo Costa, the vice-president of the Italian Alpine Club, were no doubt told the whole tale by Desio, and Bonatti was given the entire blame. The ambassador's enquiry was held to refute the story of Mahdi's desertion by Compagnoni, while hushing up Bonatti's alleged misdemeanour in the interests of international harmony and the reputation of Desio and his expedition. Indeed, it was so effectively hushed up that Bonatti himself remained blissfully ignorant of his secret trial and conviction until ten years later when Giglio's articles were published in Italy.

Significantly, although Mahdi was the central character in the drama, he was not invited by the ambassador to give proxy evidence from his bed in the hospital at Skardu. This would have brought his accusations against Bonatti out into the open, which was the one thing the Italian officials wanted to avoid at all costs.

There seems no reason to doubt Desio genuinely believed Bonatti guilty. He presumably did for the rest of his life. There can be no other explanation for his obduracy. And the Italian Alpine Club would of course accept Desio's decisions without question. This is why Bonatti was never asked for his side of the story. It was all too convenient. Mahdi was frost-bitten and Bonatti was condemned, but the expedition could claim resounding success at all levels and the glory of Italy was intact. Desio's reputation was unbesmirched, and Compagnoni and Lacedelli were famous. Why should anyone worry about young Bonatti? He was only an idealistic lad, and therefore expendable.

Compagnoni's Role

Professor Desio was a stickler for protocol and order. It is inconceivable he would accept Mahdi's accusations against Bonatti at face value: he would have to check and double check any allegation as serious as this. He must have called his climbing leader in at once and confronted him with Ata Ullah's story: not to do so would have been completely out of character.

There is therefore one final question. Everything that happened later hinges on it. Why did Compagnoni not immediately defend Bonatti and tell Desio Mahdi's accusations were absurd? No one could have known better than he did that Bonatti and Mahdi had no masks and regulators for the oxygen packs – Compagnoni himself had them. So he knew Bonatti could not have used any of the oxygen, even had he wished to. He also knew perfectly well an unprotected bivouac at that altitude would be very likely to prove fatal. No one but a madman would have deliberately set out to spend the night in the open at over 8,000 metres with the intention of attacking the summit next day.

Why did he not tell Desio this? The answer can only lie in Compagnoni's character, which must be judged by what he said and did during and after the ascent of K2. He claimed repeatedly in the press, on television and even in court not only that Bonatti had tried to reach the summit first and intended to keep the oxygen for himself, but also that he had used some of it during his night in the open to avoid frostbite and then deserted Mahdi to save his own skin. But quite apart from all this, he insists he and Lacedelli set off from Camp 9 at about 4.15 am and descended more than 100 metres to pick up the oxygen, which ran out at 4 pm, 200 metres below the summit. He says they then carried the empty cylinders up this last 200 metres in only two hours. Simple arithmetic makes this impossible to accept – but apart from this, what is one to make of the accusations against Bonatti?

It was undoubtedly Mahdi who was the source of Bonatti's so-called 'plot to reach the summit first', but *not* the story that he used some of the oxygen during the night – Mahdi specifically denied this ten years later. He also denied he had been deserted by Bonatti next morning. So Compagnoni himself must have been the source of these last two accusations. When questioned by Desio, he not only confirmed Mahdi's story of Bonatti's 'plot' but went even further. He must have told Desio the same tale he was to repeat for the next forty years – that Bonatti had used some of the oxygen during the bivouac and then deserted Mahdi. Why? What motive could he have had?

In 1954, Compagnoni was 40 years old – a thickset, tough, senior Alpine guide from Cervinia, a veteran of many Alpine seasons. He was almost old enough to be young Bonatti's father. It goes without saying that he and Lacedelli, as well as all the other climbers on the expedition, dearly wanted to reach the summit of K2, which was the focus of all their hopes and dreams. Although they were among the best Italian climbers of the day, they were not world-famous until after their first ascent of the second highest mountain in the world. Years later, their names are still household words in Italy. The honour of being first to climb K2 was one to be jealously guarded.

Compagnoni said to Bonatti at Camp 8 'you might have to replace one of us for the final assault'. Was this offer genuine or was it merely used as a bait to induce Bonatti to carry the oxygen up to Camp 9? It was, after all, the same prize that Bonatti dangled in front of Mahdi next day. But the changed site of Camp 9 was scarcely calculated to make it any easier for Bonatti to reach. Even more significantly, Compagnoni and Lacedelli ignored Bonatti's increasingly frantic cries for help and then, when they did answer, instead of coming to his aid, they brusquely dismissed him and re-entered their tent, leaving Bonatti and Mahdi to the elements. At best this was thoughtless and insensitive, but at worst it was totally irresponsible for them to assume this ill-assorted pair needed no help. Why would two mountain guides behave so badly? And why had they changed the summit plan and placed Camp 9 on the far side of the slabs? No doubt one reason was to avoid the risk of avalanches, but since they knew perfectly well their companions were trying to reach them, why were they not listening intently for Bonatti's shouts? They took a very long time to answer him. It seems they did not wish Bonatti to spend the night with them at Camp 9 – they gave him no option but to dump the oxygen and descend to Camp 8. Was this to ensure they alone would be able to attempt the summit next day?

Perhaps Compagnoni simply disliked Bonatti or was jealous of his climbing reputation, regarding him as a young upstart and deciding that, whether or not he reached the summit himself, Bonatti would not if he could prevent it. Regrettably, this has happened on other expeditions. He might even have interpreted Bonatti's brief illness at Camp 7 as being faked, seeing it as a ruse by Bonatti to rest and save himself for a later summit attempt. Bonatti's arrival at Camp 8, 24 hours later, miraculously now in good health, could well have seemed to Compagnoni proof he had never been ill. This sort of thing has also happened on other expeditions, sad to say.

And there are other possibilities. The Austrian climber Hermann Buhl had climbed Nanga Parbat, another 8,000-metre peak in Pakistan, the previous year, solo and without oxygen, in defiance of the expedition leader Dr Karl Herligkoffer. The bitter arguments between Buhl and Herligkoffer were front-page news in the European newspapers not long before Desio's expedition left Italy, and Buhl's astonishing performance was the talk of the mountaineering world. Bonatti was just the sort of man who might have contemplated repeating Buhl's extraordinary feat. Perhaps Compagnoni and Lacedelli were worried that if Bonatti got as far as Camp 9 he would try to emulate Buhl's exploit by attempting K2 next day without oxygen. It would have completely overshadowed their success if another climber had reached the top without oxygen on the same day they climbed it using respirators.

Also, Bonatti had misgivings when they were all at Camp 8 planning the assault and thought he might need to replace Compagnoni. If Compagnoni had any inkling of this it would have added further fuel to the fire. Bonatti says Compagnoni 'seemed to read my thoughts' – there must have been some suspicious glances exchanged.

Compagnoni told Bonatti 'you might have to replace one of us at Camp 9'. But the events of the following day, when he put Camp 9 well and truly out of Bonatti's reach, indicate he did not take his own offer too seriously. As for Lacedelli, he seems simply to have gone along with Compagnoni that evening, and was willing enough merely to tell Bonatti to go back to Camp 8, then re-enter the Camp 9 tent and ignore his further entreaties for help.

All in all, it is difficult to avoid the conclusion Bonatti was not welcome at Camp 9, despite the agreement made at Camp 8 the previous evening. Compagnoni no doubt presumed that, having failed to reach Camp 9, Bonatti and his companion would go back to Camp 8 in the dark. Not in his wildest dreams would he have expected them to bivouac in the open – he had every reason to believe such an action could end only in disaster. He probably was quite certain the other two had gone down after dumping the oxygen – he had left them no other choice.

He must have been horrified when he got back to Camp 8 and discovered what had happened the previous evening. Mahdi testified Compagnoni 'did not seem to be on bad terms with Bonatti in Camp 8 after the summit day', and indeed he must have felt very relieved Bonatti was still alive. But Mahdi's terrible injuries would certainly have made Compagnoni uneasy and worried he would be blamed, particularly if he felt even partially responsible for the bivouac. In his deposition, Mahdi also made the gratuitous comment 'Compagnoni and Lacedelli were not on speaking terms' at Camp 8 after their victory. One would surely have expected them to be bubbling with joy. What were they worried about?

So Compagnoni reached Base Camp with mixed feelings – elation he had reached the top, but uneasiness because his summit plan had backfired with what could have been fatal results. He must have felt extremely threatened when Desio questioned him about Mahdi's injuries. But Mahdi's allegation that Bonatti had plotted and then actually tried to get to the summit first must have produced an explosive reaction. Compagnoni then had a perfect excuse to lay the entire blame for Mahdi's injuries on Bonatti and claim he himself had been merely an innocent bystander. The more indignant he could let himself become about Bonatti's 'treachery' the less he would have to blame himself for any part he might have played. As in all such situations, the greater the guilt feelings, the more the outrage. It acts as a convenient psychological defence mechanism.

Compagnoni had seen a solitary figure going down to Camp 8 and discovered later that, although Mahdi had severely frost-bitten feet, Bonatti was unscathed. Compagnoni himself had frost-bitten fingers and no doubt refused to concede Bonatti could merely withstand cold better than other people. So instead of defending Bonatti, he went further: not only did he confirm Mahdi's story but also he told Desio Bonatti had used some of the oxygen during the bivouac to avoid frostbite and then deserted the Hunza porter. He embellished his own dramatic account of the end of the oxygen supply by bringing it back from 6 pm to 4 pm. Indeed, a little extra drama involving empty oxygen cylinders being carried to the peak made a good story even better. With this masterstroke, he portrayed Bonatti as a devious and treacherous competitor for the summit, a cheat who used precious oxygen, a coward who gave none to Mahdi and then abandoned him to his fate, and a liar who then had the effrontery to pretend his loyalty to the team. Poor repayment for a man who had risked his life and by almost super-human efforts had brought Compagnoni the oxygen essential for his success. *But since this is the precise story that Compagnoni told Nino*

Giglio ten years later, it is what he must have told Desio in 1954.

A few weeks later the Karachi press erupted with accusations that Compagnoni had ordered Mahdi to stop climbing only a few metres below the summit and so caused his frostbite. How ironic that Compagnoni had to appear before the Italian ambassador to refute this charge. It must have been galling for him to (more or less) support Bonatti's story at this hearing – but no one could be blamed publicly for Mahdi's injuries, and therefore Bonatti's 'treachery' could not be mentioned. However, Desio and the Italian Alpine Club had long since decided (without questioning him) that Bonatti was guilty of disloyalty, irresponsible behaviour and worse.

Undoubtedly Bonatti told Minister d'Acunzo of the bait he and Abram had held out to Mahdi; but the ambassador had already been told the 'true' story by Desio and Compagnoni, and would privately have 'known' Bonatti was a liar. Significantly, the Ambassador's report presented merely a watered-down version of events, which did not mention exactly what inducements Bonatti offered Mahdi. Compagnoni's accusations were not made public until Giglio's articles appeared a decade later, but perhaps the other climbers in the K2 team were told confidentially of Bonatti's 'treachery' after they got back to Italy. Ultimately they sent Bonatti to Coventry, and no doubt many other Italian climbers followed Compagnoni's lead because he was a senior and now very famous member of their fraternity. No wonder Bonatti became progressively more and more isolated in Courmayeur and ultimately resigned from the company of guides.

It is even possible Compagnoni somehow convinced himself over the years that his allegations were true. People racked by guilt and spurious indignation are quite capable of even greater excesses of self-deception and wishful thinking. But on another level, he knows it is all lies and humbug. In particular, he knows exactly when the oxygen *really* ran out.

However, it is plain Compagnoni must have had some very powerful reason in 1954 for not clearing Bonatti when beyond any shadow of doubt he knew Mahdi's accusations were preposterous. He could only have justified his attitude by convincing himself that since Bonatti was guilty of other peccadilloes he thoroughly deserved whatever happened to him.

Is it possible to give Compagnoni the benefit of the doubt? Are all these theories no more than fantasies?

The most charitable construction that can possibly be put on the affair is that Compagnoni selfishly put Camp 9 out of Bonatti's reach and ignored his calls for help without considering the implications. He then felt worried and guilty when he later found Mahdi had gangrenous hands and feet, and feared he would be held responsible (as he later was by the Karachi press). If he wanted above all to be cleared of any possible complicity in the near disaster and was willing to see Bonatti blamed with no concern for the consequences, he might, acting on impulse, have taken the easy way out and blamed Bonatti when questioned by Desio about the affair. But this scenario would make it impossible to understand what induced Compagnoni to unburden himself to the press ten years later. To make this old accusation public after so long can only indicate either he believed it (!?), or he hated Bonatti very deeply, or both. One can only conclude he was very angry when Bonatti's autobiography first appeared in 1961. In it, Bonatti implied (with considerable restraint) that Compagnoni and Lacedelli had left him for dead at Camp 9. With Ata Ullah present in Italy to confirm his accusations, Compagnoni felt it was safe to pillory Bonatti in the press. He also knew Lacedelli would back him up, and Desio was on their side. But he must have been unpleasantly surprised by what happened later in court.

It is clear Bonatti's account is all too true, and the official version really is 'mere words and humbug'. What a sorry commentary on such a wonderful achievement!

Conclusion

So there was the entire unholy mess. Poor Bonatti! Those condemned by Star Chamber methods can never defend themselves because they are never accused directly. He made a very convenient villain and an ideal sacrificial goat. The fact he became severely depressed after he had been repaid for his devotion to duty by being condemned unheard was a matter of no concern to the establishment. Not to a government hungry for success and national pride after a disastrous war, nor to the Italian Alpine Club, nor to the Military Geographic Institute. They were all well able to present a united front against the protestations of a young upstart.

As for the Italian press: newspapers are interested only in what will sell papers – never in truth for its own sake. Continued accusations against such a controversial national figure as Walter Bonatti will certainly boost circulation, even years later. Imagine if Bourdillon and Evans, the first team to attempt the assault, had reached the summit of Everest in 1953, and Tensing had staggered down to base camp frost-bitten, accusing Hillary of trying to forestall the other team. What a bonanza for the press that would have been. What a feast for scandal-mongers!

The Italian public turned out in Genoa 40,000 strong to welcome Desio's team when it got back to Italy in 1954, and the whole country basked in the reflected glory of the ascent of K2. Desio, Compagnoni and Lacedelli became national heroes, and any attempt to denigrate them would prove very unpopular, even years later. Bonatti, on the other hand, made an ideal target for those who enjoy cutting famous people down to size. The people of Italy are no different from those of other countries – some ready to believe the worst, others full of good will; some stupid, others intelligent; some evil, others good, but mostly interested only in a good story and not caring too much about truth in the abstract. Certainly not caring too much about Walter Bonatti!

Regrettably, the same can be said about all the other interested parties in this affair.

At the end of the day, the K2 expedition emerges as a sad business. It really was 'miserable and sordid', just as Bonatti says, and the aftermath was even worse.

It all started because Mahdi thought he and Bonatti were making an independent attempt on the summit. He would not have been too surprised. Mahdi had seen Hermann Buhl do exactly the same on Nanga Parbat in 1953 – he had himself carried the frost-bitten Buhl down the mountain. After his experience on K2 the very next year with Bonatti he must have concluded this was how European climbers always behaved.

Compagnoni changed the proposed site of Camp 9 not because of the risk of avalanches but so that Bonatti would not be able to reach it. He and Lacedelli did not care what happened to Bonatti and were even less concerned about how he was going to get back to Camp 8. So they ignored his frantic calls for help and left him for dead.

Next day, Compagnoni and Lacedelli left Camp 9 at about 7 am, crossed the couloir, retrieved the oxygen from the bivouac site and climbed K2. The oxygen did not run out at 4 pm; it lasted until they reached the top of the mountain. Compagnoni's graphic description of the end of the oxygen rings true enough, but it happened on the summit at 6 pm, *not* 200 metres below it and two hours earlier. No doubt he believed Bonatti and Mahdi had gone back to Camp 8 the previous night: he must have been thunderstruck when he got back to Camp 8, heard about the bivouac and saw how terribly Mahdi had been frost-bitten.

When they all got back to Base Camp, Ata Ullah questioned Mahdi and was told Bonatti had tried to get to the summit before Compagnoni and Lacedelli and had intended to use the oxygen 'if necessary'. Ata Ullah confronted Desio, who in his turn questioned Compagnoni. The climbing leader jumped on the anti-Bonatti bandwagon and confirmed the allegations because he felt guilty about his own part in the affair and wanted at all costs to protect himself from blame for what had happened to Mahdi. Perhaps he also resented young Bonatti and wanted to see him cut down to size – so he told Desio Bonatti had also used some of the oxygen during the night and deserted Mahdi next morning. He modified his account of the summit day to fit this story. He placed the bivouac site more than 100 metres lower down than its real position (and therefore almost out of earshot from Camp 9, which neatly accounted for the previous night's 'misunderstanding'). It also conveniently explained how he and Lacedelli could not possibly have helped Bonatti that night, nor could Bonatti have reached them. So Bonatti alone was responsible for the bivouac and for Mahdi's injuries – Compagnoni was just an innocent bystander. He put the departure from Camp 9 at 4.15 am, and the exhaustion of the oxygen at 4 pm. This was to become the official version of the ascent.

So, right from the day he arrived at Base Camp, Bonatti was tried *in absentia* by Desio and found guilty. All three of his companions had condemned him – first Mahdi, then Compagnoni and Lacedelli. How could he be other than guilty?

It is almost possible to forgive Desio, but not quite – he should at least have given Bonatti a hearing. As it was, he decided the young climber was a traitor, a liar and a cheat. When they got back to Italy Bonatti was ostracised, because the last thing Desio wanted was unsavoury publicity and debate to sully his precious expedition. He therefore did not confront Bonatti with his 'crimes'. It was much easier just to hush the whole thing up and pretend it had not happened. No doubt he expected the guilt-ridden Bonatti would be glad to let the whole affair of the bivouac be forgotten. He must have been furious when the 'traitor' had the effrontery to tell a different story seven years later, and presumably dismissed the contents of Bonatti's book as a barefaced lie – though the Tribunal of Turin, of course, decided in 1966 it was all true. The Italian Alpine Club, believing its own elder statesman, desperately wished to underplay the whole affair, and would even now prefer Bonatti would simply be quiet and go away. For this reason, his protestations have been ignored by the club and the map-makers. If they so much as answered his letters it would re-open the whole can of worms with a vengeance. Much better to do nothing!

It seems a great pity no one was ever willing to re-examine all the evidence 'quietly and competently with all its aspects each in its proper place'. If only the search for truth and justice had been everyone's first concern, things would have turned out very differently. Even now the CAI could still re-open the matter and conduct a judicial enquiry, but it no doubt prefers to avoid besmirching the prime achievement of Italian mountaineering.

It might seem strange the success of Bonatti's libel action in 1964 against Giglio did not convince Desio, the Italian Alpine Club and the entire mountaineering establishment they had all gravely misjudged him and owed him an abject apology. But one must remember court cases the world over are seldom reported in full, and Desio would certainly not have been in court throughout the entire case. Everyone knows clever lawyers can clear the guiltiest defendant. No doubt Bonatti's detractors presumed the decision of the Tribunal had nothing to do with the true 'facts' and Bonatti's victory was a miscarriage of justice – after all, such things have happened before. Even Abram and Gallotti, who gave evidence, would merely have attended court and left immediately afterwards. Very few people would have followed the entire proceedings, apart from Bonatti himself.

The ultimate irony of this whole unsavoury affair is that if Compagnoni had simply remained silent, his infamous behaviour would never have been discovered. There was no need for him to lie to Desio about the oxygen running out early. He had already earned life-long fame by climbing K2. His reputation was secure and nothing could harm him. But it was not enough for Compagnoni merely to have denied Bonatti any chance of reaching the summit; he wanted to destroy his rival completely.

Neither did he need to renew his attack ten years later, but he was determined to rid himself once and for all of this irritating trouble-maker who had dared to tell the truth in *Le Mie Montagne*. If he had said nothing to Nino Giglio, the newspaper articles accusing Bonatti of treachery would never have appeared. Bonatti would have lived on in blissful ignorance of his secret trial and conviction ten years earlier. There would have been no libel action. Mahdi would never have given evidence. Neither *Trial on K2* nor this commentary would ever have been written. The incriminating summit photographs which finally came to light in 1993 would have stayed buried in the archives forever, and the official story of the first ascent of K2 might well have prevailed for a hundred years. Compagnoni has now not only been unmasked as a liar but also, far worse, his lies were specifically designed to destroy the very man who, at the risk of his own life, made his victory on K2 possible.

The conquest of K2 changed many lives. Ardito Desio of K2, like John Hunt of Everest, became famous and went on to greater honours. Compagnoni and Lacedelli of K2, like Hillary and Tensing of Everest, have enjoyed lifelong fame for their achievement.

And Bonatti? If he had not been tempered by K2, would he have become the questing spirit who, driven by his private demon, conquered the 'Bonatti pillar', survived the disaster on the central pillar of Freney, and climbed the 'direttissima' on the north wall of the Matterhorn in winter? He might have developed a very different personality had he not felt the need to 'prove he was not finished'.

It is interesting to contemplate alternative scenarios …

What would have happened to Bonatti over the next four decades if he and Mahdi had reached Camp 9 that night?

Or suppose he had been able to make his proposed Alpine style solo attempt on K2 the following year without oxygen, 25 years before Messner's solo ascent of Everest?

It seems very likely he would have succeeded if he had been able to try; and in that case, who knows where his destiny might have led him?

Even more intriguing – what would have happened if Compagnoni and Lacedelli had found Bonatti and Mahdi dead and frozen in their bivouac that morning, as well they might have done? Would they have taken the oxygen and climbed on, or not? The earlier death of Mario Puchoz at Camp 2 had not stopped the expedition, so why should another tragedy? But obviously, if Bonatti had died that night, the aftermath of the conquest of K2 would have been very different. No one would have had the faintest idea Camp 9 had been moved from its proposed site, or that the death of the two oxygen bearers was anything more than an unfortunate accident. It would have been thought merely that Bonatti and Mahdi had over-reached themselves and perished in the snow, and many crocodile tears would no doubt have been shed. The conquerors of K2 would still have enjoyed lifelong fame.

But not Bonatti – he would now be just another talented young climber who might have achieved great things had he survived. The name 'Walter Bonatti' would be one more entry in the far too lengthy list of dead Himalayan climbers. No doubt he would be remembered by a few people in Italy for the brilliant beginning of his career – his 1951 ascent of the north face of the Grand Capucin. But who would now recall his epic bivouac? Does anyone nowadays know, much less care, who carried the oxygen up Everest for Hillary and Tensing?

Unfortunately, *Processo al K2* had made no great impact in Italy and there seemed no prospect of a new edition containing the commentary being published. And there the matter rested for the next eight years.

Confirmation

The scenario of the conquest of K2 just depicted was never made public, because at that time there was no second edition of *Trial on K2* in which my commentary could have been included. But there was still to be one last dramatic and quite unexpected development seven years later – a development that brought the whole K2 affair to a head.

In mid-1993, as the 40th anniversary of the first ascent of K2 was fast approaching, while leafing idly through my own copy of the 1955 issue of *The Mountain World*, an annual Swiss publication of the 1950s and 60s (now defunct), I glanced at the original article by Ardito Desio describing the conquest of K2 (published soon after his expedition had returned to Italy and long before his official book *The Conquest of K2* appeared). It included two full-page summit photographs.

I had seen these pictures many times during the previous four decades, but in the 1950s had known nothing of the accusations against Bonatti, and these illustrations had seemed no different from a thousand other Himalayan summit photographs. Nor were they. They were so familiar that, as on previous occasions, I barely noticed them.

But suddenly I realised what I was seeing. In one photograph, Compagnoni is standing on the summit of K2 next to his discarded pack with its three oxygen cylinders. Tibet can be seen in the background. His mittens are lying in the snow. He is taking off his inner gloves to photograph Lacedelli in his turn.

Opposite
Lino Lacedelli on the summit of K2. Though his face is not in sharp focus, as the magnified inset shows, his mouth is covered in ice, indicating he has been breathing in a face mask until very recently.

He has thrown back his hood. But he is still wearing his face mask, two hours after he is supposed to have ripped it off to avoid suffocation. The knurled connecting tube still attaches the mask to the cylinders at his feet. The photograph is sharp and clear. There is no possible doubt. Compagnoni is standing on the summit of K2 and the oxygen is still running.

In the other photograph the background is the same, though the angle is different because the camera is lower. Compagnoni's discarded face mask and tubing are now lying on the oxygen cylinders at Lacedelli's feet. The two climbers have changed places. Lacedelli has taken off his inner gloves to take the earlier photograph and now has his bare hands in his pockets. He is not wearing his face mask, but his moustache and beard are rimed with a circle of frost. He has been breathing hard into a confined space so the water vapour from his lungs has frozen.

I stared at the two photographs, completely bemused. How could everyone, including myself, have read Desio's book and failed to see the obvious? The pictures completely contradicted Compagnoni's story about the end of the oxygen supply. When I consulted *The Conquest of K2* the mystery was solved at once. The summit photographs are *not* the same as those in *The Mountain World*. The picture of Compagnoni is missing. In its place is a rather blurred photograph of much inferior quality showing him from side on – and he is no longer wearing his oxygen mask. The identical picture of Lacedelli is there, but the ice on his beard is not of itself so obvious a casual observer would be likely to notice it or realise its significance.

In both publications, Compagnoni and Lacedelli's own account of their climb spells out what happened 'at 4 pm' on the summit day in specific detail: 'Suddenly, at intervals of a few seconds, we both experienced a horrible sensation. We found ourselves gasping for breath, an oppressively hot feeling enveloped us from head to foot, our legs grew weak, we could no longer stand. We were very alarmed at first – we were so out of breath we had a ghastly feeling of complete prostration. Then

Another photograph of Lacedelli on the summit of K2. Initially the author considered that the prescence of frost around Lacedelli's face and beard would have been unlikely if he had been climbing into the blazing sun of a Karakoram afternoon without wearing an oxygen mask. The ice on his face seemed to suggest that it was more likely that he had just removed his face mask. But during a conversation with Jim Wickwire, who climbed K2 on 6 September 1978 (the third ascent and first American ascent, with Louis Reichardt), Wickwire pointed out that he and Reichardt had followed the route taken by Lacedelli and Compagnoni during the final stages of their climb, and had been in shadow until the last few metres, when they emerged into the sun. The author's original idea was therefore invalid. Wickwire suggested a much more plausible explanation. On their climb, Wickwire used supplementary oxygen to the summit, but Reichardt's set had failed about 350m from the top: he dumped the set and climbed on, thus making the first ascent of the mountain without supplementary gas. At the summit, Reichardt's face was covered in rime. By contrast, when he removed his mask, Wickwire's face showed only a few specks of ice where the seal between mask and face had not been complete. Wickwire's view, now supported by the author, was that the distinctive circle of rime on Lacedelli's face had been caused by an ill-fitting oxygen mask, suggesting that he had been wearing his mask all the way to the summit. In the photograph above, the circle of rime can again be seen.

Opposite
Achille Compagnoni on the summit of K2. He is very obviously still wearing his oxygen mask.

Above
The photograph in Ardito Desio's book on the K2 expedition. The photograph is blurred, an inferior shot. But Compagnoni has removed his mask.

we realised what had happened. Our supply of oxygen was exhausted. At once we snatched off our masks, inhaled deeply, and tried to pull ourselves together. And in fact, little by little, that terrible feeling of constriction disappeared.'

They make it perfectly clear that, even standing still, they could not breathe until they had removed their now useless face masks. And as for climbing – impossible! Once the oxygen was exhausted, the face masks had to go: and the summit was still 200 metres above them and two hours away. 'So they say!' to quote Bonatti. It is not too difficult to guess why the photograph that appeared in *The Mountain World* was discarded.

So here, against all expectation, was definitive proof that Bonatti is right: the oxygen lasted right to the summit, which was reached at 6 pm. This confirms the two climbers could have left the bivouac site 'absolutely no earlier than 8.30 am' (for oxygen sets lasting about ten hours) – just as he insists. How ironic that in the end their own photographs should provide the most damning evidence imaginable. So much for the official account of the climb. 'Mere words and humbug', indeed, to use Bonatti's description of the official account.

As far as I was concerned, the photographs merely confirmed what I had long since believed, for reasons amply discussed in Chapter 5. But here at last was overwhelming, objective proof that the story of the oxygen running out at 4 pm is a lie. And as Bonatti had always said, this was the linchpin of the whole libellous article written in 1964 by Giglio: if the account of the missing oxygen was false, how could anyone believe anything else Compagnoni said? Objective evidence such as this could not be doubted. There was no longer any need to study the arguments in minute detail – one look at Compagnoni and Lacedelli's own summit photographs was enough to prove Bonatti had been telling the truth all along. When I sent him the pictures he was just as astonished as I had been to realise irrefutable evidence proving the official account to be a tissue of lies had been there all the time for anyone who cared to look.

Bonatti's great friend Mirella Tenderini suggested to him that this discovery should be publicised immediately, and the prestigious Italian mountaineering magazine *Alp* duly published the incriminating photographs, together with the commentary I had written eight years earlier. The result was a furore: the national press took up the story with great enthusiasm, and all the major newspapers and magazines printed long articles about the affair. Compagnoni, now 80 years old, angrily insisted to the reporters who interviewed him that he had put the mask on his face on the summit merely to 'protect my face from the cold'. But he fared very badly in the press debate that ensued, and there were repeated calls for a judicial inquiry – though without response from the CAI.

In January 1994 the CAI did issue a statement about K2, but it was conciliatory at best, and refrained from making any specific reference to the matters being debated furiously in the press at the time. The Committee was clearly anxious to dampen down the controversy without irretrievably blackening its own, and also Italy's, reputation by admitting that the blue ribbon event of the first ascent of K2 had indeed been a matter of 'Lies and Treachery'. It was against this background that an announcement by the CAI President, Roberto De Martin, appeared on 22 January 1994.

STATEMENT RATIFIED BY THE CENTRAL COUNCIL OF THE CAI

Forty years have passed since the first ascent of K2 and the CAI celebrates the anniversary, remembering with gratitude the tremendous efforts of all the participants at that time in this national enterprise, which gave so much momentum and prestige to Italian mountaineering. But like national expeditions from other countries, ours too had a 'zone of shadow' which today the passage of the years allows us to think about more calmly.

Back in the fifties, the CAI acted to address the unpleasant events relating to its financial organisation, as evidenced by the numerous articles published in our monthly journal between 1954 and 1958, which clarified all the aspects with complete accuracy. These events are now filed away and no one remembers them any more. It remains to address the internal discrepancies in the accounts of the final phase of the ascent, which at that time the CAI left as matters to be discussed between the climbers involved.

Today we realise that this was a mistake, because the lay press seized on the affair, creating disputes and pushing the protagonists into extreme positions which ended in a court case. Following this, for fear of re-igniting the polemics, the CAI did not intervene officially to clarify the true history of K2. Perhaps this was of little concern to the outside world, but it was important for the international mountaineering world and to the protagonists themselves.

Today, to celebrate the anniversary with full dignity, the CAI wishes to remove this last shadow from the affair and has given a hearing to Walter Bonatti in its official records, in homage to those 'moral responsibilities' which the CAI itself assumed at the time on behalf of the mountaineering aspects of the expedition.

Roberto De Martin

Bonatti responded to this announcement by thanking the CAI President in an open letter, as follows:

> Ten years ago, driven by the irreconcilable events that accompanied the thirtieth anniversary of the conquest of K2, I wrote and published *Processo al K2*. In it I consigned to the mountain my full testimony about what happened there.
>
> In that book I discussed everything that concerns me, and I believe that from now on the responsibility rests with all those who have poisoned or hushed up the truth about the affair.
>
> I confess that until now I believed the truth would never be recognised as the last forty years had been given over only to incomprehension and a progressive degradation of the facts. I was mistaken, and I am happy to be able to say so in the context of this responsible official action the CAI has now taken.
>
> I wish to recognise the honour and the credit due to those who have today demonstrated sensibility, courage and determination – it is never too late for such virtues – in their wish to confront and resolve such an odious and complicated affair, which was certainly not their fault, but merely one which they inherited.
>
> I thank President Roberto De Martin, the Central Council of the CAI, and all those who have set this process in action with such admirable responsibility and sense of justice.
>
> Walter Bonatti

However, despite repeated articles in the press about the matter, there was no further action from the CAI and, pleased though he was in some ways, many of these articles infuriated Bonatti because they constantly referred to his 'rehabilitation' by the CAI. Their authors asked repeatedly why he was still not satisfied, wondering why he had not attended the 40th anniversary celebrations in Cortina in August. For his part, Bonatti objected strenuously that he had done nothing whatever that required 'rehabilitation' and that as long ago as 1966 the Court in Turin had definitively decided the allegations made against him by Nino Giglio were false. He insisted that if anyone or anything needed 'rehabilitation' it was the CAI, *not* Walter Bonatti.

The spate of such articles misrepresenting the point continued, so in 1996 Bonatti published a new book, *K2 – Storia di un Caso* (*The Story of a Court Case*). The first half was a reprint of *Trial on K2*; the second half included the summit photographs and my commentary, as well as many excerpts from articles written by Italy's major mountaineering journalists, and an account of the fortieth anniversary celebrations at Cortina d'Ampezzo in 1994, which he had declined to attend. His concluding comments were:

> To sum up, I must say again that, even if not really lacking in good will, there was at least an inability on the part of the Alpine Club to confront the most embarrassing aspect of the affair. It has therefore neither illuminated, nor expressed a clear judgement on the lie about the oxygen, nor has it exposed the web of slander and lies which arose from it. I might finish by saying this was an imaginary 'revision'. The only logical deduction is that no one has ever really wanted either to confront or to resolve the whole false history of K2, nor to expose the one terrible lie which is also the most blatantly obvious. However things might turn out in the future, for myself the story of K2 ends on this page.

Over the next few years, as the millennium approached there was no change in the situation and, wishing to do whatever I could to help, I busied myself in preparing a definitive translation of Bonatti's climbing career, including a section on the K2 affair. This was published in the USA as *The Mountains of my Life* in 2001, and offered at least some consolation that the story of Bonatti's travail would be known by people outside Italy, whatever might happen in his own country.

In Italy, on the other hand, things were rather different. The publication of Bonatti's new book and the hubbub in the press seemed to fall on stony ground as far as officialdom was concerned, with the CAI remaining completely mute after the hopeful-sounding *pronunciamento* in 1994. The official façade relating to K2 still mirrored the veneration extended by the British to the conquerors of Mount Everest, and in 2001, on his 104th birthday, Ardito Desio was honoured by a ceremony conducted at the Quirinale, the Presidential Palace in Rome. Bonatti was intensely irritated by this and was moved to write the following letter to President Ciampi, enclosing a copy of *K2 – The Story of a Court Case*:

Monte Argentario, April 18th, 2001

To the President of the Republic CARLO AZEGLIO CIAMPI
    Quirinale Palace, Rome

Signor President,

I have just seen on the Television News the ceremony at the Quirinale in honour of Professor Ardito Desio for his 104th birthday. Your Excellency awarded him a most prestigious award, which assumed the greatest possible value precisely because it was delivered by your Excellency in person. I, like many others, have the greatest respect for the personal achievements of Professor Desio and his scientific work; but I believe his worth as the leader of the historic Italian expedition to K2 in 1954 is quite another matter.

I respect you very much, Signor President, and it is for this reason that I take the liberty of sending you this book of mine, hoping you will find the time to read it: it is the historic obituary of this great National expedition, in which I took part.

It is not so much my personal story that I wish to bring to your Excellency's attention – being as it is an addition to the affair – but rather my wish to inform you about the false history still contained in the reports and in the official documents concerning the conquest of K2: an historic lie now recognised as such all over the world. I therefore believe that an eminent person like yourself should be totally informed on the subject, given that the official position on this event certainly does no honour to our country.

With the utmost respect and admiration,

Walter Bonatti

A month later he received the following somewhat oblique and soothing reply:

The Secretary General of the President of the Republic, March 18, 2001

Dear Signor Bonatti,

The President of the Republic has received your letter and thanks you for your expressed esteem and for your book, which describes a remarkable exploit.

The Head of State wished to celebrate with Professor Ardito Desio his reaching 104 years of age, expressing to him thanks for his contribution to science through his work and his expeditions.

The credit attributed to him in no way detracts from the support you provided to the conquest of K2 which, even after such a long time, is still recognised by everyone.

Please accept, in the name of the President and my Department, the most cordial good wishes,

Gaetano Gifuni

However, there were at least some hopeful signs that people were coming to see that Bonatti had been badly dealt with for years. A long article was published in *La Repubblica* on 27 June 2001 summarising yet again the events on the summit of K2 and describing Bonatti on K2 as *'a lad condemned to death by freezing powdered snow, by unstoppable tremors of both arms, by the fear of a collapse of the ice cliff above, by the hypocrisy of Grande Italia. This letter from the Secretary General was enough to bring back the anger of a man who just last year was granted the title of Officer of the Order of the Legion d'Honneur by Jacques Chirac, the President of France.'* (Bonatti had been made a Member of this Order in 1961 after saving Pierre Mazeaud's life on the Pillar of Freney – see Chapter 2 – and his rank has now been upgraded from 'Member' to 'Officer'.)

In August 2001 two articles written by Charlie Buffet were published in France in successive issues of *Le Monde* after a long interview with Bonatti. They were simultaneously published in Italy in *La Stampa*. In these articles Buffet gave a detailed account of the whole long-drawn-out affair which was totally sympathetic to Bonatti: he went so far as to describe the events leading to the K2 bivouac as 'an attempted homicide'.

But accurate reporting of this sort was a rarity. As anyone who has had intimate knowledge of any *cause célèbre* knows only too well, press reports in every country have a regrettable tendency to print versions that read well and sound impressive but are all too often utterly divorced from the true facts. The K2 story is a perfect example of this melancholy truth, as was amply demonstrated in December 2001, when Professor Desio died at the age of 104 after fracturing his femur in a fall.

The news of his death was reported – on *Italian* television – as the demise of 'the first Italian to reach the South Pole'. Though true enough, this comment is somewhat misleading. It seems to suggest that Desio went there as an explorer, whereas in fact he simply visited Antarctica as a geologist in 1961 at the invitation of the USA National Science Foundation. He visited the stations of McMurdo, Byrd and Amundsen-Scott at the South Pole, and the Wright valley (one of the Dry Valleys in Victoria Land). In *The Times* of London, Desio was described at some length as 'the man who survived the epic bivouac on K2 in 1954 during the first ascent of the second highest peak on earth' (!!) One can only marvel at such ineptitude.

Nevertheless, the following year some long, very perceptive articles about K2 did appear in American mountaineering journals, notably by such correspondents as John Thackray in the *American Alpine Journal*, and Rob Buchanan in *Climbing*. Buchanan interviewed Bonatti at length in Italy after reading *The Mountains of my Life*, which caused him to conclude that the K2 affair was 'a story of confusion, betrayal and shameless hypocrisy unparalleled in the annals of alpinism. After reading the book I began to understand why the tumult was still going on even 40 years later'.

Buchanan's final paragraph summed up the whole situation; at the end of the article describing his interview with Bonatti he wrote:

> But when I told him he had won this public relations battle, and that it was therefore not very important what was written in a couple of dusty tomes in the CAI library, his eyes widened. *'All that counts is the official historic record'*, he hissed between clenched teeth. *'In the end, that's the only important thing. In a hundred years, when someone wants to read about the first ascent of K2, what will he find? A conspiracy of ambiguity, of lies, and of silence.'*

But the demands of these journalists received nothing but disdain from those responsible for the whole disastrous problem. 'If Bonatti had to bivouac,' said Compagnoni during a telephone interview with *Le Monde*, 'it was because he had spent too much time resting at Camp 8.' (?) And he went on: 'I'm proud of what I did … Bonatti thinks he can throw mud at heroes'. Then when the same publication queried Lacedelli's illogical answers, he cut his questioner short, saying: 'I don't care if you say it's unbelievable, that's what's written!' This remarkable and quite illogical comment certainly serves to reinforce Bonatti's view that only the official record matters because it defines history.

And Ardito Desio was no less slippery in his turn: he hid behind his own advanced age and had his daughter say: 'You can't disturb a man of 104 years with things like that'. And when the *Le Monde* investigator insisted and reminded Desio's daughter about the gravity of the accusations they were discussing, she cut him off arrogantly and abruptly, saying: 'The President of the Republic has answered already [by inviting him to the Quirinale Palace]'.

In 2003, as the 50th anniversary of the first ascent of K2 was approaching, Bonatti's definitive book *K2 – La Verita (K2 – The Truth)* was published in Italy. It included many articles about the K2 affair that had appeared over the previous decade in the Italian press: Bonatti hoped this would finally produce some action by the Club Alpino Italiano to amend the official account of the climb, but in vain. There was no response whatsoever from the CAI, which no doubt was still hoping desperately that the controversy would subside spontaneously.

But in 2004, the 50th anniversary year, there were three dramatic new developments, which served to resolve all doubt: they confirmed absolutely the truth of Bonatti's story and, at the same time, the complete accuracy of my own speculations about what really happened on K2 in 1954.

First, in February 2004 Roberto Mantovani, the editor of the prestigious journal *Rivista delle Montagne* (*Mountain Review*) and curator of the Mountaineering Institute in Turin, wrote an open letter to the Italian Alpine Club: it was published in his magazine and co-signed by 24 other eminent Italians from various walks of life. The letter referred to Bonatti's most recent book about K2, and demanded that the Club immediately conduct an inquiry into the matter so that an official revised version of the climb could be published in time for the 50th anniversary celebrations in July. Rather surprisingly after 20 years of inaction, the CAI responded immediately and appointed three eminent senior authorities, *i tre saggi* (the three wise men), to examine the matter by consulting all the available evidence – Professor Fosco Maraini, Professor Luigi Zanzi and Professor Alberto Monticone.

These three experts duly conducted an enquiry and published a comprehensive report in April 2004. It comprised 39 pages of closely reasoned argument. They decided that the true version of the events of the summit eve was precisely as set out in Walter Bonatti's autobiography *Le Mie Montagne*, and that the version given in the official account was completely misleading. They concluded there had been 'two victories' on K2 in 1954 – the first by Compagnoni and Lacedelli in reaching the summit, the second by Walter Bonatti in performing prodigies by carrying up the oxygen necessary for the summit climb, then surviving an unprecedented bivouac at 8,100 metres.

This report of the *tre saggi* concluded with a very strong recommendation that the CAI should publish immediately a new official history of the Italians on K2 to set the record straight. But despite this advice from its own committee of enquiry there was no action at all by the Club at that time.

Second, after 50 years of silence, Lino Lacedelli has at last published a book, *K2 – Il Prezzo della Conquista* by Lino Lacedelli and Giovanni Cenacchi, Arnoldo Mondadori Editore 2004, Milano [now also published in English as *K2 – The Price of Conquest*], written by a journalist and based on some long interviews with Lacedelli. In the book Lacedelli does a quite stunning about-face and completely repudiates Compagnoni. He totally – or almost totally – confirms both Bonatti's version of events and the scenario depicted in my commentary.

It is difficult not to feel a little sorry for Lacedelli, who emerges as a simple man embroiled in matters largely beyond his control: who for years simply remained quiet and tried to avoid becoming involved in arguments about K2. He admits frankly that he was terrified of Ardito Desio, and thought he would be 'destroyed' if he as much as opened his mouth. Nevertheless, it is impossible to condone the fact that he said nothing for 50 years when he could have cleared Bonatti's name at any time with the greatest of ease, and chose to speak out only after Desio was dead. The silence is even more difficult to understand when it is noted that on Lacedelli's own admission in his book it was Bonatti who massaged his fingers after the summit climb. If that massage was a reason for Lacedelli suffering so little permanent damage to his fingers, then his silence was a poor way of expressing his thanks.

In his book, Lacedelli bitterly criticises Desio. He says the expedition leader was hated by all the climbers except Compagnoni, and that even during the approach march the whole team was on the verge of mutiny, to the point that this national expedition almost ended, there and then, in 'shipwreck'. He insists Desio knew nothing about climbing and was simply not fit for his role as leader: he had a closed mind and constantly flew into rages; he was authoritarian, impossible to talk to, centralised all merit to himself, and demanded all publication rights; he tried to confiscate the diaries of all the climbers after the climb – though Lacedelli kept his; he issued ridiculous, arbitrary 'Orders of Service' as well as stupid daily orders, which Lacedelli says were posted each morning on his tent flap by Compagnoni and were then uniformly ignored by the other climbers; he treated Lacedelli and the other climbers as 'no better than Balti porters'; he was completely uncaring about the death of Mario Puchoz at Camp 2; he was totally insensitive to the needs of the climbers and patronisingly referred to them as his 'children'. Lacedelli describes how Desio congratulated Compagnoni after the ascent but ignored him completely. He adds: 'I was infuriated! I could have throttled him!'

Lacedelli also notes that back in Italy there were no fewer than four court cases as a result of the expedition: Compagnoni sued the CAI for compensation for his frostbitten fingers as a result of taking photographs on the summit; the CAI sued Desio in an attempt to recover several million Lire missing from the expedition coffers; Desio sued the expedition photographer, Mario Fantin, over some missing film (which had in fact been taken quite legitimately by one of his own scientists); and, of course, Bonatti sued the *Gazzetta del Popolo*.

As far as Compagnoni is concerned, Lacedelli is absolutely scathing. He insists Compagnoni should never have been appointed head climber. He describes him as 'malleable', 'persuadable' and 'moveable' – as a complete sycophant who 'sucked up to Desio at all times'. He even accuses Compagnoni of dishonestly secreting a much needed high altitude tent in his own tent at Base Camp 'as a present for his children'. He describes giving Compagnoni his own left glove on the summit when one of Compagnoni's gloves blew away and his fingers were going white, but never receiving the slightest thanks. Most of all, he describes his fury when Compagnoni told a reporter soon after their return to Italy that he had 'pulled the totally exhausted Lacedelli up to the summit'. He confesses that the story of the climb in the official account was based solely on Compagnoni's diary and that he, Lacedelli, had signed it even though he knew it was inaccurate – because he wished at all costs to avoid controversy.

Concerning the events of the summit eve and summit day, Lacedelli confirms Bonatti's version of events in almost every respect. He agrees Camp 9 was supposed to be placed 'as low as possible' – that is, at 7,950 metres – to enable Bonatti to reach it with the oxygen. He says Compagnoni insisted on putting it higher against his (Lacedelli's) wishes, and that Compagnoni then also insisted on crossing the couloir to place Camp 9 in

Opposite
Lino Lacedelli fixing his crampons at Camp 9 on summit day. Compagnoni claims the two men started the climb to the top at about 4 am. But the sun did not rise on K2 that day until just before 5 am. Bonatti claims that he saw no movement in Camp 9 at 7 am when he started his descent from the bivouac. The photograph was taken when the light was already very good, certainly more consistent with Bonatti's time than the half-light of early dawn that Compagnoni claims, or even the 6 am that Lacedelli claims.

what Lacedelli describes as a 'most dangerous and stupid position'. He insists the traverse was actually far more dangerous than the risk of ice-fall from above, and indeed was a 'useless waste of time'. He agrees with Bonatti that the bivouac was just across the couloir from Camp 9 and at almost the same altitude, and says that in their tent at Camp 9 Compagnoni told him quite explicitly he did not want Bonatti there, saying 'nobody but the two of us' were going to attempt the summit next day. Lacedelli believes Compagnoni was afraid Bonatti would be fitter than he was, and might replace him in the summit attempt next morning. He says Compagnoni would not leave the tent to speak to Bonatti that night and sent him out instead.

Lacedelli flatly denies Compagnoni's story of them leaving Camp 9 next morning at '4 to 4.30 am' and ventures the opinion that their departure was perhaps at about 6.00 am. However, he admits this is only an estimate because he 'did not look at his watch all day': Bonatti, of course, insists he could see no one moving on the slope when he last looked up towards the bivouac site at 7.00 am. Lacedelli's book even contains a photograph taken by Compagnoni, which shows Lacedelli sitting outside the Camp 9 tent putting on his crampons in broad daylight – certainly well after dawn. And he agrees he saw Bonatti descending while he and Compagnoni were putting on their crampons, which completely fits in with the independent stories of both Bonatti and Mahdi.

Lacedelli also agrees they took an hour and a half to reach the oxygen bottles at the bivouac site, but insists they left for the summit at 'about 7.30 am' (though this too is merely 'an estimate' because again he did not look at his watch). According to Lacedelli the oxygen *did* run out 'just before we reached the summit at ten to six', the only time he did look at his watch. This time of 'ten to six' is of course verified by Bonatti and others who could see the summit from Camp 8. He puts the altitude where this happened at 'between about 8,500 and 8,550 metres' – that is, some 60 metres below the summit.

Lacedelli refers repeatedly to my commentary throughout his book, and agrees that all my speculations were correct – except the conclusion that the oxygen must have lasted right to the summit. He insists the oxygen did run out 'just below the summit', and speculates that perhaps the supply may have been exhausted early because they had been 'breathing too hard on the way up'.

As for the summit photograph of Compagnoni still wearing his oxygen mask, he too says that Compagnoni replaced the mask on his face for five minutes merely to 'protect himself from the cold'. (But if this were true, surely the straps of Compagnoni's face mask would have to be visible outside his cap? The summit photo from *The Mountain World* clearly shows that the straps are hidden under his white woolen cap, where they were placed when the oxygen apparatus was first donned at the bivouac site.)

Lacedelli's co-author Cenacchi insists that the story of the oxygen lasting to the summit must be accepted and asks: 'Why would Lacedelli lie about such a relatively minor matter of a few minutes?' On reflection, the answer to this question seems obvious. The time the oxygen ran out is by no means 'a relatively minor matter', but is indeed the linch-pin of the whole controversy, just as Bonatti has always insisted. Lacedelli undoubtedly wishes to preserve at least some scraps of his own integrity and heroic reputation as the conqueror of K2. He portrays Compagnoni as the villain of the piece and himself as a mere bystander who simply went along with the story because he really had no option. If, however, he were to agree that the central dramatic picture of them reaching the summit gasping for breath is a lie, he would be totally discredited and revealed as a fraud. So he must insist that the oxygen *did* run out on the way up. And, on the assumption (made also by Bonatti) that the bottles must have lasted for ten hours, his conveniently 'estimated' departure time of 7.30 am from the bivouac site would have seen this happen just below the summit, because $7.30 + 10.00 = 17.30$. And the summit was, of course, reached at

17.50. In other words, Lacedelli's 'estimate' of the time they left Camp 9 and the time they set off from the bivouac site was reached by working back from the time of their arrival on the summit at ten to six.

Lacedelli also agrees there was a plot hatched after the event between 'Desio, Compagnoni and Ata Ullah' to discredit Bonatti and that Bonatti was indeed made a 'sacrificial goat'. (However, as described in my commentary, any involvement of Ata Ullah in a plot against Bonatti seems most unlikely: it seems quite clear that Ata Ullah must merely have accepted the story he was told by Mahdi and in turn confronted Desio.)

Notwithstanding all this, Lacedelli states in conclusion that Bonatti was a completely honourable man and under no circumstances would have contemplated using the summit oxygen even had he been able to do so – but in any event he also confirms that he and Compagnoni had the oxygen masks at Camp 9 while Bonatti and Mahdi had none.

One final comment in the book is most interesting. Lacedelli refers to a visit he and Compagnoni made to Pakistan in 1994 to celebrate the 40th anniversary of K2, and says that Compagnoni said to him as they arrived: 'Let's hope Mahdi doesn't talk!' He asked Compagnoni what he meant by this strange comment but got no answer.

Third, and last, some new and crucial information about the oxygen bottles has now come to light. Late in 2004 Bonatti received a letter from Erich Abram, the engineer who was in charge of the oxygen bottles on K2. Who knows why Abram had remained silent for the past 50 years, but after reading the report of the *tre saggi* he volunteered some startling information about the oxygen bottles. His letter makes it absolutely clear that the rate of supply was completely invariable because the control tap was a simple on-off affair, unlike modern bottles in which the rate of flow can be varied. Heavier breathing would merely increase the amount of outside air drawn in, but the rate of oxygen flow would be unaffected. This completely negates Lacedelli's suggestion that perhaps the oxygen supply ran out earlier than expected because 'we had been breathing too hard on the way up'. Actually, the fact that the two packsaddles became exhausted simultaneously (according to both summit climbers) speaks volumes for the Germanic precision with which they functioned and indicates that they were full.

But the real bombshell is Abram's news that there were two different types of bottle. The Italian bottles destined for use at Base Camp were indeed scheduled to last ten hours, but the German Dräger bottles for the higher camps were filled at a higher pressure and supplied oxygen for twelve hours! So, even if one were to accept Lacedelli's story that they started their climb from the bivouac site at 7.30am, there would still have been one and a half hours of oxygen left in the bottles when they reached the top – though actually, since they set off at 8.30 am, it was a matter of two and a half hours.

Ironically, it therefore seems that Compagnoni's story is at least partly correct. The oxygen did perhaps run out on K2 at 8,400 metres or so, 200 metres from the summit, just as he has always insisted – but if so, this must have happened on the way down, *not* the way up!

In late 2004, there was a final sad postscript to the K2 anniversary year. Just before Christmas, Bonatti was invited by the President of Italy to attend the Quirinale Palace on Christmas Eve to be granted the 'Grand Cross of the Knights of Italy' – the very highest Italian civilian award. He was delighted and surprised. However, when he arrived at the palace for the ceremony he was disconcerted to find himself face to face with Compagnoni, who was to be presented with the same honour. One must presume that both awards were granted by the President on the recommendation of the CAI, which no doubt hoped Bonatti would at last be satisfied and cease his embarrassing agitation. Lacedelli, after the publication of his scurrilous book, was conspicuously *not* invited.

Bonatti was outraged, but held his peace during the ceremony out of respect for the office of the President. However, next day he sent the medal back to the palace with an icy note to explain why he was rejecting it. This *all'italiana* ending seemed at least in some sense, after 50 long years, a fitting climax to the entire unhappy story of the first ascent of K2.

Recognition

The Central Committee of the Italian Alpine Club had received the report of the *tre saggi* in 2004, but nothing happened for the next three years and it seemed that the whole affair might well remain in limbo forever. However, Annibale Salsa, the current President of the Club, was determined that something must be done to solve the problem once and for all, and worked tirelessly to convince those members of his own Council who wished to do nothing that the K2 affair must be settled once and for all.

And so finally, in late 2007, quite unexpectedly, an official publication finally appeared, entitled unequivocally *K2 – Una Storia Finita* (*K2 – A Final Report*), endorsed by the CAI as the definitive official account of the first ascent of K2 and correcting the version originally provided by Ardito Desio. It had taken Professor Salsa three long years to achieve his aim.

The book consists of five sections – a preface by Salsa himself, an introduction by Enrico Camanni, Director of the prestigious magazine *Alp*, followed by the report of the *tre saggi* (which is reproduced in full here in the appendix). Professor Luigi Zanzi, one of the *tre saggi*, then provides a meticulous discussion and clarification of that report (summarised below), and a final summing-up is given in a postscript provided by Roberto Mantovani, the Director of the National Mountaineering Museum in Turin, whose letter to the CAI in 2004 had started the whole enquiry.

PREFACE

The publication of this book marks the release in print of the report prepared by the *tre saggi* – Fosco Maraini, Alberto Monticone and Luigi Zanzi – who were nominated by the Italian Alpine Club after its discussion of 14 February 2004 to clarify aspects of the crucial events of 30 and 31 July surrounding the first ascent of K2 achieved by the 1954 Italian expedition.

The task given to the *tre saggi* also included the aim of providing complete satisfaction to the writers of an open letter prepared by a group of mountaineers together with a number of journalists. The letter was published in the magazine *Alp* Number 220 in January/February 2004 and also in the *Mountain Review* Number 270 in 2004. It requested the CAI to use the 50th anniversary of the first ascent of K2 to conduct an investigation into the Italian expedition in order to provide a definitive, critical historic clarification of several questions that had been the source of complex disputes and arguments, and which arose from the official account of the climb written by the expedition leader, Professor Ardito Desio.

The dispute had begun principally in relation to several depositions documented and rigorously argued by Walter Bonatti, partly, but not only, in response to accusations made against him. He had responded by initiating an action for libel, that had been decided in his favour, and his version of events was given complete endorsement by the court.

Confronted by occasional outbursts of polemics of this nature, the CAI for a long time believed it should refrain from taking any official stance on the matter and should merely allow the debate to run its course. The Society was convinced that it should avoid anything that might detract from the historic memory of such a prestigious success achieved by Italian mountaineering.

However, the duties placed upon the *tre saggi* resulted in a renewed awareness of the primary cultural duties of the CAI, that is, the assumption of full responsibility for the promotion of initiatives or actions required to obtain clarity and understanding of those key critical-historic or cultural facts that are most significant to the Club.

By initiating the review the CAI had intended to reaffirm its own responsibilities and, following its fundamental aims, to definitively research and edit the history of the climb. This, it hoped, would stimulate and cultivate an interest in alpinism and the culture of the mountains, something that can only be achieved by an open and transparent debate that gives due consideration to the various opinions and different points of view that have been expressed.

Given that on 17 January 1954 the Council General of the CAI had adopted the role of patron, and assumed full responsibility, both moral and financial, for the Italian K2 expedition, the present council 50 years later wished to respond to the need for a clarification and reconstruction of the truth of the expedition, a need that could be deferred no longer.

With that background, the Club set the *tre saggi* their task fully understanding that to do other than fully investigate the events surrounding the climb would be to permit the continuation of inappropriate and drawn-out arguments which could only diminish the value and standing of a great mountaineering feat.

The *tre saggi* Commission finished editing its own report on 28 April 2004 and delivered it to the CAI on 30 April 2004. On 22 May 2004 the report was received by the Central Council of the CAI, which unanimously approved the decision to 'accept the critical-historic report concerning the ascent of K2 provided by Fosco Maraini, Alberto Monticone and Luigi Zanzi' together with the need for an 'adequate circulation of the document'.

I believe it is extremely significant that the contribution of Fosco Maraini – honorary life member of the CAI, outstanding alpinist, explorer, ethnologist and authoritative writer – was to be his final task, and to its fulfilment he committed his usual generosity and intelligence, together with his alpine experience and common humanity.

To conform to the need to provide wide, adequate distribution of the report, it was the subject of a press conference in Milan on 3 May 2004, and was reproduced in summary in communications to various magazines – including *Lo Scarpone* (*The Boot*) and *La Rivista del CAI* (*The CAI Review*). The report of the *tre saggi*, after setting out and explaining all the preliminaries of the issues surrounding the expedition, then integrated – and, when necessary, corrected – the previous official report, signed at the time by Professor Ardito Desio, the leader of the expedition.

A critical-historic truth emerges from the report, which in many respects and on many specific points differs from the official version, which has remained unaltered for the 50 years since it was presented.

The salient points of this critical-historic truth now presented to the CAI, those which have been used to rectify, or to be integrated with, the official version of the Italian expedition to K2 in 1954, can now be briefly listed:

Camp 9 was arbitrarily moved by Compagnoni and Lacedelli from the agreed site to a different and rather higher position, too difficult for Bonatti and Mahdi to reach, loaded as they were with the oxygen supplies for the final assault on the summit.

Compagnoni and Lacedelli's climb to the summit of K2 was achieved with the use of oxygen, which lasted to the top – contrary to what Compagnoni and Lacedelli themselves stated.

The role of Bonatti and Mahdi is now recognised as the decisive and absolutely essential factor for the success of the expedition.

These are unequivocal, distinct conclusions, which will form the new official version of the ascent of K2 achieved by the Italian expedition of 1954.

The Italian Alpine Club considers that these new conclusions are now incorporated into the story of an event of major importance in the history of our culture – not merely of alpinism.

In my role as President General I wish to highlight the following:

The proposals of my term of office following the duties entrusted to the *tre saggi* were accomplished as planned.

Apart from the recognition of the crucial role which fell to Walter Bonatti in this affair (which, in some respects, had already been recognised in the dossier of the May/June 1984 issue of the CAI Review – a special number published on the occasion of the 40th anniversary of the K2 climb), there had been expressed in the earlier Official Version some historic falsehoods, which would always have spoiled its credibility.

An historic truth has now been established, which brings even more to the fore the idealistic enthusiasm of Walter Bonatti, independently of the diverse roles played by the other members, beyond any human misunderstanding and ambiguity. He emerges as the very quintessence of team spirit.

The official version of the K2 climb concerning the work of the Italian expedition has now, therefore, been integrated with the report of the *tre saggi*. The actual events of the final assault on the days of 30/31 July 1950 must be considered as having been re-written in accordance with the critical-historic facts established by the report.

The CAI is the entity responsible for the acquisition and preservation of historic documentation concerning the K2 ascent by the Italian expedition, and on 17 January 1954 it assumed the 'full moral and financial responsibility' for the expedition. In this regard, and again from my position as President General of the CAI, I must mention one last consideration. This concerns the conjecture that the *tre saggi* intended to make comprehensible the testimony on which Achille Compagnoni and Lino Lacedelli have always insisted: they state that they suffered an indisposition caused by an interruption of the oxygen they were breathing at a place quite far below the summit with two hours more of climbing ahead of them. Only recently, after a period of 50 years, and following the report of the *tre saggi*, Lacedelli has reduced the timing of this event to 'a few minutes from the summit'. The report of the *tre saggi*, in terms of documented historic truth, has rejected this conclusion, which they consider incompatible with the facts.

To derive such an exclusion from historic truth, the *tre saggi* have conjectured how compatible it would be with their assessment that the final interruption of respiration of oxygen – an interruption that affected Compagnoni and Lacedelli in a manner so grave as to make them forget exactly where they were – could have occurred practically on the summit. The conclusion of the *tre saggi* is that in the absence of any reasonable proof of this having been provided it cannot be accepted as part of the history of the climb of the Italian expedition on K2.

The *Tre Saggi* Report is therefore clear on this issue: the historic truth is that the summit of K2 was reached by Compagnoni and Lacedelli *while using oxygen right to the top.*

Any alternative version cannot form part of the story of the ascent of K2 as definitively set down by the CAI. (This does not imply that the CAI can also ascertain the human reasons which, beyond strict historic truth, leave open a route of understanding, which perhaps might redeem a stubbornly insistent error.)

In setting down this particular clarification I have intended to clearly align myself with the position expressed over the years by Walter Bonatti.

In conclusion it can be stated that in accepting the report of the *tre saggi* the Italian Alpine Club has set down the critical-historic truth of the events of the summit climb of K2 completed on 31 July 1954 which formed part of the expedition led by Professor Ardito Desio, patronised by the CAI and concluding with the success of the team. In its basic truth it honours the history of

Italian alpinism, of which the CAI is custodian, in the spirit of an incessant search for truth.

Everyone should consider the great philosophic words of the ancient classics – *Amicus Plato, sed magis amica Veritas.*

Annibale Salsa
Milan, October 31, 2007

INTRODUCTION

I believe that those who asked the CAI to carry out an examination of the mountaineering and 'political' issues relating to the 1954 K2 expedition can finally feel satisfied because clarification has been achieved and the story can never again be the same. There will be no further need for hagiography, for the confusion of legend with truth, conspiracy of silence with goodwill, and satisfied smiles with good faith.

In alpinism it happens. It always happens. The reason is that usually it is mountaineers themselves who write about themselves, rather as if Del Piero were to write the history of Juventus or Chirac the history of France. It doesn't work. It has never worked. Every scientific elaboration (and history is a science just like others) demands competence, professionalism and detachment, and should relate to methods of investigation, to research documents, to the comparisons of testimonies, and the verification of sources.

History cannot be entrusted to the protagonists unless they present themselves as mere witnesses. If it is, the results will differ from historic analyses. We will see the self-celebration of some personage, of an event, of a climb, of an expedition. There are sometimes better outcomes, honest though risky attempts at the reconstruction of history in which merits and defects are divided equally between the protagonists so as not to lay blame on anyone. Then the romantic flavour of the mountain is not spoiled by rivalry, conflict or overwhelming attitude and the story is miraculously free of the black marks and lies which, inevitably, can stain every human event.

In the case of the K2 expedition of 1954 it was clear right from the very beginning that the official account could not stand close examination. When men like Riccardo Cassin are thrown out of a team one is forced say that there is something going on which is a great deal more powerful than alpinist idealism or sporting aim. And there was indeed – the future of a country in need of redemption: post-war Italy. With apparently noble and disinterested motives, the men who were fortunate enough to climb the second-highest mountain on Earth for the first time, aware of it or not, satisfied the interests of an entire political class, of an enormous organised publicity machine, of the machinery of power, which extended way beyond their merits or their alpine limits. In other words, the story of K2 is not simply the story of a climb but the story of Italy, as it then was, struggling in a world of complex and contradictory power games.

This explains why for a good 50 years the official account of the expedition has concealed that other story, rather less noble and triumphal, that today recognises the contribution of Walter Bonatti, something that all observers with a little experience of high altitudes have known for at least 30 years. Namely that Bonatti was the strongest member of the team and would have been able to overshadow the success of his companions if he had not been marginalised during and after the expedition. This explains why his tireless exhortations concerning the truth of the matter were ignored and put aside for so long, apart, that is, from a general understanding which did nothing in terms of clarifying official facts and responsibilities. Finally it explains why, conditioned and protected by rules and overriding regulations, none of the climbers involved in the case has until now apologised, as would have happened in any respectable family, even if one of the two summiteers, Lino Lacedelli, on the 50th anniversary, has produced a book-interview which clarifies many facts and confirms the conclusions that the *tre saggi* of the CAI had reached with their parallel inquiry.

A mere handshake between the climbers would have been enough to end 50 years of accusations, court cases, humiliation, ugly situations. It would have triggered a release of pride and honesty there, at the base of the mountain, to reaffirm that the honour of a climber should not be corroded by power games and a code of silence, that no victory makes sense if it compels you to conceal the truth, that friendship is worth more than a pay cheque or a medal.

But climbers are men, no more, and like other men they make mistakes, confuse the issues, confuse themselves.

Because of this, historians are needed – they sort things out.

Enrico Camanni

The report of the *tre saggi* is reproduced in full in Appendix 2, but the clarification supplied by Professor Zanzi in *K2 – Una Storia Finita* explains the much longer full report and is in turn summarised below:

CLARIFICATIONS AND CONCLUSIONS
It seems to us that that the CAI has finally come to realise that Ardito Desio's report of the expedition lacks the integrity of historic evidence for which only Ardito Desio himself can be responsible (though his book does note that Chapter 8 'The assault on the summit' was merely accepted by Desio as reported by Achille Compagnoni and Lino Lacedelli). The matters discussed in our report diverge profoundly from the report of expedition leader Desio, finding that his account does not cover all relevant issues and includes others that are unacceptable.

Recapitulating the critical-historic truth that now emerges in respect of the final act of the K2 climb during the Italian expedition of 1954, it is possible to state that conclusions can only be recognised as acceptable if they fulfil the criterion of being compatible with other, irrefutable and incontrovertible facts. It is therefore possible to group points under the headings of **'dubious'**, **'historic falsehoods'** and **'critical-historic truths'**.

The dubious matters concern:
The arbitrary and unjustified alteration by Compagnoni and Lacedelli of the site chosen for Camp 9, which was placed much higher (about 250 metres – from 7,900 to 8,150 metres) in a zone on the far side of a difficult rocky traverse and invisible to Bonatti and Mahdi, who had climbed up from Camps 7 and 8 carrying the essential oxygen supplies for the final climb.

The incomprehensible lack of any meeting up between Compagnoni–Lacedelli and Bonatti–Mahdi, who were completing the incredible feat of climbing up from Camp 7 – to which Bonatti had descended from Camp 8 – carrying on their backs the crippling load (some 19 kilograms) of oxygen, without which it would have been impossible for Achille Compagnoni and Lino Lacedelli to reach the summit.

The even more incomprehensible lack of communication or understanding between Compagnoni–Lacedelli and Bonatti–Mahdi for an interval of about five hours, during which time Bonatti and Mahdi were perfectly visible to Compagnoni and Lacedelli while they were climbing up the 'shoulder' of K2 with their heavy load of oxygen: a lack of contact which forced Bonatti and Mahdi into the gravest risk of the entire climb – spending the night at 8,150 metres, in a storm, with no protection whatever.

The version of the contact which happened on 30 July between Compagnoni–Lacedelli and Bonatti–Mahdi while the latter two were climbing up along the shoulder is full of gaps and is unacceptable. The first contact was at 4 pm: Abram testifies there was one new contact before he left Bonatti and Mahdi: then nothing until 10 pm; at 10 pm the request to go down, leaving the oxygen bottles, in response to Bonatti's calls for help.

These gaps in contact are mysterious, but cannot be doubted, as confirmed indeed in the *report* recounted by Desio in no more than three or four lines in his version.

The historic falsehoods are:
The claimed time of departure of Compagnoni and Lacedelli from Camp 9 at 4.30-5.00 am, whereas they left in fact not before about 7.00 am, reaching the oxygen bottles left by Bonatti and Mahdi at about 8.00, leaving for the summit between 8.00 and 8.30 – and *not* at 6.00-6.30 as they stated.

The claim of Compagnoni and Lacedelli to have climbed from about 8,400 metres to the summit without oxygen after a presumed cessation of the oxygen flow when the supply was exhausted. This happened simultaneously to both of them (a simultaneity which of itself is extremely unlikely to the point of being unacceptable and challenges the entire version of events) at about 4.00 pm. This means that, according to them, having taken ten hours to climb from about 8,150 metres to 8,400 metres they then achieved the incredible miracle of climbing from 8,400 metres to 8,616 metres in two hours, without oxygen, but with 19 kilograms of bottles on their backs – a useless burden seeing that, so they say, there was no more oxygen left in the pack saddles.

(*Author's note: the simultaneous exhaustion of the oxygen sets of Compagnoni and Lacedelli does not in fact challenge the entire version of events. The oxygen system employed by the Italians was 'free flow', the rate of supply of gas being independent of the breathing rate of the climbers. Therefore it would be expected that the two sets – indeed the three bottles in each of the two sets – would exhaust almost simultaneously, and that is just what happened. What the simultaneous exhaustion does challenge is Lacedelli's story that the oxygen did not last as long as expected because the two had been breathing hard. That version appears to have been set down to support the idea that the gas did not reach the summit.*)

The critical historic truths that have emerged are highly significant to the history of the 1954 Italian expedition to K2, particularly concerning the decisive phase of the climb to the summit: as such they cut right across the production of an Official Version of the history of a mountaineering exploit that produced such an outstanding result.

This historic truth, while recognising that there are issues that are ambiguous and others that are difficult to understand in some phases of the climb, restores full dignity and respect to the memory of a great mountaineering achievement. In particular it recognises the 'team spirit', of the very greatest merit, which inspired Walter Bonatti to devote himself to the extraordinary exploit he achieved with the help of Erich Abram and the Hunza Amir Mahdi on 30 July 1954.

The final section of the CAI book is devoted to this amended, new Official Version of the story of K2, now at last accepted as the truth after 53 years.

POSTSCRIPT

History cannot be written by protagonists, as Enrico Camanni says in this book. That is sacrosanct. And it must be added that even less can it be entrusted exclusively to their recollections. These are obviously important but they are not enough. Any sort of memory, even the most precise and detailed, constitutes for the historian only one of the sources to be considered in the reconstruction of any particular event. To become a 'shared memory' – that is, history – the opinions of witnesses must be subjected to verification by a rigorous methodology, supported by documented truths, and set down in relation to other events.

'The nature of his trade as an historian', insists the great French mediaevalist Georges Duby, 'is to reassemble the facts in an attempt to get as close as possible to the truth and to remove anything that can undermine the evidence'.

Any fact in the flux of events that characterises human events has its own place and its own explanation in the great panorama of History. The ascent of a mountain is no exception. As with other activities, it can be broken down into the ideas, projects and outcomes which entwine to support a great historic event: to a multiplicity of meanings able to explain its reason for existence and even its most intimate essence.

But let us return to the central theme of this book. Given the premises, it is clear that it would be unpardonably ingenuous to reduce this epic of the so-called 'conquest' of an 8,000 metre giant to a purely sporting ambit, or to a simple drive for exploration, without investigating the possible connections with the panorama that characterised civil life, the economy, politics and international relationships in a world that had just emerged from a war like no other.

And even if it is true that the story has now definitively changed in the telling and the facts have become more equitable, it is still necessary to comment on the incomprehensible slowness with which it was investigated. It is not enough to point to its complexity – this was an event which, in the post-war years, had important implications for the countries involved in a race to the highest peaks in the world.

In fact it was not necessary to wait such a long time before asking questions about a page of history which, in the Europe of the 1950s, had seen alpinism become an international challenge, one which could be seen as a return match between nations that, until a few years earlier, had been confronting each other with weapons of war.

It is in this difficult political and cultural climate – one characterised by the transition to democracy – that the 'Himalayism' of conquest can be placed. And it is really within that logic that extraordinary mountaineering exploits find their explanation. But it is also a logic that tends to regard the conquest of the summit as worth any price. Even the traditional mountaineering schools, far from the tentacles of the politics of that time, became captives of the culture of international competition. In this way, each country had its 8,000 metre reference point: the Germans, Nanga Parbat; the English, Mount Everest; the French, Annapurna. Americans and Italians aimed at the summit of K2. It was as if the war had been transferred to another venue.

The ascent of K2 was no exception: in those days victory over the mammoth of the Karakoram came to be seen by many as the settlement of an account left unpaid for too long.

It was the demonstration that Italians too were capable of achieving great things on their own. The climb became a symbol of national redemption.

However, in relation to the Italian expedition, understanding this frame of reference should not exempt historians from investigating with great care the unfolding events which reached their conclusion on the summit of K2 on the evening on 31 July 1954.

The requirement to contrast and clarify some questions definitively has existed for a long time now. For too long these questions have been defined merely as 'arguments'.

Only after a very grave delay has the subject of this book (the *Tre Saggi* Report in the spring of 2004) allowed the Italian Alpine Club to acquire the critical-historic truth of the final phase of the first ascent of K2.

The final section of Mantovani's contribution is devoted to this amended, new version now at last accepted as the true, official story:

Notes for a new account.

The questions examined and the historic truths reached in the 2004 report, together with the work of Professor Zanzi, now allow a version of events which is accepted by historians to be summarised. This summary covers the salient facts concerning

what happened on 30 and 31 July 1954 on K2 between Camp 7 at 7,345 metres and the summit.

Mid-July 1954. For about two months the expedition had been involved in climbing the Abruzzi spur of K2. One after the other six high camps were established along the route, and the route had been equipped with fixed ropes. On 18 July two ropes – Compagnoni/Rey and Lacedelli/Bonatti – installed 700 metres of fixed rope up to the shoulder. Camp 7 was installed at 7,345 metres, at the site where in 1953, Camp 8 of the American expedition headed by Charles Houston had been placed. During the same period Camp 6 was relocated 100 metres higher up the mountain for reasons of safety. And, profiting from a break in the bad weather, the climbers also were able to furnish the high camps with food and equipment. The work was carried out by the in-form climbers: Abram, Bonatti, Compagnoni, Floreanini, Gallotti and Rey, helped by a few Hunza porters.

On 28 July, when the weather improved, the group of climbers set up Camp 8 at 7,627 metres: a single tent in which Compagnoni and Lacedelli spent the night.

The next day, these two made an attempt to establish Camp 9, the last before the summit, but were forced to stop. They were blocked by a wall of ice which overhung the camp and by the deep snow. So after they had left their rucksacks at the highest point of their attempt, Compagnoni and Lacedelli returned to camp, determined to resume their efforts the following day.

Meanwhile, in the morning, Bonatti, Gallotti, Abram and Rey set off towards the high camp with food and equipment for the final attempt. Only the first two managed to reach Camp 8. Their companions, worn out by the effort, had to go down; Abram descended only as far as Camp 8, but Rey had to go right down to Base Camp.

At this point it was clear that the date of the summit attempt would have to be postponed. Bonatti and Gallotti had managed to carry up a tent and some food and fuel. But they did not have the backpacks with the oxygen bottles, which had been abandoned a little above Camp 7, at a height which is identified in the report as between 7,375 and 7,400 metres.

At Camp 8, after they had set up the tent and eaten a little food – they had not eaten since morning – Bonatti and Gallotti crawled into the tent of their companions, and discussed with them what strategy should be adopted the next day. It was decided that on 30 July, while Compagnoni and Lacedelli climbed up to establish Camp 9, Bonatti and Gallotti would go down to recover the oxygen bottles. The Camp 9 tent, which would be set up as the final camp before the attempt on the summit, would however have to be installed at 7,900 metres, 100 metres lower than had been proposed originally, in order that the two ropes could meet: in fact, it was clear that this provision of vital equipment would demand a very significant effort: 220 metres of descent and 500 metres of climbing (which in the end, as we will see, was to become 700 metres), carrying on their backs the trestles of oxygen, which weighed some 19 kilograms – and this certainly was no joke.

In the meantime, that evening, two very strong and fit Hunza porters, Mahdi and Isakhan, arrived at Camp 7 with some new loads.

From this point, rather than setting down the differences that exist between the official version and Bonatti's story, as has been done in the recent past, we will try to follow the development of the climb by simply setting out in chronological order the facts that have been ascertained by the report of the tre saggi.

On the morning of 30 July, at the place where the day before the bottles of oxygen destined for the final assault had been abandoned, that is, at a height of about 7,375 to 7,400 metres, five men met almost at the same time: Bonatti and Gallotti, who had left at 8.00 am from Camp 8, met Abram and the two Hunza porters, who a little earlier had set off from Camp 7.

By common accord the group resumed the climb towards the high camp. Worn out by the effort, Gallotti and Isakhan had to give up at Camp 8. After a frugal meal of chicken soup and stock cubes, only Bonatti, Abram and Mahdi were left to share the task of carrying the oxygen, and they resumed climbing at 3.30 pm. They followed the tracks of Compagnoni and Lacedelli, taking turns to carry the heavy bottles. Their path led them up into a zone of shadow, and the temperature started to fall.

The three men overcame the crevasse at the base of the ice cliff and at 4.30 pm arrived on the slope above. But where was Camp 9? They called loudly to their companions, who answered and told them to follow the tracks. So they went on climbing, but were unable to see the bright orange tent. At about 5.30 to 6.00 pm Bonatti and Abram shouted again. This time, the answer they received seemed to be coming from near a huge rock above them.

Meanwhile, the sun had disappeared behind the summit ridge of K2, and the cold began to make itself felt. One of Abram's feet was completely numb, but after a massage to restore the circulation he was able to continue climbing.

By 6.30 pm, Abram had turned back to Camp 8. Bonatti and Mahdi went on by themselves, following the line of tracks towards the great hogback ridge that separates the east and south faces of K2. It would be dark in half an hour and still they did not know where the tent might be. Mahdi showed signs of panic. Bonatti shouted again. No answer. They headed towards the huge rock. Meanwhile the slope steepened and became dangerous, while the weight of the bottles became unbearable.

More shouts for help: still silence. Bonatti shed his load and climbed up to the big boulder. But the Camp was not there, the tracks went on towards the left.

At a height of 8,100 metres, 20 metres above the boulder (one of the projections on the slope that leads to the 'Bottleneck') and to the right of a series of rocky slabs, Bonatti and Mahdi were forced to stop. It was dark, and their flashlight didn't work. The slope inclined at about 50 degrees and the Hunza porter, now desperate with fear, was at risk of falling.

Every new cry was followed only by silence. Bonatti dug out a small step on the slope with his ice axe. With no shelter at all he was forced to spend the night on that steep pulpit with Mahdi, under the scourge of a wind that raised gusts of snow and made the bite of the cold unbearable. An awful, terrifying experience, above all after such an exhausting day: the young Lombardy climber had gone down 227 metres to retrieve the bottles, then climbed up 700 metres – an unheard-of feat.

More desperate shouts. Suddenly, at about 10 pm, a light appeared a little higher up over to the left. A voice – Lacedelli's – asked Bonatti if he had brought the oxygen, then told them both to go back down. A few words, then the dialogue ceased, and at once the darkness and silence returned. The drama for the two men curled up on the tiny icy terrace then commenced in earnest.

The reconstruction of the historians allows us to confirm that the camp of the summit pair was higher than had been arranged (250 metres higher, in fact) at about 8,150 metres on the far side of a difficult and dangerous traverse over treacherous rocks. 'The actual site of Camp 9', we read in the *Tre Saggi* Report, was changed, it seems, according to the direct testimony of Lino Lacedelli, not without some divergence of opinion, 'from the snowy hogback of the shoulder to the far side of some steep and delicate … rocky slabs to the left.'

Bonatti emerged from that experience miraculously unharmed. Mahdi, however, was scarred by severe frostbite of his hands and feet, which caused grave mutilation.

At 5.30 am on the morning of 31 July Mahdi started to descend to Camp 8, followed a good deal later, in full daylight in fact, by Bonatti who, before going down (he reached Camp 8 at 7,627 metres at 7.30 am), had dug out the trestles of oxygen bottles, which had been half-buried in snow. Bonatti left the bivouac site between 6.30 and 7.00 am.

After leaving Camp 9 at a time estimated by the *tre saggi* as about 6.30/6.45 am, Compagnoni and Lacedelli reached the place where the trestles of oxygen bottles lay between 7.15 and 7.45; roughly at the same time Bonatti reached Camp 8. They adjusted the respiratory apparatus and loaded the heavy trestles onto their backs. Then the two climbers – according to the 2004 report – took off for the summit at a time which can be estimated as 8.30 am ('at about 8.00 to 8.30 am'. But in his clarifying note #4, Luigi Zanzi specifies: 'most probably about 8.30 am').

The Open Circuit Dräger bottles used for the final ascent were chosen as the best available by the technical expert of the expedition, Erich Abram, and were filled to a pressure of over 220 bars with 1,700 litres of pure oxygen, and were prepared by the manufacturer's technicians to guarantee a supply for about twelve hours.

Without following the climb step by step, we know for certain that on 31 July 1954 Compagnoni and Lacedelli reached the summit in the late afternoon, a little before 6.00 pm. In the chapter signed by the two summiteers and included in the official report of the expedition leader, it is stated that the oxygen ran out at a height of 8,400 metres at about 4.00 pm; from that moment, without discarding the heavy pack-saddles, the two climbers carried on up to the summit of K2, covering the remaining slope in only two hours. They therefore completed the first part of the climb   300 metres of altitude, from 8,100 metres to 8,400 metres, in ten hours; while the final stretch – 200 metres of altitude – took them only two hours (without any oxygen).

From the *Tre Saggi* Report it emerges first of all that Compagnoni and Lacedelli reached the summit after about ten hours of climbing (nine and a half if one considers that their departure from 8,100 metres took place at about 8.30 in the morning), compared with the 1954 version, which described a little less than twelve hours in total for the climb.

In their summing up, the *tre saggi* also concluded that the first conquerors of K2 had reached the summit with the help of oxygen, which had lasted throughout their climb (cf. also the note of clarification by Prof. Zanzi #3). Apart from this, the climb was also concluded with a residue of oxygen in the bottles (cf. paragraph 2d of Zanzi's report, #3). How much? If we re-calibrate 'in a completely conjectural and prudent manner' the availability of the oxygen reserves from twelve to ten hours, 'the supply of oxygen … would have lasted right up to the summit of K2, with a reserve capacity of at least half an hour' (cf. paragraph 2d in Zanzi's report #3). But since the re-calibration to a minimum of ten hours of oxygen supply is a 'conjectural and prudent' eventuality, concerning a 'proposed technical guarantee' of twelve hours it is also possible to work out a hypothesis of a maximum, which allows us to increase the duration of the reserves of oxygen to two and a half hours. In his note (#5) Zanzi in fact speaks specifically 'of a *minimum* of 30 minutes (compared with a predicted theoretical *maximum* of two and a half hours)'.

The 'convergence' of the *tre saggi* 'on a critical-historic result of reaching the summit of K2 with the use of oxygen' in fact has no relevance to any question of 'sport'. At the time of the 'conquest' of K2 the use of respirators was considered normal and necessary: only after the first ascent of Everest without oxygen by Reinhold Messner and Peter Habeler in 1978 did the use of oxygen become a discriminating factor in the evaluation of a Himalayan climb. In the particular case with which we are concerned here, the reference to the duration of the oxygen supply on 31 July 1954 merely furnishes a fundamental measuring stick to reconstruct as accurately as possible the temporal sequence of some fundamental events, and to identify the correct altitude of the places in which the salient facts of the final acts in the 'conquest' of K2 took place.

Roberto Mantovani

As may well be imagined, Bonatti more than anyone was overjoyed to find the CAI finally re-writing the history of K2. He has now finally won the battle he started in 1964 and the lies about the summit day have finally been laid to rest. He has now been able to write this final chapter for his new anthology *Ricordi* (*Memories*):

Today, 18 October 2007, the Italian Alpine club, through the announcement of its President General, has completely fulfilled the need claimed by myself to repudiate the lies and foul play involved in the crucial sections of the official account of Ardito Desio, the leader of the K2 expedition. So at last, even though it is now 53 years since the conquest of K2, the true story of what happened at that time is established once and for all.

Honour and credit is due, first of all, to Professor Annibale Salsa, President General of the CAI, because his achievement in bravely committing himself to replace the lying official version with the truth has demanded that he had to fight against a certain persistent resistance present even in the Central Committee of the Society itself.

I would also like to express my praise and thanks to Professor Luigi Zanzi, who had already served as a member of the *tre saggi* committee. During the following three years he has shown the same perseverance and has persisted with his researches until he could establish the true story of every moment and every condition of the final assault on K2.

I also wish to give specific and significant credit to Reinhold Messner, quite apart from my wish also to thank him for his public statements in Trento in 2004, when he made some very pertinent comments about the true story of K2 during an evening session of his Film Festival.

Here are some of the comments made by Messner – during discussions, or published later in the press: *If the conquest of K2 had its own father in Ardito Desio, then it had a second father in Walter Bonatti.* And brushing away the arguments he also said *Bonatti had no masks, so he couldn't have used the oxygen, but in any case he had not the slightest intention of making a summit attempt. Anyway, if he had wanted to try he wouldn't have gone down to Camp 7 to fetch the oxygen bottles, which demanded an enormous effort. Instead, he gave his all, and risked his life to allow the Italian expedition to succeed'.* He added later *True alpinists have always known this. I'm happy for Bonatti, but his merits have never been in doubt. Today, what Professor Salsa has written is most important for the reputation of Italy overseas: the CAI was the only organization that went on supporting the official account, which clearly is just not credible.*

Then, speaking of himself, Messner commented further: *'The same sort of ugly bastardry suffered by Bonatti on K2 was heaped on me concerning Nanga Parbat: with K2 they screwed him twice – at the time, then again later. They trapped him, and they wounded him very deeply. And now, after 53 years, the CAI has agreed he was right all along: but we mountaineers knew this already. Desio and Compagnoni were Fascists, and they formed an alliance because of this. Bonatti was the best and easily the youngest man of the team – just ripe for sacrifice.*

The leader of the German expedition, Karl Herrligkoffer, who doubted my story about Nanga Parbat, was a Nazi.

Signor Marco Onida, Secretary General of the Alpine Convention of Bolzano, wrote this about the CAI book in a press release on 19 March 2008:

This is an act of great responsibility which has restored credibility to our country: with the publication of *K2 – Una Storia Finita* the Italian Alpine Club has taken the final step to correct the errors and omissions contained in Ardito Desio's account of the Italian expedition he led, which in 1954 conquered for the first time the second highest mountain on Earth – K2, 8,616 metres. Walter Bonatti has now been recognised definitively and unequivocally as playing the key role which allowed Compagnoni and

Lacedelli to make their assault on the summit. He provided them with the essential oxygen bottles, descending from Camp 8 to Camp 7, then climbing again to Camp 9, which had however been placed by Compagnoni and Lacedelli at a different site from that previously agreed. This meant that Bonatti and Mahdi were forced to bivouac in the open in a storm at a height of over 8,100 metres. Bonatti survived this ordeal unscathed, but Mahdi had to undergo various amputations of his hands and feet. Apart from being a victim, Bonatti was later made the object of absurd accusations and suspicions concerning his 'presumed true intentions' and was forced to take (successful) legal action.

With this gesture the CAI has put itself forward not as a defender of the presumed 'truth' which would have sat comfortably in an historic period during which Italy was trying to regain the international esteem it had lost in the first half of the century, but rather as a custodian of a 'demonstrated and documented critical-historic truth'.

We must not forget that the expectation for a rectification of official versions has long since passed beyond the borders of Italy. This publication by the CAI restores credibility to Italy in the mountaineering world and in the high mountain culture of the entire planet.

Sadly, Bonatti is still a little less than completely content concerning this final denouement of the K2 scandal which has filled his life for so many years because many press reports, as so often happens, completely missed the point of what had occurred and insisted still on referring to Bonatti's *rehabilitation* (*sic!*). Here are his final comments in *Ricordi*:

Conclusion
To make what follows more comprehensible, I will recapitulate the events of the past ten years. In 1994, on the 40th anniversary of the first ascent of K2, the Italian Alpine Club announced 'Bonatti has been rehabilitated'. In everyone's eyes this admission appeared intentionally

soothing – undoubtedly for the Society itself, which with this press release evidently was trying to resolve the age-old, burning questions about K2 with a minimum of fuss. But if we wish to analyse the matter we must immediately ask ourselves: 'Bonatti rehabilitated? From what? For what crime? What terrible thing did he do?'

There are two possible answers:

First, one must note that, if today (as was also the case yesterday during the fortieth anniversary) the CAI pronounced me 'rehabilitated', this would imply that the Club believed me guilty of something: but this would mean it had reached this conclusion without ever having subjected its accusations to any analysis or criticism. So it would all be groundless.

The second possibility, perhaps more probable but even more improper, would also originate from the CAI and would presumably relate to the story invented by Compagnoni and Lacedelli, who accused me of consuming a good part of the bottled oxygen intended for their use. But I took that story to court for damages in a libel action, which succeeded.

So, what did the CAI actually mean? It cannot behave as if it were a tribunal investigating a crime. More than that, this is not a matter which concerns today, nor even the fortieth anniversary – the whole affair happened a good 54 years ago and the CAI of those days treated me somewhat less than helpfully.

But beyond this expedient use of the word 'rehabilitation', which has persisted for years unresolved, there is the false and serious account given by the summit pair, which I have always opposed vehemently. Quite apart from the version in the now discredited original official account, Compagnoni and Lacedelli (clinging desperately to the non-existent fact that the oxygen ran out at 8,400 metres) have continued to repeat the absurd lie that they continued to climb under their own steam right up to the summit.

This was the great, basic lie later added to by one thing after another – places, times, equipment and its use. This is what I have fought incessantly to combat ever since 1967, and it was certainly not in the hope for any personal compensation that I kept putting this forward though, sadly, even today some people still continue to hold this against me. On the contrary – I have pursued truth and justice with the aim of restoring dignity to the historic events of the conquest. And thank goodness, these aims have now finally been achieved. But only thanks to the steadfast will of right-thinking men, Professors Annibale Salsa and Luigi Zanzi, the authors of *K2 – Una Storia Finita*.

The comment I have heard most often these days is from those who congratulate me for having been 'rehabilitated' by the CAI after 54 years. Well, many thanks – even if, as seems obvious, these well-meaning people have been unable to read the true revelations contained in the CAI's reparative book. But that's how things have panned out, thanks to the quite terrible information system operated by the media. So I still have to keep repeating that the revolutionary change from negative to positive in the history of K2 must be attributed solely to the advent of a frank, definitive recognition of what really happened on the mountain on that 30th and 31th of July so many years ago. In this new CAI book the lie about the oxygen presented as the truth in Desio's official book is denounced and blame finally rests where it belongs. It is established that the bottles did *not* run out and that the two climbers reached the summit of K2 after using oxygen for the entire duration of their climb, which took nine and a half hours from when they left the bivouac site at half past eight.

Nevertheless, look what was reported instead these days in a great part of the national press: in newspapers like *La Stampa*, *La Repubblica*, *Il Resto del Carlino* and associates, *Il Messagero*, *Il Giornale*, *Il Gazzettino del Nordest* and still others from the Italian provinces, not to mention some confused and inexact *ANSA* reports. They are all much the same and quite repetitive – here are some of the contents:

'Bonatti rehabilitated. He did not abstract oxygen from the bottles Compagnoni and Lacedelli carried to the heights'.
'Bonatti has been rehabilitated by the CAI. He is now recognised as playing the key role which allowed Compagnoni and Lacedelli to succeed in their climb'.
'It emerges from the *tre saggi* report that the bottles were carried up by Bonatti'.
'For years Bonatti has fought, even in court, to have his contribution recognised'.
'Bonatti has finally had his revenge. The CAI has officially recognised his contribution to the conquest of K2'.

But, when all is said and done, not the least mention about oxygen being used right up to the summit. Not one line about the scandalous lies that accompanied the two of them right up to the top. Not a single word about the lies in their account considered until yesterday to be the true official story.

So there it is, still, for the umpteenth time – a garbled opinion forced down readers' throats by an information service that shows itself to be not merely inattentive but ignorant. But still, these are no more than the views of an Italy which again and again displays its same old superficiality. What really matters is that, finally, complete historic truth and all due dignity have been restored to this Italian achievement and, after 53 dismal years, has now awakened once more in our country a sense of national pride and joy.

Walter Bonatti
31 March 2008

Compagnoni's Reaction

The imposing edifice of lies erected by Desio and Compagnoni in the 1950s had seemed quite impregnable for many years, and Bonatti's successful libel case in the 1960s had raised no more than a ripple of public interest. His book *Processo al K2* (*Trial on K2*), published three decades after the climb, mounted the first assault on the official story, but nothing really changed until ten years later when the summit photos were published in *Alp* on the 40th anniversary. The ensuing controversy saw the first cracks appear in Compagnoni's stronghold, but another decade had to pass before the frontal assault of the Tre Saggi on the 50th anniversary completely breached its ramparts: the crumbling walls finally collapsed in complete ruin three years later, when in 2007 the CAI itself published its new official history.

However, soon after the Tre Saggi Report was presented in April 2004, Lacedelli had finally deserted his fellow conspirators when his book *K2: Il Prezzo di Conquista* (*The Price of Conquest*) was published. In it he totally repudiated the account of the climb given by Compagnoni in Ardito Desio's official book and made bitter accusations about his climbing partner's motives concerning Bonatti. So in August 2004, Compagnoni was interviewed by the *Corriere della Sera* (*The Evening Courier*) immediately after the Cortina d'Ampezzo celebrations of the K2 50th anniversary. He was livid with rage, and furious with Lacedelli. In response to questions about Lacedelli's book, he said:

> I've read his book and I don't want to hear any more about it. It throws mud on the victory. Now, fifty years later, it's all just one huge argument, an accusation, a disgrace – and now the CAI has joined in and wants to review the truth that

was recognized then. But I put the national flag on the summit. I lost two fingers taking photos and spent a hundred days in hospital. I will not allow this!

I read Lacedelli's book in one night. At first I was astonished, then shocked. He has humiliated me, if it were possible to be humiliated by such false accusations. How could anyone imagine I alone decided to move Camp 9? The tent couldn't be set up in that place. It was too dangerous – we were below a very threatening ice cliff.

[*Author's note: But it wouldn't have been dangerous to put Camp 9 on the 'shoulder' at 7,900 metres, as had been agreed the evening before.*]

So we moved away onto a ridge to the left.

Bonatti couldn't make it on time. Our appointment was for three thirty in the afternoon, but at that time he was still inside his tent at Camp 8, or perhaps he had just left. Everyone gives what he can. Bonatti did a great deal. I did even more.

Bonatti was my friend. He was a guest in my house here in Cervinia. Every year we were together in Courmayeur on 21 June, the anniversary of the death of our companion Mario Puchoz. On one occasion, I think it was the seventh time; we were dining at Ubaldo Rey's home. Suddenly Bonatti got up, excused himself, said he had to go, goodbye! That was the last time I ever saw him. Immediately after that he started his accusations.

[*Author's note: And these accusations have now been acknowledged as completely justified by the CAI: the report of the* tre saggi *has accepted Bonatti's version as the absolute truth.*]

Lacedelli and I were friends for fifty years; and now he makes up all this poisonous rubbish – I don't want to hear from him any more. It isn't true that we arrived on the summit still breathing oxygen. The bottles were empty. We hadn't taken them off because we were still telling each other that there must still be a little oxygen left. A lie, to give ourselves courage.

[*Author's note: Yet another variant – this is completely at odds with his original version.*]

Compagnoni's spurious indignation during this interview in 2004 was conspicuously unsuccessful in defusing the outrage aroused in informed Italian mountaineering circles by the Tre Saggi Report and confirmed now by Lacedelli's revelations. Nevertheless, for the next three years the CAI Council, despite having formally accepted the Tre Saggi report, did nothing further, although President Annibale Salsa was working hard to convince his Central Committee that the Club must recognise officially that Ardito Desio's official K2 account was inaccurate. Finally, in 2007, Salsa succeeded; *K2 – Una Storia Finita* was published by the CAI and the true story of the first ascent of K2 emerged at last. In a final desperate attempt to save his reputation, Compagnoni was moved to write an article, which was published in the March 2008 issue of the Italian magazine *Trekking*. It was called *Il Mio K2* (*My K2*):

On July 31 1954, when I was almost 40 years old, Lino Lacedelli and I conquered K2. I am now 93 years old and note with great bitterness that I have been subjected more and more, particularly in recent years, to an increasing barrage of criticism against myself and Ardito Desio. Very little has survived of that group spirit which allowed us to conquer K2, and this has left space for a never-ending conflict, not lacking in deliberate personal attacks; by some members of the expedition more than the rest. These eternal accusations relate exclusively to the highest camps, where problems were created whose further investigation went on into the depths; to the foot of the mountain. It has been by climbing K2 again figuratively with Mario Fantin that I have started to understand where these problems all started, and I was gratified to read his book *K2 Sogno vissuto* (*K2 – A Dream Brought to Life*) Tamari, Bologna 1958. This book, rather than being merely a diary, is a very real *'naval-type log-book, and is therefore not susceptible to changes, nor to the involuntary distortions made inevitable by human nature when written much later as a result of suggestions or recollections.'*

Particular thanks are due to Fantin for the tables he punctiliously produced day after day concerning the daily movements of each climber, from which the strategy of each emerges. As a whole the writings of Mario Fantin represent a *'breath of fresh air, with news from 50 years ago'*. Today, however, I wish to reaffirm vehemently that the conquest of K2 was due to the entire climbing team and to Ardito Desio who – thanks to his iron-fisted control – knew how to manage and transform all of them into a united group; from the most individualistic to the most unselfish.

I wish to record the efforts of Puchoz in setting up Camp 4 at an altitude of more than 6,500 metres; this outstanding alpinist was then struck down by pneumonia. I also want to record the generosity of Rey: I quote from my book *Uomini sul K2* (*Men on K2*) the events of the nights of 26 and 27 July at Camp 7 – *'Bonatti did not have a sleeping bag so Rey and I, for one night each, gave him our own bag and slept without. During the first night I was woken by a terrifying sensation of oppression: I became aware that I couldn't breathe.'* Who knows if that night of generosity was fateful for Rey and caused the sudden illness that compelled him to give up the following day?

I also must note the generosity of Lacedelli, who offered me his glove on the summit in an attempt to save my frozen fingers: my own had been blown away by the wind. There were also the extraordinary efforts of all the other climbers, but in particular those of Gallotti, Viotto and Abram. And Bonatti too, who back in Italy came to visit me in hospital, smiling and without the slightest sign of rancour.

This was my K2! This was the spirit of the Italian victory over K2!

That huge mountain was vanquished because it was enmeshed in a web of fixed ropes, and thanks to nine camps established and adequately supplied by all of us. Every member of the expedition climbed up to and down from the various camps many times to install stretches of fixed ropes, or to carry up tents, oxygen bottles, ropes, pitons, cooking stoves and other equipment: all in very bad weather, buried in snow up to their waists or climbing up impressive slopes of sheet ice.

I, Achille Compagnoni, took part in that expedition, and it was I who directed the summit attack on K2. This responsibility was entrusted to me officially on July 14 1954 by Ardito Desio; I had by then spent 50 days climbing on the slopes of K2, and he evidently had identified me as the man for the job. I quote: *'From the Order of Service number 12, July 14 1954 ... In conclusion of what is set out above the following duties are allotted to:*
a) To Achille Compagnoni the role and responsibility of directing the attack on the summit ... sig. Ardito Desio.'

And I carried to its conclusion this task that had been entrusted to me – I conquered K2. I acclaim with great pride my role and my exertions, to confront those who (even in the pages of this magazine) have said I found myself on the summit of K2 'by chance'. On the slopes of that mountain I gave my whole heart and soul without sparing myself. I set up a good seven of the nine camps with various companions. I climbed up and down the slopes of K2 so many times that I accumulated in all, with ascents and descents, more than 16,000 metres – more than any other member of the expedition – as set out in the table provided by M. Fantin in his book *K2 – Sogno Vissuto*, quoted above. Adding it all up, I climbed and descended K2 more than four times, from Base Camp (4,970m) to the summit (8,611m).

Every day I committed myself totally to the success of the expedition, never sparing myself except for the pauses forced by the fury of storms. Unlike some others, I never even considered the need to acclimatize myself and so preserve my energies for a possible final assault. At critical moments of the the expedition my sole aim was to carry on and bring the enterprise on which we had embarked to a successful conclusion. I would not go along with useless modifications or spiteful confrontation of Ardito Desio's orders, because this would have meant only one thing – failure.

TABLE OF THE CLIMBERS' MOVEMENTS ON K2
M Fantin

Compagnoni, Achille	16,110m
Gallotti, Pino	15,272m
Lacedelli, Lino	14,106m
Rey, Ubaldo	13,462m
Viotto, Sergio	12,597m
Abram, Eric	12,481m
Soldá, Gino	12,361m
Bonatti, Walter	11,577m
Floreanini, Cirillo	10,049m
Puchoz, Mario (died on June 21 1954)	7,120m
Fantin, Mario	5,518m
Angelino, Ugo	3,998m
Pagani, Guido	3,988m

Achille Compagnoni

Readers will note many omissions and inconsistencies in this self-serving diatribe. Compagnoni makes no mention whatever at this stage of his role in the controversies of the last 50 years. In contrast to his interview four years earlier in *Corriere della Sera* (see above), he now says nothing at all about his decision to change the site of Camp 9; nothing about the time when he and Lacedelli left Camp 9 next morning; nothing about his original fabrication of the oxygen supply running out two hours below the summit; nothing at all concerning the accusations he levelled at Bonatti in 1964 or of the court case two years later. There is not one word now about the Tre Saggi Report, nor any mention of the 2007 CAI publication (*K2: Una Storia Finita*), which flatly rejected his account of the climb to the summit; neither does Compagnoni now deign even to mention Lacedelli's totally damning accusations in *K2: The Price of Conquest*.

But it is also interesting to see how this article mounts a varied and quite subtle attack on Bonatti. Apart from presenting himself as a heroic donor of his own sleeping bag to Bonatti at Camp 7 (which is a direct lie), Compagnoni also suggests it was Bonatti depriving Rey of *his* sleeping bag that caused Rey to become ill, give up the climb and turn back to Camp 7. He also implies Bonatti was a hypocrite because he visited Compagnoni in hospital in 1954 'smiling'. But of course at that stage Bonatti knew nothing whatever of the kangaroo court in Pakistan, which had condemned him of trying to get to the summit, stealing the oxygen and then deserting Mahdi. That story emerged only ten years later, and during the 1950s, after the team first returned to Italy, Bonatti was simply trying to make the best of things.

In contrast to his own spotless integrity (!), Compagnoni also refers to those 'others' who attempted to sabotage Desio's orders, and in particular those who chose to 'preserve their energies for a summit attempt' (who else can this mean but Bonatti?). Finally, the table of the altitudes climbed by the various climbers is quite interesting because, on the dubious authority of the expedition photographer, Compagnoni lists Bonatti as almost the lowest achiever, whose contribution to the expedition exceeded only that of the medical officer (Pagani), the photographer (Fantin) and three climbers, including one disabled by illness (Angelino) and one who died (Puchoz).

As one would expect, Bonatti was most unhappy when he read this article in *Trekking* – he wrote at once to the publishers as follows:

Dear Sirs,

I was surprised and disillusioned to read on pages 18 and 19 in the March 2008 issue of *Trekking* an article signed by Achille Compagnoni: a man whose repeated lies have by now been unmasked by assiduous clarification all over the world.

Let us carefully examine his arguments one after another. Compagnoni says on Page 18 '*Bonatti did not have a sleeping bag so Rey and I, for one night each, gave him our own bag and slept without.*' Well, not only on K2, but also during every other expedition, I always slept only in my own sleeping bag. Everyone regards this particular piece of equipment as strictly personal and every climber always carries his own bag everywhere in his own rucksack. To use anyone else's would, as everyone knows, be like wearing someone's soiled underpants. But apart from that, I spent *four* nights at Camp 7 (25, 26, 27 and 28 July), all of them in my own sleeping bag. To clarify the matter even further, I should add that on the morning of July 28 Compagnoni, Lacedelli, Rey, Abram and Gallotti all left Camp 7 and went up to establish Camp 8; Rey had to turn back to Camp 7 a little later because he was completely exhausted; he stayed there with me in the same tent, wrapped up in his own sleeping bag, naturally enough, and the following morning set off and went back down to Base Camp. On that same afternoon of 28 July Abram and Gallotti also returned to Camp 7. On the other hand, when Compagnoni and Lacedelli had set off from Camp 7 to establish Camp 8 they had obviously taken their own sleeping bags with them in their rucksacks. Even though this story about the sleeping bags seems absolutely ridiculous it does have some importance, because it shows how this fellow, hell-bent on bringing me into disrepute, talks the most utter hogwash.

Turning to the table on page 19 of *Trekking*, there is a great deal to which I could object concerning the various loads I carried above Camp 5. The figures are incomplete and completely inaccurate. But enough of that. Let us now speak of Mario Fantin, the expedition photographer and author of *K2 Sogno Vissuto*. It is certainly Fantin himself who must be held responsible for all the omissions, blunders and errors contained in that book of his, and also for those in the film *Italia K2*. However, no less responsible than Fantin are those who for the past 50 years have used and have continued to use these same omissions and falsehoods – even using them as a shield as the need arose – and doing so without ever making the most minimal attempt at verification or critical analysis.

But with these tables published in his book and now reported in part in *Trekking*, it is Fantin himself who is finally responsible that errors like this have never been forgotten and now have even managed to assume the aura of historic truths on which any commentator can draw. And many have done so, writing and speaking about K2 for more than fifty years. *Trekking* itself stated, concerning *K2 Sogno Visto*: '*This book, rather than being merely a diary, is a very real naval-type log-book, and is therefore not susceptible to changes... .*'

Referring to these graphic tables, the fact is that between 28 March and 12 July Fantin had been to Camp 1 no more than four times, each time going up and down the same day. After 13 July he then did reach Camp 2 and stayed there for six days, then went on up to Camp 4 (6,560m), where he stayed for a few more days. But he went no higher than this at any time. So I must comment: in all that time, never having visited any of the four upper camps (5, 6, 7 and 8), which were notoriously problematic in the demands they made on climbers, how on earth could Fantin have seen anything that would enable him to testify what went on up there? And indeed, how could he have known anything about what happened above Camp 4 except what he was told by others? I have to say that this 'knowledge' and 'information' of Fantin's could only have come from someone else – perhaps a Compagnoni, for example? It was he who had also made up the same lies that one reads, strange to say, on page 200 of Fantin's book, where it says just this: '*July 31. At four, Compagnoni and Lacedelli were already on their feet. At five they left their tent and set off down to the oxygen respirators. The weather had closed in. K2 was surrounded by a heavy cloud cap.*' And again, further on, on page 202: '*For the last two hours they had been without oxygen. Disconcerted by the physical reaction provoked by the unexpected lack (of oxygen) they set off again, incredulous that they were able to resist (...) On the conquered summit, stretched out on the ground, they finally freed themselves of the heavy respirators.*'

But there is still one other matter to enrich the *curriculum vitae* of Fantin and also that of Compagnoni. The feature film *Italia K2*, mostly derived from shots taken for the most part by the official photographer Fantin, was presented in public for the first time at the Barberini Cinema in Rome, in the presence of the highest Italian authorities and personalities. Well, as far as the final assault on the summit was concerned, the film contained not the slightest mention, neither on film nor in the commentary, of my efforts at very high altitude to supply the summit pair with oxygen; nor was there a single word about my enforced bivouac that night in the storm. I protested, and after that the film was changed.

Thirty years went by, and I found myself a guest on a television programme together with the director who had produced that film – Marcello Baldi. Poor Marcello; with understandable embarrassment he felt duty bound to tell me that, in the course of the production of *Italia K2*, no one had ever told him what had happened to me that night of 30/31 July up there in the storm at over 8,100 metres. But the real surprise for me was to be told that the film's director, Marcello Baldi, had been supplied with two consultant historians – Mario Fantin and Achille Compagnoni.

Must this tainted story go on and on forever?

Walter Bonatti

Regrettably, but all too clearly, the Italian press for the most part had never been very well informed about the K2 saga, and the repeated, exasperating comments about Bonatti's 'rehabilitation' have often left him frustrated and at times infuriated. But at least this time *Trekking* was moved to consider Bonatti's letter and a journalist actually took the trouble to read the new CAI book. In May 2008 a long article by Michele Dalla Palma appeared in *Trekking* to set the record straight at last. *K2 Una Storia Finita* was extensively quoted and Compagnoni's views were utterly rejected. Dalla Palma's critique was illustrated by a large photograph of the CAI's book cover and was entitled:

L'Opinione
K2: una storia finita

In 2004, on the 50th anniversary of the first ascent of the most demanding mountain on the planet, the unresolved arguments which have muddied this magnificent exploit exploded yet again. The climb had been accomplished by a group of wonderful mountaineers at a very difficult time in Italian history.

No one, at any time, had ever instigated any discussion concerning the conquest of K2 on that 31st of July 1954. The aberrant gestation of the disgraceful description of the climb produced by the leader of the expedition, Ardito Desio, produced a compound of lies, wickedness, false accusations and fabrications. His report manages to debase the efforts, the suffering and even the tragic outcomes for some men who left part of their lives on the mountain, transforming an exceptional event into a squalid *all'italiana* farce. (I say this with all good will towards those who may be indignant about my judgement in comparing the methods and modalities of this story to the worst and darkest events of our national life in the last half century.)

The K2 affair developed quite quickly from a mere mountaineering chronicle into a series of court cases and, despite the history, the established facts and the long since forgotten evidence, the 'Little General' managed to manipulate and distort the true story right up to the time of his death.

For my part, I have already expressed my thoughts about this milestone of alpinism and, unfortunately, also about the intellectual dishonesty of some people, in two articles published in this magazine in 2004. Today, after four long years of delay, the official document signed by the Italian Alpine Club has finally appeared. It finally renders long delayed but complete justice to those who made victory possible fifty years ago but received in exchange nothing more than infamy and offence.

At the same time, and with the obligatory soberness due towards an institution like the CAI, one must identify as 'historic falsehood' the account provided by the two principal authors of the official version, Ardito Desio and Achille Compagnoni. Until now this has been accepted as the only exhaustive documentation concerning the conquest of the mountain. For the past fifty years, and to the bitter end, this 'Desio-truth' has been held up as accurate, and it is difficult to avoid attributing to the CAI a great responsibility for this. Nevertheless, the current President of the Club has made his own intervention in the matter abundantly clear.

For the record, it must be noted that a document signed by the senior mountaineer Achille Compagnoni was published in the last issue of this magazine. In substance he repeated, with considerable rhetoric and emphasis, the same story he has told for the past fifty years. In the light of the new official document now provided by the CAI, this grates even more and leaves room for anyone to make his own judgement about the honesty of this man.

Apropos of this recent article in *Trekking*, and referring explicitly to Desio, Compagnoni and Lacedelli, the CAI President Annibale Salsa specifies in his introduction of the book: 'This does not imply that the CAI can make judgements about *human* factors which, apart from matters of strict historic truth, leave open a path of *understanding*, which can perhaps redeem a persistently perverse error.'

FACTS AND HISTORY

From today, and surely everyone will allow me the pleasure of saying 'finally', Desio's vituperative 'absolute truth' about K2 assumes the precise shape of a deliberately false story. Personally, I grant to Desio too acute an intelligence to think of all this as an error committed in good faith. Rather, in the light of what went on in the years following the ascent of K2, it is easy to discern a scrupulously detailed plan, consistent with the style of a scientist, to derail every investigation or request for clarification about what had to remain his personal 'victory'.

But now let us examine the outcome, now published as an official book, as presented by the Tre Saggi – Fosco Maraini, Alberto Monticone and Luigi Zanzi – who were recruited by the CAI in 2004 to shed light on one of the most notorious 'Italian Intrigues'.

[*Author's note: Here follows a long series of quotations from* K2: Una Storia Finita.]

Dalla Palma's article continues:

WALTER BONATTI ON K2, FIFTY YEARS LATER

I know, from many years acquaintance with Bonatti, that he is regarded as one of the great legends of alpinism. I regard him as one of the straightest and toughest people I have ever met, always inclined to drive himself mercilessly on a matter of 'principle'. His last letter to *Trekking* a few days ago touched me greatly. He referred word for word to the affirmations made by Compagnoni in the March issue of this magazine, and with precision bordering on the maniacal he specified and contested every last detail – just as if the matters he was discussing had happened yesterday and not fifty years ago.

This rare if not unique talent is what has allowed him to become Walter Bonatti. Many other people, perhaps most, would have 'let it lie' long ago when confronted by what seemed a futile battle, purely a matter of philology and third-rate quibbles. Oxygen bottles yes; oxygen bottles no; a metre of altitude more or less on the infinite pyramid of K2. These seemed quite childish preoccupations for a giant that the whole world has regarded for at least four decades to be one of the greatest interpreters of alpinism.

But even among the most 'single-minded', many people have misunderstood his tenacity, which for a long time seemed devoid of any possibility whatever of successfully dismantling the falsehoods of the Official History of K2 as recounted by Desio and Compagnoni.

It seemed perhaps to be the presumption of an already great man demanding recognition of yet another achievement, yet another victory. But this isn't so! Walter has not been fighting for his name and his honour – he has no need to do so because they are both immense. Neither does he need to add another summit, however enormous, to his curriculum vitae – he has been fighting for what is defined in the Tre Saggi report as *Historic Truth*. This stands aside from human richness and poverty, and remains universally fixed in time; it cannot be made subservient to the machinations and interests of individual men.

Even if all Walter Bonatti's exploits were to be forgotten, he should be remembered for this – to have pursued for half a century the affirmation of historic truth, which is not a matter of emotions, sensations, misunderstandings and lies, but of deeds and incontrovertible facts.

This is where he has committed his whole being, even risking ridicule when many people have asked themselves 'But what does this fellow Bonatti want?' without understanding that the issue is not a squabble about dates and days but concerns the very essence of *historic truth*. For a long time the mountaineering world has recognised Bonatti's merits, but men pass on – while history, written in books or in stone, remains.

This mountaineer, who has made integrity the only wall one must not violate, demonstrates to all of us that truth is a chimera worth fighting for with all our strength. Because at times it becomes reality.

So today, finally, Walter Bonatti has written the final page of his story of K2.

Postscript

Readers may well ask how it is that *K2: Lies and Treachery* came to be written by an Australian surgeon who has never climbed a mountain in his life, but I hope this book is acceptable as a completely unbiased analysis of what happened on K2 in 1954. The final conclusions reached are quite certainly accurate, as certified by the Italian Alpine Club itself – however, some explanation seems appropriate.

I first became a dedicated armchair mountaineer many years ago when I read Fosco Maraini's wonderful book *Karakoram*, a description of the 1958 Italian expedition to Gasherbrum IV. That expedition, led by Riccardo Cassin, had seen Walter Bonatti and Carlo Mauri reach the summit, and soon afterwards I chanced to come across Bonatti's first instalment of his autobiography, *On the Heights*, in a bookstore in Melbourne. I was enthralled and became completely fascinated by the world of the high mountains: I soon was an avid collector of mountaineering books. I also started to study Italian at the same time because I had a great number of Italian patients and, as part of the learning process, bought Bonatti's climbing books in Italian and translated them.

I was also driven to become an enthusiastic trekker and visited the Himalaya many times, but I knew nothing of what had happened on K2 apart from the original account in *Le Mie Montagne* until, once again by pure chance, I came across *Processo al K2* in 1985 and read for the first time about the libel case of 1966. I realised immediately what had really happened on K2 and wrote the commentary reproduced here as Chapter 5. I later visited Bonatti and came to understand how very badly he had been treated: the need to see his name cleared soon became an obsession.

Through a combination of most unlikely events, in 2004 I found myself invited to speak at three separate mountaineering conventions, in Lugano (Switzerland), Banff (Canada) and Leeds (UK), where at last I had the opportunity to make public the matters discussed in this book. I recall that in Leeds I somewhat emotionally described the whole disgraceful affair as 'a piece of typical Italian Machiavellian bastardry' – and I see no reason to change that judgement.

It goes without saying that Italy produces not only villains but also men of complete integrity, and Walter Bonatti is certainly one of those men. He has, however, for the last half-century been treated shamefully, in a way that beggars belief. It is very interesting to contrast what happened during the K2 affair with the behaviour on other climbs carried out by other nations. Needless to say, there have been plenty of examples of friction (or worse) on other expeditions – such as the ill-fated 1971 'International Everest' team that disintegrated completely and even had disaffected climbers throwing things at each other and leaving in a huff. The leader of that expedition, Colonel Jimmy Roberts, shed some light on the fiasco in his memoirs. He noted regretfully that a disability had prevented him going beyond Base Camp and added that this had certainly not helped matters. His restrained comments on the debacle that ensued leave little doubt concerning his views about the whole unhappy affair:

The International Expedition of 1971 is probably remembered now mainly for the walk-out of the four so-called "Latins" in protest about concentrating all our efforts on the South-west Face climb. In fact the seeds of failure had already been sown when a spell of appalling weather followed the quite unnecessary death of a well-loved Indian member. The expedition was if anything strengthened by the departure of the dissidents (three of whom were in any case probably somewhat too elderly for very high altitude work), only to be decimated by an outbreak of apparently infectious fever. Despite all this, we did not do too badly and my main regret was the loss of a childish and innocent personal belief that mountaineers of a certain calibre and reputation must also be gentlemen (to use an out-moded expression). After the expedition had failed the mutual personal abuse and accusations which broke out among some of the members (and not only the Latins) were quite extraordinary and continued for over two years. At the same time, encouraged by the press, some normally well-respected Himalayan pundits were unable to resist the heady satisfaction of having a personal cut at the expedition corpse.

By contrast, the British assault on Everest in 1953 provides a graphic example of what happens when a good team is properly led. John Hunt was clearly an ideal leader and organiser who for his own part was perfectly content to act as a mere load-carrier between the lower camps and selected a New Zealander and a Sherpa as the successful summit team. There appears to have been no sign of any unhappiness or rancour whatever, and the whole enterprise apparently went like clockwork.

But Desio's K2 expedition the following year can only be described as a disaster, despite the fact that the mountain was climbed successfully. If we can accept the evidence of Lacedelli and others, and there is no reason why we cannot, Desio's leadership was catastrophic. The disgraceful sidelining of Riccardo Cassin before the Italians had even left Italy did not bode well for the future, and in the Karakoram Desio appears to have behaved as a complete martinet who treated his climbers like children or servants – to the point where they were 'ready to mutiny'. Even so, his behaviour as a leader on the mountain pales into insignificance when compared with what happened later in Italy. He first condemned Bonatti out of hand without even questioning him, then for the rest of his life refused even to discuss the matters raised in the press about K2. The accusation by Reinhold Messner that Desio was a 'fascist' may or may not be true (though Desio had certainly risen to his Professorship during Mussolini's time in power), but he certainly seems to have been an autocrat of the worst type who was perfectly willing to see Bonatti's reputation destroyed for reasons of pure political expediency.

Compagnoni's behaviour was far worse. It is abundantly clear that he was driven by envy, greed and grasping ambition to abandon Bonatti and Mahdi without caring in the least what happened to them. He then compounded this felony by telling Desio a pack of lies about Bonatti using some of the summit oxygen, and repeated this story ten years later to Nino Giglio. His behaviour towards his rope-mate Lacedelli was no better, and he is depicted in Lacedelli's recent book *K2 – The Price of Conquest* as a most selfish, unpleasant character. He appears all too clearly as a classic font for the development of a *storia all'italiana*, concerned solely with self and to Hell with anyone else: the very antithesis of anything that could even remotely be described as 'team spirit'.

Lacedelli played a lesser role and is best described as a mere 'fellow traveller'. It was not his idea to put Camp 9 out of Bonatti's reach that night, though he seems all too willingly to have followed Compagnoni's orders when he merely told Bonatti to 'leave the oxygen and go down'. But in the light of his present revelations it is absolutely unforgivable that he remained silent for the next 50 (!) years until, driven by who knows what motive, he finally decided to speak out. He now at last has confirmed everything Bonatti had been saying for years (with the one exception of the time the oxygen became exhausted – and that, it seems abundantly clear, is merely because he wants desperately to come out of the affair with at least some shreds of dignity). He emerges as a man who for half a century has been concerned above all else with his own preservation and not at all with the fate of his younger team-mate.

At the conclusion of *K2 – The Price of Conquest*, Lacedelli and his co-author attempted to excuse his silence for 50 years in this way:

> Lacedelli is right when he says that telling the truth about K2 at the time would have been a waste of time. He would have been destroyed by Ardito Desio, who held a monopoly on the official story, secured by his rigid discipline of the other team members, and controlled the power of the media. If Lacedelli had tried to oppose Desio he would have ended up like Bonatti, an isolated, Don-Quixote figure, forlornly tilting at windmills.

What a sad comment, particularly in the light of current developments. Despite Lacedelli's continued protests that the oxygen ran out before they reached the top, the Italian Alpine Club at last now agrees with Bonatti that the summit pair did use oxygen right to the top of K2. This forthright decision by the CAI has vindicated Bonatti's statements concerning what he has always referred to as 'the mother lie'. Don Quixote? Maybe so: but, unlike Cervantes' character, Bonatti has now won his particular 'forlorn' battle and flattened his windmill at last.

Ironically, simple arithmetic has all along made Compagnoni's entire dramatic fabrication about the oxygen and Bonatti's 'treachery' totally unacceptable. His original version had it that he and Lacedelli left the bivouac site at about 6.00 am, and that the oxygen stopped flowing at 4.00 pm – that is, ten hours later. Almost everyone, including Bonatti, had always accepted that the cylinders were designed to last for ten hours, though now it is clear that actually they ran for twelve hours. So at least it should have been obvious to the meanest intelligence that Giglio's accusations (*vice* Compagnoni) of Bonatti using oxygen during the bivouac were absurd – whatever anyone might care to believe about the subsequent two-hour climb to the summit carrying the empty bottles claimed by the summit pair. Lacedelli's modified version of events now has them leaving the bivouac site at 7.30 am, and ten hours of supply thus has the bottles becoming empty at the (very convenient) time of 5.30pm, just twenty minutes or so before they reached the top. This once again makes the accusations against Bonatti absurd – as Lacedelli now agrees. But Abram's news that they were twelve-hour bottles (or rather, to be completely accurate, three four-hour bottles in each respirator pack) changes things completely, especially as everyone, including the CAI, now recognises that Lacedelli's so-called '7.30 am start' is also a fairy tale and that they actually left the bivouac site at 8.30 am. It now seems clear that when they reached the summit at 6.00 pm there must have been two hours or more of oxygen left, and one can only wonder whether they left the bottles where they lay or used them for the first part of the descent: Compagnoni's graphic description of what happened when the oxygen was exhausted would seem to suggest the latter.

Apart from the main players in this sordid affair, the supporting cast, comprising the other members of the K2 team, also emerges with no great credit: Bonatti's team-mates were all too willing to bow meekly to authority and stay mute. Certainly none of them did anything whatever to help Bonatti's quest for justice and some, for example Floreanini, have been quoted in the press as 'wondering what all the fuss is about'. Even the two with whom Bonatti has remained very friendly, Gallotti and Abram, have always stayed completely aloof from proceedings – though they surely must always have known exactly what was going on. It seems completely incomprehensible that Abram, in particular, waited almost twenty years after the publication of *Processo al K2* before he volunteered the crucial news that the summit oxygen bottles lasted for twelve hours – not ten, as Bonatti had always believed. Did Abram even bother to read Bonatti's book when it was published in 1985?

The Council members of the CAI were quite content for years to let the whole matter slide in a vainglorious attempt to allow the controversy to simmer down. They cared nothing for

Bonatti's anguish and wished simply to avoid besmirching in any way Italy's glorious achievement of climbing the second highest mountain on earth and in this way restoring Italy to a place of international respect. They preferred the reflected glow of fame to honesty and truth.

The Italian press, as in most countries, is interested only in publishing what will sell – the facts are neither here nor there. Much the same can be said about the readers of such accounts: people in the main are interested only in a good story rather than truth in the abstract. In fairness it must be said that the Italian press is certainly not alone: newspapers the world over also at times produce astonishing gaffes on any subject one cares to nominate – including mountaineering. When Ardito Desio died in December 2001 at the age of 104 it was reported in *The Australian* on 18 December that England's most prestigious newspaper (*The Times*) had published an obituary in which it was stated that 'Desio and the rest of the team had stopped a few hundred feet below the summit while Compagnoni and Lacedelli climbed to the top'. It would seem that the whole sordid story of K2 has become inextricably confused over the years to the point where no one knows or cares what really happened.

The only public figures to emerge from this sorry saga with credit and enhanced reputations are those who have been willing to take up arms in the service of truth – Annibale Salsa, Luigi Zanzi, Alberto Monticone, the late Fosco Maraini, Enrico Camanni, Roberto Mantovani and his colleagues. These honest, strong-minded men demonstrate that, thankfully, not all Italians are concerned only with their own preservation at all costs.

All the available evidence seems to point in one direction. If Ardito Desio had been a different man – perhaps a man like John Hunt – the story of K2 (and of Walter Bonatti's next 50 years) would have been very different. If he had behaved judicially and questioned Bonatti, Mahdi and Lacedelli in 1954 the truth would surely have emerged at once. But he chose to adopt the role of a martinet who cared nothing for individual members of his team and thought nothing of throwing young Bonatti to the wolves. He was instead obsessed with his own image, which now ironically seems somewhat tarnished.

The mills of fate, grinding slowly as always, have finally seen the saga of K2 reach its end. Bonatti has always insisted that 'the official record is the only thing that counts': two hundred years from now, just as he had always hoped, historians curious about the first ascents of the 8,000 metre peaks in the twentieth century will be able to examine the 'dusty tomes of the official records' of the CAI and discover the true story.

By then the unfortunate comments in the Italian newspapers about 'rehabilitation' will have been long forgotten. But for the present, the incompetence and misinformed conclusions of some sections of the press will prevail and, regrettably, Bonatti will just have to live with the residual false impressions of the controversy. These misconceptions seem likely to persist for some time yet – the 'lies and treachery' of the K2 affair have left a long, long shadow.

Appendix One

The Ambassador's Report

On August 26, 1954 the Italian Embassy in Pakistan received a letter in which Islam Salmani, a student at the 'Sind Muslim Law College' of Karachi, enclosed a copy of a letter he had written to the editors of the major Pakistani newspapers. In this letter he sent out his own ideas concerning the conquest of K2 and the Hunza porter Amir Mahdi and asked for an explanation. We note that this letter gives all the credit for the success of the Italian expedition to the porter named above. He accuses the two Italian climbers who reached the summit of having compelled Mahdi to stop only 100 feet lower down. They did this to prevent him from sharing in their glory, exhibiting the most flagrant example of ugly, sly and selfish human nature.

We note that the reporters present at the Karachi airport on August 30, in the course of interviewing the climbers after their arrival from Lahore, asked questions almost exclusively referring to the Hunza Mahdi, indicating how much Islam Salmani's letter had impressed the public and how much discussion it had been able to generate.

The undersigned, Dr. Benedetto d'Acunzo, Italian ambassador to Pakistan, has concluded that it would be appropriate to investigate the facts concerning the final phase of this Alpine exploit and in this way establish, in an unequivocal manner, just where the Hunza Mahdi set foot, where he carried his load, how he comported himself and what help he provided other than purely as a porter.

To this end I have brought together in the embassy the Italian protagonists of the so-called final phase of the climb:

Walter Bonatti,
Achille Compagnoni,
Lino Lacedelli,
in the presence of these officials:
Colonel Ata Ullah, the Pakistani liaison officer who accompanied the expedition, Commendatore Amedeo Costa, Vice-President of the Italian Alpine Club, Dr Guido Pagani, the expedition medical officer.

The undersigned put several questions to them, from which it transpired that the expedition had established Base Camp at 4,950 m, and had set up in the course of the climb nine camps, of which the seventh, eighth and ninth had been the site of the final phase of the climb. Between the seventh and eighth camps there was an altitude difference of 400m; between the ninth camp and the summit a further distance of more than 500m. Of the ten Hunza porters present at Base Camp only nine reached Camp 4, seven Camp 5, six Camp 7, and two (to be precise Amir Mahdi and Isakhan) Camp 8. They were then invited to give an account of what happened on 30 July 1954 on the so-called 'shoulder' of K2. From this account, clarified and put in order by the undersigned with appropriate questions, then put down in writing, the result was as follows:

On the 28th Compagnoni, Lacedelli, Abram and Gallotti established Camp 8 between 2.00 and 3.00 pm, putting up a K2 tent for two people furnished with mattresses, down sleeping-bags, provisions for two days, bottles of propane gas and stoves. These loads were carried exclusively by these four climbers. Towards 4.00 pm Abram and Gallotti set off again for Camp 7. On the 29th, Compagnoni and Lacedelli left between 5.00 and 5.30 am to establish Camp 9 at an altitude of about 8,000m. They were carrying with them, without any help from the porters, a light 'Super K2' tent weighing 3kg; a small bottle of propane gas with a little cooking stove, provisions for two meals, as well as two down sleeping bags. When they had gone halfway to their destination they were confronted by an ice wall, preceded by a transverse crevasse. They had to turn back to get round this obstacle and continued to climb. They continued until 3.00 pm. After resting for about ten minutes, they left their rucksacks there and starting to back to Camp 8, which they reached between 4.00 and 4.30 pm. They did not set up a camp at the place they had reached because Lacedelli, to complete his work of compressing the snow without too much fatigue, had earlier abandoned his rucksack which contained the food and his sleeping bag. Half an hour after they had returned to Camp 8, Bonatti and Gallotti arrived from Camp 7 bringing a two-man 'Himalayan' tent, two mattresses and two sleeping bags. Nothing else. They had left Camp 7 about 8.00 am together with Abram and Rey with the task of carrying up to Camp 8 all the material mentioned above and their own personal equipment, as well as two respirators each furnished with three bottles of oxygen, as well as some replenishment stocks of food. Halfway up Abram and Rey, who the day before had carried loads from Camp 7 to Camp 8, felt too tired to go on and decided to go back to Camp 7. When he turned back, Abram left the oxygen apparatus that he had carried up. Bonatti too abandoned his load of respiratory apparatus before resuming the climb to Camp 8, carrying instead the tent which had been abandoned by Rey. That same day, the 29th, while coming up as arranged, Floreanini and the Hunzas

Mahdi and Isakhan had left Camp 6 carrying up to Camp 7 another two respirators and a box of provisions. It had been expected that the Hunzas would return that same evening to Camp 6 and that the following morning, the 30th, the two respirators would be carried up to Camp 8 by the two climbers of the four who had climbed up there on the 29th who that same evening had gone back down. Those two were Abram and Rey. They didn't feel certain that they would be able to carry this load up by themselves the following day and took along the two Hunzas to help them. On the 30th, while Compagnoni and Lacedelli were setting off up their track of the previous day to set up Camp 9, Bonatti and Gallotti went back down again towards Camp 7 to pick up the two respirators left mid-route the day before. On reaching them, because they were able to communicate by voice with Camp 7, they were able to call out to Abram (Rey and Floreanini had gone down to Camp 6) and ask him to carry up some provisions, some sleeping bags and some propane instead of the other two respirators which now did not seem any longer to be strictly necessary. Abram with the two Hunzas named above then left and arrived at Camp 8 between 1.00 and 1.30 pm. The condition in which at that moment they found the occupants of Camp 8 was:

the Hunza Isakhan exhausted,
Gallotti very tired,
Abram tired,
Bonatti tired,
the Hunza Mahdi tired.

They ate a meal and rested for about two hours, then decided that Isakhan and Gallotti would stay at Camp 8; that Bonatti and the Hunza Mahdi would carry the respirators up to Camp 9 while Abram accompanied them and helped for as long as he was able, consistent with the need for him to go back to Camp 8 before night. Bonatti, despite the fact that he had found it necessary to make many promises to the Hunza Mahdi to induce him to follow him to Camp 9, intended they should both stay at Camp 9 that night and next morning, his physical condition permitting, prepare the first part of the trail Compagnoni and Lacedelli would have to follow to make an attack on the summit by compressing the deep snow with the help of Mahdi. At 3:30 pm Bonatti, Abram and the Hunza Mahdi left Camp 8 carrying only the two respirators. They followed the trail beaten by Compagnoni and Lacedelli. Three hours later, at about the three-quarter mark of the trail, Abram left them to return, arriving at Camp 8 at about 5:30 pm Bonatti and the Hunza Mahdi continued their ascent as dusk fell because, following the track, they were sure to reach Camp 9. However, at the point where they were convinced it should be, they found no sign of it.

From there, the way followed by Compagnoni and Lacedelli could not be followed because those two, to avoid an area of snow threatened by avalanches, had turned off over some rocky terrain – unfortunately impractical in the dark. At this point, Mahdi gave clear signs of wanting to go back to Camp 8. Bonatti, believing a descent very unwise, especially because of the state of agitation that Mahdi was demonstrating, decided to spend the night where he was, and to demonstrate this decision to his companion he started to dig out a hole in the snow for protection.

While the Hunza Mahdi was anxiously trying to make out the path to follow across the rocks, Bonatti's voice pleading with him to desist was carried by a current of air to Camp 9, inducing Lacedelli to come out of the tent and signal with a pocket torch. [Authors note: This fanciful, soothing description of events is so far from the truth that it would be laughable if the implications were not so serious.] In the conversation established between Lacedelli and Bonatti across about 200m in a direct line, the former advised the latter to put down the respirators and go back to Camp 8. Bonatti answered with a somewhat muffled phrase to express his prior intent to spend the night where he was and his concern about Mahdi, who still showed no sign of accepting the situation. From this arose the misunderstanding by virtue of which Lacedelli, convinced that Bonatti had accepted his advice to turn back to Camp 8, switched off his torch and went back into his tent. It was probably the disappearance of the light that induced Mahdi to turn back to the place where Bonatti was and resign himself to take off his load and settle down into the cavity dug out by Bonatti.

At Bonatti's insistence he also decided to take off his crampons, the straps of which could compromise the circulation of blood to his feet during the hours of inaction they were preparing to follow. Until 3.00 am of the 31st the two managed to keep themselves warm by embracing each other and furiously rubbing each others limbs. Bonatti however, on two occasions, had to stop Mahdi taking off to go back down towards Camp 8. At 3.00 am a storm arose and the wind soon blew the snow over them so that they were buried and had to dig themselves out again. At dawn Mahdi showed renewed determination to go back to Camp 8 and Bonatti after some further attempts to stop him doing so, at least until the sun rose, had eventually to let him go. But about an hour later Bonatti, leaving the respirators at the bivouac site, also descended towards Camp 8. From the moment of their reaching that camp no other attempts to reach Camp 9 were made either by Bonatti or by Mahdi. From what precedes all this, it is evident that:

Camp 9, situated at an altitude of more than 8,000 metres, was established by Compagnoni and Lacedelli, without the help of any porters;
Bonatti and Mahdi did not reach Camp 9, but stopped at a lower altitude;
the porter Mahdi caused Bonatti great concern by his wild behaviour and his

unwise and undisciplined attempts to get out of their predicament;
Bonatti decided to spend the night where he was partly through the fear
Mahdi's agitation would cause an accident while descending in the dark, and
partly in the hope of being able to reach Camp 9 next morning with the two
respirators:

he managed to restrain Mahdi during the night, but not after dawn;

he then followed Mahdi down to Camp 8, leaving the respirators at the
bivouac site (as Lacedelli had advised him to do the previous evening,
shouting this to him across the space which separated them);

Compagnoni and Lacedelli on the 31st had to descend from Camp 9 to
fetch the two respirators before starting their climb towards the summit.

The undersigned has written this deposition and it has been read in its Italian
text by all present and in its English translation by Colonel Ata Ullah. It has
been approved and signed by all present.

Walter Bonatti
Achille Compagnoni
Ata Ullah
Amedeo Costa
Guido Pagani
Dott. Benedetto d'Acunzo
Karachi, September 1, 1954.

Appendix Two

The Tre Saggi Report

This is the full text of the report the *tre saggi* supplied to the Committee of the CAI in April 2004. The Italian of the original is extremely formal, with interminable sentences which occasionally fill an entire page and include numerous sub-clauses. Translation into smooth English is not only difficult, but loses some of that formal sense. Through author choice, the translation has not, therefore, been over-edited.

Report on K2, 1954

by

'The Three Sages' appointed by the Italian Alpine Club

Professors Fosco Maraini, Alberto Monticone and Luigi Zanzi

The Central Council of the CAI conferred on us the task of 'historic clarification' of the K2 affair in a letter from the Director General dated 23 February 2004. This letter also made explicit reference to an attached document provided by a designated adviser, which set out a clarification of the Central Council's own responsibilities. In preparing ourselves for this task it seems appropriate that we formulate some preliminary remarks to clarify the aims and principles with which we proposed to develop and conduct a rigorous research project.

First, we believe our precise and limited duty was to discover the 'truth proved by documents' using sound 'written historic' methods – that is, to investigate the so-called 'historic truth' concerning the controversial issues in the official account of the climb from Camp 7 to the summit of K2 on the 30 and 31 July 1954. Over the course of half a century this 'historic truth' has been filtered and dissected by critical debate of complex testimony made public by the chief protagonists of the K2 affair. We have now reconstructed this in a brief, conclusive summary after noting what emerges from the 'common view' of experts in the history of mountaineering, in particular 'Himalayan' climbing. In the broad sense this obviously includes expeditions in the so-called 'Karakoram', where K2 lies.

An appeal was sent recently to the CAI by several eminent men and journalists close to the world of mountaineering: it was also published in *The Mountain Review* No 270 of 2004. Being limited to a rigorous, critical search for 'historic' truth on such controversial issues, we wished to re-interpret this appeal. On the other hand, we have left unanswered the request for new preliminary investigations formulated in the appeal. What follows later explains this in more detail, but above all we believe that such investigations could start new arguments, which would be harmful as well as fruitless.

Second, we wish to confine our attention rigorously to the issues dealt with below. We believe we should not air new 'written history' investigations concerning these issues. We have taken into account the present state of the available documentation, not to mention the community of those who have studied these questions – that is, all those able to reach a conclusive judgement. (This same judgement also seems to be dominant in the public at large.)

Even more, we believe our role should radically exclude providing any instructions whatever. Such suggestions would be appropriate only to a 'Commission of Inquiry' convened to investigate and decide on the demands and disputes of the participants. In this context we must observe that the 'written history' process we have used can never elevate itself to become any type of 'judicial tribunal'. Even less can it judge presumed and more or less secret aims and intentions, or individual behaviour, nor re-interpret such matters. It should aim only to reconstruct factual truth through the complex paths that have come to light little by little as time has passed and the experiences of different witnesses have been compared.

The so-called 'historic' truth is therefore always relative to the documentation on which it is built: it claims no other merit and can be recognised only in this way. However, although one can never be sure of the complete truth, historic truths can, and therefore should, acknowledge that at times some truths are incontrovertible on the basis of documents that leave no room for interpretation and are confirmed by common knowledge. In the present case these crucial truths are those that have been extracted and highlighted below: but we have omitted further analysis of other aspects about which there is no dispute and so are not called into question.

We must also stress that our cautious methodology included a 'decoding' of the 'narrative' mode of the complex accounts, versions, inquiries and testimonies about these events. These various accounts often were structured as a 'hagiography' of adventure or a celebration of 'conquerors' – at times also with a 'nationalistic' tendency.

Observing such criteria, we have also tried to avoid the risk of provoking unhappy after-effects of arguments that could poison the final memory of such an event as the first ascent of K2, which was an event of great importance – an emotional and image-making issue in the long-term tradition of alpinism.

Third, therefore, we believe it is our duty to reject radically any attempt to search for new 'truths' and produce more or less sensational 'revelations'. On the contrary, our principal intent is to make critical, open, transparent 'written history' comparisons of the various opinions about the climb and their reception by the CAI. We must also take adequate, official action about any incontrovertible factual truths. The CAI itself has already done this (in an indirect, informal manner) in 1994, by adopting a somewhat different position in a text published in 'The CAI Review'.

Because of this we thought it both superfluous and unnecessary to seek new evidence even from the main surviving protagonists of the K2 affair, even though these people have made various announcements recently. Firstly, we believe the critical 'written history' outcomes we describe are unarguable and need no further testimony. Secondly, we do not consider that we should introduce further 'revelations'. By their very nature these would have been kept surprisingly secret for many years. In one way, they would be irrelevant to the reliability of the facts established below in this report. In another, they would provoke further inquiries in depth because it would be difficult to have much faith in exclusive, 'critical written history' concerning 'revelations' kept hidden for so long.

Fourth, we do not believe we should set out any rectification of Ardito Desio's account, which was prepared in his role as expedition leader. He was the only person entitled to formulate a 'reference account' for the official archives of the CAI, the institution that promoted the expedition. Ardito Desio's account remains what it is, as do other documents available for 'written history' reconstruction – its role is as the 'reference account' of the 'expedition leader'. Ardito Desio remains exclusively responsible for the account because he gave it to the CAI and it was subsequently made public in a book entitled *La Conquista del K2*, published in Milan (Garzanti) in December 1954.

However, in our opinion this does not exempt the CAI from its duty to acquire officially in its archives a text in which some incontrovertible, 'critical written history' comparisons are summarised. These should be facts peculiar to the CAI itself in whatever official posture the club intends to adopt in future. The CAI sponsored the expedition and so became the responsible depository for the official history of the climb.

This aim would be well worthwhile and fulfil every principle, because it follows the statutory and cultural scope peculiar to the Italian Alpine Club. Deplorably, claims and references to the 'reference account' of Ardito Desio have been divulged just in the past few days. Until today it was assumed to be the unique official CAI version, implicitly confirming in this way any other account as unacceptable for the 'true history'. Such drawbacks demand an urgent and effective remedy.

We have therefore set out not only to show our 'critical written history' results in brief, precise form, but also to demonstrate by comparison those incorrect and unacceptable points which need integration into the 'reference account' of Ardito Desio, the expedition leader.

We know very well that the diary and notes of Ardito Desio's personal archive are still locked up and secret. We must therefore stress that we do not believe it necessary to set up specific reservations in anticipation of any later disclosures. Firstly, such sources could not invalidate the points established below. Secondly, it would be very surprising if denials of the 'reference account' were to emerge from that same document which Desio wrote in his capacity as expedition leader. In fact, this would be a case of authentic and until now hidden self-criticism, and this would make any such reports rather dubious.

Incidentally, we must stress that, surprisingly, the chapter in Desio's 'reference account' concerning 'the assault on the summit' was equivocal, because Desio added a warning that the chapter was an account written by Achille Compagnoni and Lino Lacedelli, with no corrections or alterations of emphasis. Actually, the chapter was specified by Compagnoni and Lacedelli to be a report from 'both of us'.

Fifth, we do not believe we need set out any specific recognition of Walter Bonatti's role in the 'K2 Affair'. This role has already been fully and definitively recognised in the 'common opinion' of mountaineering experts in all its decisive relevance, but has become even more obvious in the 'written history' critique below. The Italian Alpine Club too has recognised Bonatti's role, though only in an informal, non-official way.

We have discovered precise contributions of great 'written history' relevance in Walter Bonatti's testimonies, which have allowed us to establish incontrovertible facts when investigating conflicting points of view. If one could establish the serene comparison between the protagonists which has been asked of Ardito Desio without him ever complying, these unarguable facts could well be included in the 'reference account' of the expedition leader.

These critical 'written history' conclusions set out below seem certain to produce the most tranquil agreement between the CAI and Walter Bonatti, and for this reason we have not attempted to initiate any rapprochement or reconciliation between them. This attitude stems from the omens that come from the whole world of mountaineering and also from inside the CAI itself.

In the light of these preliminary remarks we have formulated our report in four distinct sections that involve precise corrections of the official version. These four aspects relate to places, to times, to equipment (and its use) and to modes of action relating to the events of the final phase of the climb to the summit from Camp 7 on 30 and 31 July 1954.

1. Places

(a) The site of Camp 9
The actual position of Camp 9 was different from what had been planned – both in site and altitude. It was originally to have been placed on a rounded snowy ridge on the 'Shoulder' at about 8,000– 8,100 metres ('below the rock buttress that cuts across the terminal dome of the great mountain', as Desio's account specifies). However, this had been planned much earlier, at a much lower altitude and with no direct information about the condition of the terrain and the state of the snow. According to a later plan, the camp possibly should have been lower, at about 7,900 metres, to allow those who were to carry up the oxygen indispensable for the final assault to reach it in good time. (This final strategic agreement had been taken the previous evening by Compagnoni, Lacedelli, Gallotti and Bonatti.)

According to the direct testimony of Lacedelli, the actual site of Camp 9 – not without some argument – was displaced left from the snowy shoulder, to the far side of some steep and delicate rocky slabs (described by Compagnoni and Lacedelli as 'very treacherous'). It was also fixed higher than had been planned, at about 8,150 metres.

Obviously only examination on site could allow one to decide on the best strategic place for the camp: on the one hand, as high as possible towards the summit; on the other, as safe as possible from the collapse of the seracs above; and, from yet another aspect, not too high, to make it accessible to the oxygen carriers.

Quite apart from any consideration of intent, this displacement of Camp 9 is the basis of later disputes between the two different groups of protagonists about their own climbs, step by step, hour after hour. These are complex issues, and it is not easy to make judgements in such a situation of uncertainty, fatigue and disturbed thought-processes at very high altitude.

But the bald declaration in the so-called 'official account' that the sole reason for displacing the camp was to put it 'as high as possible' seems unacceptable. Compagnoni and Lacedelli explicitly declared that 'we tried to climb up as high as possible', and one can well understand this as a strategic choice to get as close as possible to the summit. But such a choice could be valid only in the context of there being no pre-arranged strategic plans – if they had complete autonomy and sure availability of all the necessary resources for the final summit attempt (including, of course, the oxygen).

They should have considered all the possible consequences of such a choice before making this decision, which turned out to have such dramatic consequences. They did not think deeply enough about other advantages and disadvantages – in particular how difficult it would be for the climbers carrying the oxygen to reach Camp 9 (as foreseen and planned by the four protagonists the previous evening). They also did not consider the further problem the oxygen carriers would have in finally trying to overcome those 'very treacherous slabs'. This lack of thought indicates the difficulty of making judgements in such a difficult, complex situation, and indeed is comprehensible only in such terms.

Mishaps of this sort cannot be kept quiet; they must be accepted as fact, without making judgements about their intent; they are part of the adventurous aspects intrinsic to mountaineering expeditions of this type.

It is important that the so-called 'official account' be modified to include these matters. In the first place, there should be a punctilious investigation of how Camp 9 came to be displaced to a quite different and much higher position (about 250 metres further up). In the second place, the altitude of Camp 9 should be corrected (about 8,150 metres and not 8,050 as indicated in Desio's account). In the third place, there should be a description of the exact position of Camp 9 on the narrow ledge just beyond the traverse of the rock slabs, in a position not visible to those who climbed over the shoulder and then up the steep slope below the 'Bottleneck'.

(b) The site of Bonatti and Mahdi's bivouac

The site of the Bonatti-Mahdi bivouac is not identified accurately in Desio's account, but is presumed to be below 8,000 metres. However, the site can be positioned precisely through various testimonies of the protagonists and in the various accounts of how events unfolded. It was about 20 metres above a large rock mass at 8,100 metres, one of the projections on the steep slope below the 'Bottleneck'. It was to the left of this large rock, and to the right of the rocky slabs beyond which, a little higher, Camp 9 was situated at about 8,150 metres.

It is also necessary to specify that the bivouac did not really take place in a 'hole dug in the snow': the two men sat curled up on a small ledge dug out in the slope as well as possible with an ice axe. It would have been impossible in those conditions to dig a 'hole' in the ice, which would have provided them with a more comfortable refuge.

In this regard it seems important that the 'official account' be integrated in a form that presents exactly the position specified above as the site of the Bonatti-Mahdi bivouac that night between 30 and 31 July 1954.

The difference in the site of the bivouac is most important in understanding the altitude difference overcome by Bonatti and Mahdi that day carrying the oxygen. In Bonatti's case this comprised 927 metres (227 metres of descent and 700 metres of ascent) with a load of about 19 kilograms on his back. The correct altitude of the bivouac is also decisive in fully understanding Bonatti's decision to bivouac in the open with no equipment for that altitude rather than descend in the pitch dark down that steep and exposed slope. He chose this course as the lesser evil (though terrible enough because of the very grave risks involved) because it was not practicable to descend in the darkness without artificial illumination. Bonatti and Mahdi had no torch at their disposal, and Mahdi at that moment lacked the necessary technical expertise and calm self-control.

If the bivouac had been lower down, where the snow slope eased off more gently towards the 'Shoulder', Bonatti and Mahdi would perhaps have been able to attempt a descent in the dark.

The exact position of the Bonatti-Mahdi bivouac at 8,100 metres is highlighted also by locating it in a place consistent with the possibility of contact, of shouts and the exchange of words and signals, between Compagnoni and Lacedelli on one side of the couloir and Bonatti and Mahdi on the other side.

It is also important, in the light of the distance they still had to ascend at the end of an extremely exhausting day, to understand how Bonatti and Mahdi continued their climb after they were first seen by Compagnoni and Lacedelli (at about 4 pm) and the first exchange of voices with them. On the basis of comparison between different testimonies, this seems to have happened for the last time at around 5.30 to 6.00 on 30 July, when Abram was still with Bonatti and Mahdi. Not much later, between 6.00 and 6.30. Abram was forced to give up and start his descent towards Camp 8. By contrast, the progress of Bonatti and Mahdi became rather wandering and uncertain from that time (5.30/6.00 pm) until about ten o'clock, when the last exchanges with Compagnoni and Lacedelli happened (strictly speaking, with Lacedelli alone). One must also note the difficulties of communication between Bonatti and Mahdi, aggravated by the altitude, by the darkness and by their related state of great anxiety [*Author's note: not to mention their lack of a common language*].

(c) The place on the track where the oxygen was left
The trestles with their bottles of oxygen were originally left near Camp 7. They were then recovered and carried up to the neighbourhood of Camp 9 – part way by Bonatti and Gallotti, then the rest of the way by Bonatti and Mahdi, with Abram's help.

Although it may seem a matter of little importance, it is necessary to correct an inaccuracy in the 'official account' concerning the place where the trestles with their bottles of oxygen were left between 28 and 29 July. In the 'official account' it refers to the place in a vague way, placed at 'the middle of the track' between Camp 7 (7,345 metres) and Camp 8 (7,627 metres) – that is, at about 7,500 metres. On the contrary, comparing this with other uncontested testimonies, one can state that the actual altitude was between 7,375 and 7,400 metres.

This figure is important in evaluating the whole ascent completed by Bonatti, first in descent and then in ascent, for the recovery of the oxygen bottles that were so indispensable for the final climb to the summit. An extra 100 metres of ascent at that high altitude, without using oxygen and with a load of 19 kilograms is most significant, and this is therefore an unacceptable error.

(d) The site of exhaustion of the oxygen bottles
A problem of 'localisation' also arises concerning the hypothetical place where one should place the exhaustion of the oxygen supply as described in the account of Compagnoni and Lacedelli. We believe this question is one of the crucial points to be confronted rigorously in preparing an accurate story of what happened during the climb to the summit. In this context we permit ourselves a brief methodological digression, which we believe is crucial in the end for a smooth reading of our work of 'written history criticism'.

The climb itself is a fact: and it is an extraordinary fact, unique and unrepeatable. It cannot be re-experienced through an experiment, but only through the memory-account of those who were there. Such a fact involves and implies other facts, which cannot and should not be considered in isolation (though this often happens when single issues are considered separately). However, the complete story cannot hold to a solitary memory of the protagonists for a single, isolated event.

When checking a memory one usually goes through the comparison of different memories by referring to different documents. But the question of where the oxygen ran out cannot be decided by the memories of anyone other than Compagnoni and Lacedelli. This is a single episode, individual and unrepeatable, of which the only direct, personal memory is that of Compagnoni and Lacedelli. But it appears in a narrative that seems not to be an autobiographical repetition of facts but rather a discourse that is in some respects no more than an anticipated response to possible controversies.

In this case it is not possible to arrange a written comparison between the memories of different protagonists (except for some differences in testimony in interviews received individually from Achille Compagnoni and Lino Lacedelli).

However, no written story can stand if supported by memory alone. History is not only memory, but criticism of memory, which translates memory into outcomes that can be documented and critically accepted in the light of experience. These outcomes must also follow explicit rules and be consistent with models accepted by the scientific community. (The crucial rule for verification appropriate to this case is consistency with analogous behaviour of others in similar circumstances, compared as far as possible, to the realities of the place and of the area; of time, actions and factual events).

It is most important that we make ourselves very clear. Even if the climb to the summit by Compagnoni and Lacedelli had been an individual achievement completely unconfirmed by the memories of anyone else, it would still be interwoven with other accounts narrated by other protagonists through other memories. Thus, such an account, even if it relates to a specific and unrepeatable event, in the context of 'critical written history' can and should be assessed against other events.

As an example, the 'fact' that Compagnoni and Lacedelli left Camp 9 at some hour rather than another can be compared with the departure of Bonatti and Mahdi from their bivouac site nearby: they were moving at much the same time, in an area which could be seen directly by two different groups of participants. The fact and the time of reaching the summit can be compared with the observations from Camp 8. The technical aspects can be compared with equipment reports, not to mention documentary evidence such as photographs. Also, even though unrepeatable, the identification of the sites can be compared (at least hypothetically) with other remembered accounts of other experiences during other climbs in the same places. So, too, a presumed time of an event in one place can be compared with another time of an event in a place nearby, at not too different an altitude, with appropriate allowances for the different altitudes, different states of health and physical fitness, and so on.

In this way a complex picture of the whole historic fact can be established, breaking it up into 'component facts' corresponding to different accounts (as opposed to simply breaking up the narrative into separate sections). Some of these 'component facts' can and should be evaluated by comparing them with appropriate experiences to make the narrative solidly acceptable. So, let us discuss the specific matter put forward here as 'fact' – that is, the presumed exhaustion of the oxygen as related in the report by Compagnoni and Lacedelli. From now on we will use the expression 'presumed exhaustion of the oxygen' to refer to the event described by Compagnoni and Lacedelli. We acknowledge that there is a problem concerning the site of this presumed event, and we wish finally and explicitly to highlight other arguments about the time, and activities that can be compared precisely with these events.

The report of Compagnoni and Lacedelli reproduced in Desio's account is very vague concerning the site of the 'presumed exhaustion of the oxygen'. They seem to have been near a 'hump' where the 'huge white slope seemed to curve', so they could believe 'the summit should be just behind that hump'. At that point, almost simultaneously (a simultaneity we will consider and evaluate later) Compagnoni and Lacedelli suddenly noticed they were short of breath – the oxygen was finished. They tore off their masks: the feeling of prostration (starting as a 'horrible sensation') disappeared; the two of them began climbing again. However, a little later, beyond the bump they suffered the bitter delusion that presented itself to their eyes as another 'very long' slope. (One can accept at this point that into their perception and desire was injected that game of illusions and successive delusions which is a common experience among those who have climbed high altitude peaks, the more so if as extreme and unknown as this one: a game that distorts estimations of distance and time to reach a goal, ceaselessly considered in an anxious oscillation between hope and despondency.)

A clearing then freed the mountain of mist and the two finished the last stretch, a 'wide ridge of snow, not steep', which soon faded out. They were on the summit. From the neighbourhood of the hump to the platform of the summit the account does not report precise identifiable sections of their climb, in the way that earlier sections of the route had been precisely described). As pointed out repeatedly in later statements by Achille Compagnoni, the site of the presumed exhaustion of the oxygen was 8,400 metres, reached at about 4.00 pm. The figures were given without any indication of how the estimations, of either time or altitude, were made.

Coordinates of places and times like this cannot be accepted in a critical historic version of such a factual account. Such accounts must be evaluated carefully, the more so when they are the result of an exclusive autobiographical memoir. They can be respected as such, but cannot be accepted if they do not conform with models of experience that allow them to be considered reasonably probable events. In any case, facts cannot be accepted if they present themselves as 'miracles' or are so prodigious as to be absurd. The identification of places and times in this account, which is presented as factual, is vague and ambiguous, and in any case is of itself insufficient for a critical appraisal. It is therefore necessary to make a theoretical comparison of the factual and technical circumstances with an appropriate model of experience.

Apart from a precise identification of the site, the definition of a place implies direct temporal comparison with the successive reaching of other places at that altitude, in particular the summit, and physical performances that are acceptable when compared with models of experience.

If such a place at 8,400 metres is reached at 4.00 pm, and if one considers that the summit is at 8,611 metres and was reached at 6.00 pm, it is neither more nor less than a 'miracle' of climbing by Compagnoni and Lacedelli to ascend 216 metres in only two hours, without oxygen and with 19 kilograms on their backs – and, even more so when it was at the end of a most exhausting day.

It must also be taken into account that, according to Compagnoni and Lacedelli, they had taken ten hours to climb 300 metres, from 8,100 to 8,400 metres, while using oxygen. The two different times taken for the two different sections of the climb described in their account are completely incongruous. Taking note of the very obvious differences in the terrain of the climb (though such differences are accentuated only in the final few metres) the quoting of 8,400 metres as the altitude of presumed exhaustion of the oxygen does not hold up when comparing the two sections of their climb – the first from 8,100 to 8,400 metres, the second from 8,400 to 8,611.

The suggested site of the presumed exhaustion of the oxygen is also unacceptable in comparison with corroborated experiences on subsequent climbs, even after allowing adequately for different available technology.

The presumed exhaustion of the oxygen could well have happened, because the most thorough respect is generated for an experience described in precise detail with lively signs of authenticity, but in a place quite different from that described by Compagnoni and Lacedelli. To establish the position of such a hypothetical site, within precise limits of probability, it is necessary to resort to comparison with other technical and factual circumstances (for example, the predicted duration of the oxygen, or the spectrum of different durations corresponding to different types of usage).

In evaluating the actual site the oxygen stopped one must, among other things, pay critical attention to position in which Compagnoni and Lacedelli found themselves. There were sudden variations of visibility (alternating cloud and clearing), then an unexpected, disconcerting experience ('a horrible sensation'). This disturbing experience compelled a pause, a conversation, a re-assessment of strategy, and then a resumption of their climb at a pace which, in the circumstances, could not be other than more slowly, even if inadvertently, because slowness was forced on them.

Amongst other things, we believe that such a worrying experience would probably have involved not less than 10 to 20 minutes of rest. The residual time available for the climb to the summit would diminish to about an hour and forty minutes if we accept the timescale of Compagnoni and Lacedelli's account, which necessitates an even more 'prodigious' outcome, and therefore an even less credible one. It therefore seems historically reasonable to hypothesise a different site for a presumed exhaustion of the oxygen. Conjecturally, this would be sited in the immediate vicinity of the summit, at about 8,600 metres, at the beginning of the final stretch of the climb as it flattened out towards the top (as can also be determined by precise comparison with consideration of timings specifically discussed below).

The difference between such an acceptable site and that of Compagnoni and Lacedelli's report is understandable and justifiable if one considers the likelihood, perhaps the inevitable, psychological amnesia of the situation.

In the light of the critical historic considerations set out above, we believe that the official version should be changed to a more appropriate form. The aim should be to avoid any even indirect identification of the presumed exhaustion of the oxygen at 8,400 metres, leaving a more probable approximate location at 8,600 metres. There should obviously also be reservations based on the lack of any possible critical consideration. We believe that such a correction cannot be omitted because it is a major input to the historic memoir concerning the expedition, which currently includes information that renders that account less credible. Failure to include the correction would allow further discussions and arguments regarding the 'miraculous' outcome of a climb without oxygen at that altitude and in those conditions.

2. Times

(a) The time of the conversation and exchange of signals between Compagnoni and Lacedelli and Bonatti and Mahdi on the afternoon and night of 30 July 1954

The 'official account' is more than usually vague and deficient on one extremely important point: when did this exchange of voices happen? Unfortunately, it was carried out in an incongruous manner, was ineffective, and was affected by probable ambiguities and misunderstandings. According to the official version the exchange happened only once, after dusk, when it was almost dark: the voices of Bonatti and Mahdi were lost in the wind blowing from the north: later ('finally') the answers of Compagnoni and Lacedelli were heard, with explicit instructions to go down at once. This version is also repeated in the first-person report made by Compagnoni and Lacedelli.

To our minds, such a version is historically unacceptable on the basis of both the comparison of different testimonies and the manner in which Bonatti and Mahdi behaved as they approached Camp 9, which had been placed in an unknown area different from the one they envisaged.

In truth, the first contact 'by voice' happened when the group climbing still consisted of three men – Bonatti, Mahdi and Abram. At about 4.30 to 5.00 pm there was a first, unequivocally agreed exchange between Bonatti and Lacedelli ('Where have you put the tent?' 'Follow the tracks!'). Then at about 5.30 to 6.00 pm Abram clearly heard another exchange of voices. A little later he started to descend, arriving at Camp 8 at about 7.30, where Gallotti was waiting.

Then there was a gap of several hours' silence from above as the final chapter unfolded – the most laborious (and for the most part unforeseen) part of the climb to carry the oxygen to a point where it could be used next day. Until about 10.00 pm Bonatti and Mahdi went on slowly into the dusk, the ever darker long hours interrupted at times by shouts and long silences. Finally, when it was pitch dark, in response to what were by now desperate calls from the two men, a light appeared and there was a final, peremptory demand from Lacedelli to go down – all this after an unequivocal dialogue at the site where the oxygen bottles were left. Then nothing more.

It seems to us that the 'official account' should be corrected to include the precise factual story reported here, without further comment.

(b) The time Compagnoni and Lacedelli left Camp 9.

The timetable of the climb from Camp 9 to the summit of K2 on 31 July 1954 was described more or less implicitly in the report of Compagnoni and Lacedelli contained in Desio's book and subsequently repeated by Achille Compagnoni in later testimony. We believe this account should be rectified on some points and in a rather important way.

In fact, in the light of the criteria explicitly set out in 1(d) above, comparing the official account with contiguous events and technical data accepted as highly probable, as well as with normal experience, one is unavoidably forced to reconstruct a significantly different timetable in a sensible critical historic manner.

Yet again we hasten to point out that the evaluations of times made by Compagnoni and Lacedelli were made without looking at a watch, which would have been difficult during the ascent. Their judgement also could have been altered by the intensely variable weather, which severely affected both the daylight and visibility. Their memory of time intervals, the initial and final sessions of each segment, the length of the pitches and so on could have been obscured, made vague or even confused.

It is also necessary to consider how the recounting of events later, at a different altitude and in a quite different situation, can cause timings to be confused, particular because of the slowness of events at altitude – for example the long duration of such things as putting on climbing boots, fitting crampons and preparing to start the climb. The actual time elapsed is likely to be underestimated, and this interferes with the eventual assessment of when things happened. We therefore believe we must reconstruct the timetable of the climb to the summit in a critical historic manner, and compare it with the individual points of Compagnoni and Lacedelli's report that we believe are unacceptable.

Sunrise on K2 on 31 July 1954 at 8,100 metres (36.00 N Latitude and 76.30 E Longitude) was at 4.54 am, and sunset at 7.08 pm. As a result of cross-checking the testimony of the different protagonists, a 'thick sea of cloud' that 'tended to rise' was present, although the sky above was clear. Compagnoni and Lacedelli's account reports how they left Camp 9 at 'five in the morning' – a time that seems to refer also to the advent of daybreak because they got moving 'as soon as the sky was clear'.

Compagnoni and Lacedelli also describe how they saw a man descending the snow slope below before they left Camp 9 (this was Bonatti, as one gathers from his own testimony).This timescale is unacceptable in a critical historic report for the following reasons:

First: it seems incontestable that Bonatti left the bivouac at about 6.30 am and therefore could only be seen descending the slope at about 6.45 to 7.00 am (Bonatti arrived at Camp 8 at about 7.30 am, a time confirmed by other accounts).

Second: if Compagnoni and Lacedelli had been moving around at 5.00 am they would have seen Mahdi leave the bivouac at about 5.30, but in that case they would certainly have been seen by Bonatti (who noticed at that time a zone of clear air around the bivouac) and he would have been able to make contact.

And one must take heed of other, seemingly incontrovertible, circumstances:

First: Mahdi left the bivouac at about 5.30 am.

Second: no reciprocal sighting by Compagnoni and Lacedelli occurred until Bonatti left the bivouac site and went down.

Third: Bonatti got ready to go down and did everything necessary to expose the oxygen trestles when it was 'a few minutes before six'.

Fourth: the operations performed by Bonatti before he went down reasonably took at least 20 or 30 minutes; so Bonatti was visible from above on the slope going down at 6.45 to 7.00 am (exactly when he recalls he was sighted by Compagnoni and Lacedelli).

One must therefore deduce that Compagnoni and Lacedelli left Camp 9 at about 6.30 to 6.45, and not earlier at 5.00. At that very moment the sun burst on the scene above the sea of cloud (from the sole testimony of Bonatti, who looked back up towards the heights during his descent and could see the trestles of oxygen bottles, recognisable 'by their vivid colours' with no men nearby).

It therefore seems necessary to correct the official version of the time Compagnoni and Lacedelli left Camp 9 – not around 5.00 am, but at about 6.30 to 6.45. It is extremely probable they reached the place where the trestles were lying with their load of oxygen near the bivouac of Bonatti and Mahdi some time after 7.00 am; a fair approximation being between 7.15 and 7.45.

(c) The time Compagnoni and Lacedelli began their climb to the summit using the oxygen

Having established the time Compagnoni and Lacedelli left Camp 9, it seems reasonable to conclude that in all probability they started their climb to the summit between 8.00 and 8.30 am. If they arrived at the place where the oxygen bottles lay at about 7.30, and if one then considers the time needed in those circumstances to equip themselves with the oxygen apparatus and then activate it, one must conclude they probably started up towards the top between 8.00 and 8.30. Consequently, the time of 6.15 am indicated in their account seems in no way reasonable. To our way of thinking this demands a further correction of the official account concerning this point.

(d) The duration of the oxygen supply

The whole timetable of the climb to the summit contradicts the specific technical data concerning the functioning of the oxygen apparatus. It is a matter of determining the normal, probable technical duration of flow based on the conditions of normal efficiency in which the bottles were maintained by a master technician such as Abram.

The oxygen flow was predicted to last not less than 11 to 12 hours. This duration must be regarded as variable (although not by very much) depending on the mode of use, the frequency and depth of breathing, and so on [*Author's note: as has been discussed in Chapter 7, the nature of the Italian oxygen equipment meant that the time the gas lasted was independent of breathing rate*]. However, the uncertainty of such variation seems not very important – according to the available technical data it would seem reasonably to be a matter of at most half an hour or so. (These data, of course, refer to the theoretical use of the equipment of 50 years ago.)

Assuming normal function in those conditions, we therefore believe that a ten-hour duration of the oxygen flow is acceptable from a critical historic aspect (with a generous margin of security of one or two hours in comparison with the provisional estimate of 11 or 12 hours). This duration can be accepted as real even on the basis of some factual comparisons taken from the account of Compagnoni and Lacedelli:

First: they themselves actually recognised this duration of 10 hours, which (according to their own timetable) lasted from six in the morning till four in the afternoon.

Second: they themselves insist the oxygen flow stopped simultaneously for them both. This makes any important difference in supply much less likely (in other words, the simultaneous cessation seems reasonably to indicate normal functioning of the oxygen flow from both sets of bottles).

Third: it is not possible to theorize any loss of oxygen from the bottles, since they were set up to deliver oxygen only when triggered by a strong enough inspiration. [*Author's note: this is completely incorrect – see Chapter 7.*]

Yet again, the normal ten-hour flow of oxygen is completely in accord with the timetable of the climb according to our critical historic reconstruction. The ascent took ten hours, beginning at 8.00 am near the bivouac site of Bonatti and Mahdi where the trestles of oxygen were lying, and ending at 6.00 pm on the summit, as has been unarguably established.

This real timetable implies recognising that the entire climb to the summit (from 8.00 to 18.00 on 31 July 1954) was achieved with the use of oxygen, which flowed for the normal duration of ten hours.

This does not exclude (in a conjectural way) accepting as true the presumed interruption of the oxygen flow. However, if this did happen, it was at not less than 8,600 metres – that is, a very short time before their arrival on the summit, a case perhaps of minutes. In the context of the new timetable proposed here this is the only acceptable thesis from a critical historic viewpoint.

(e) The total duration of the climb to the summit

Considering the timetable asserted here, it follows that the times of the various phases of Compagnoni and Lacedelli's climb to the summit need correction. The timetable they propose is unacceptable – that is, of ten hours for the first 300 metres (from 8,100 to 8,400 metres) and only two hours for the next 211 metres (from 8,400 to 8,611 metres).

Complex technical considerations make such a timetable completely unlikely and unacceptable; the more so if one considers the first section would be completed with oxygen and the second without. It therefore seems necessary to correct the times of the climb, so that the account becomes coherent and critically acceptable.

This does not exclude recognising that the experience of the two summit climbers was quite extraordinary. Nor does it exclude the possibility that their normal perceptions were disturbed, and this could have led them to comprehensively revise the timetable, interpreted dramatically as either shorter or longer according to the different perspective they had at the time.

The revised account should omit any such arbitrary dramatisation of the story. Their adventure was of itself so highly dramatic that there is no need to introduce 'miraculous' facts with all their 'heroic' aspects.

The historic critique of itself completely fulfils its duty concerning a quite extraordinary achievement, by presenting the bare facts with simplicity, consistency and the most stringent fidelity.

3. Equipment and its use

(a) The integrity of the oxygen resources available to Compagnoni and Lacedelli

Following the technical assertions already decided in court, it appears certain that the oxygen cylinders transported by Bonatti and Mahdi were perfectly intact – apart from anything else, they did not have any equipment to access the oxygen in the bottles. This is also important as the basis for confirming the normal ten hours of oxygen being available during the entire summit climb (or, as in the last conjecture above, to just a few metres from the top).

In Desio's account (and also in Compagnoni and Lacedelli's story recapitulated by Desio as Chapter 8 of the official account) no adequate emphasis is put on the transport of the oxygen bottles in a single day from 7,375 to 8,100 metres, nor on the fact of their perfect integrity, which guaranteed a flow duration of ten hours, nor on the fact that Compagnoni and Lacedelli alone had the equipment necessary to use the bottles. Such an omission is historically unacceptable.

We believe a precise, critical historic account of such facts is most important. The perfect integrity and full ten-hour availability of the oxygen for Compagnoni and Lacedelli's summit attempt was crucial to the success of the expedition. Without the transport of oxygen, first by Bonatti and Gallotti (from just above Camp 7 to Camp 8), then by Bonatti and Mahdi with the help of Abram (from Camp 8 to 8,100 metres), the summit of K2 would never have been reached.

(b) The use of oxygen masks to the summit by Compagnoni and Lacedelli

We have very carefully examined and compared the different suggestions relating to theories about the presumed exhaustion of the oxygen. The hypothetical location and time of this event has been fully discussed above. We believe we must now examine the possibility of unorthodox use of the oxygen masks – not as breathing apparatus for the delivery of bottled oxygen but purely to protect the respiratory tract from the freezing, thin air and to humidify inspired air by acting as a diaphragm.

This speculative use of the masks could only arise if one accepts that the oxygen flow ceased very close to the summit. However, one then would still need to justify Compagnoni and Lacedelli using the masks up to the summit. This emerges from the well-known photographic documentation precisely analysed by Robert Marshall.

Still, one must note that such a conjecture about the use of the masks on the summit meets some contextual difficulty (as do all speculations about the oxygen running out before they reached the summit – however close this might have been).

First: Compagnoni and Lacedelli's account refers quite precisely to 'tearing off the masks' and not to using them in any unorthodox way.

Second: suddenly using the masks to protect their faces could not have prevented a grave interruption in their upward progression. There would still have been a sudden change in the ambient air from about 6,000 metres to 8,600 metres. This makes such a conjectural use of the masks appropriate only for a very short time, and on rapidly flattening terrain.

Third: the summit photographs show Compagnoni on the summit using a mask still connected to the oxygen apparatus. This makes it impossible per se to decide whether this is orthodox or unorthodox use of the masks by Compagnoni and Lacedelli.

To recapitulate: to make the use of the masks on the summit consistent with the presumed interruption of the oxygen flow, one needs to postulate unorthodox use of the masks for the protection of natural respiration. But this is a non-documented hypothesis which can apply only with regard to the last minutes of action along the summit crest, by now flattening out.

As already noted, one particular difficulty with investigating written history in a case like this relates to the technical equipment of the past, used only once, in a remote situation. In such a case it is not possible to arrange experimental repetition by using that equipment in those abnormal conditions. So it did not seem possible for us to attempt such an experiment, because it would have been difficult to reproduce the actual conditions at that altitude, etc.

However, these difficulties involve further (perhaps too many) conjectural complications. We have examined this matter with scrupulous historic critical methods, and have also compared it with other analogous cases involving other climbers on similar occasions. We do not believe this unorthodox use of the masks was really practised by Compagnoni and Lacedelli. There seems to us to have been too little time involved and almost no compulsion to do so.

Finally, one cannot exclude the possibility that there might have been other events consistent with the successive putting on and taking off the masks – the full and coordinated control of operations being much more difficult at that altitude, in that condition of fatigue, and so forth. But such purely conjectural events would remain without any documentation whatever and must be excluded from critical accounts. Among other things, it is noted that they have been neither narrated nor discussed (not even indirectly) in the official account; nor are they mentioned in Compagnoni and Lacedelli's report.

In fact, even in the account of Compagnoni and Lacedelli recapitulated in Desio's book there is nothing to indicate the re-use of the masks. Neither, to be scrupulously critical, is there any sign in that text of unorthodox use of the masks to protect natural respiration.

On the contrary (and this presents a final, grave inconsistency with the factual account) the report of Compagnoni and Lacedelli refers explicitly to 'making haste' in 'ripping off the masks' without any reference to other use of the masks – and this 'ripping off the masks' is refuted by the photographic documentation.

Such inconsistencies and excessive conjecture cannot be accepted as 'normal' from a critical historic aspect. On this point, one cannot refrain from observing that this raises grave doubts whether the conjectural interruption of the flow of oxygen before reaching the summit is acceptable (the only residual hypothesis is that this might have happened very close to the summit, at 8,600 metres).

4. Modes of Action

(a) Contacts between Bonatti-Mahdi and Compagnoni-Lacedelli in the late afternoon, evening and night of the 30th of July 1954

One question relevant to the critical historic method has scarcely been mentioned. This relates to the manner in which contact was made between Compagnoni and Lacedelli (who had advanced to establish Camp 9) and Bonatti and Mahdi (who were attempting to reach them with the oxygen by a long, exhausting climb from Camp 8 to Camp 9).

The unexpected displacement of Camp 9 and the timetable of the various contacts between the two groups have been discussed above. Apart from that, it seems important to discuss the crucial modes of action involved and their consequences (above all, those relevant to Bonatti and Mahdi's forced bivouac with no preparation for such an extreme undertaking).

First: the manner in which contact was made appears to have been quite different from what is indicated briefly in Desio's official account. This mentions only some calls from Bonatti and Mahdi 'at dusk' when 'night was now approaching' – calls that reached Compagnoni and Lacedelli only with difficulty because of the wind blowing from the north. According to that account, some time later (by which time it was pitch dark) Bonatti and Mahdi would have heard the calls of Compagnoni and Lacedelli that told them to 'go down as soon as possible' (one notes that by now this would have been in impenetrable darkness).

Second: contrary to the version set out in Desio's official account, the contacts 'by sight' and 'by voice', the calls, signals and exchange of messages happened several times, started in the afternoon (as confirmed by Abram's testimony – see above), then continued on into the evening. After a long, incomprehensible pause the calls resumed in the night, when they were initiated by Bonatti and Mahdi and finally answered by Compagnoni and Lacedelli.

Third: according to the intentions of a programme agreed on by the two groups the previous evening, as stated explicitly in Compagnoni and Lacedelli's account: 'It had been established that before evening Abram, Bonatti and one of the Hunzas would reach us carrying the bottles of oxygen'. The way these plans were then ignored from 4.00 pm until late twilight is most surprising. At that stage, when night was approaching and it was so dark they could not see very well, Compagnoni and Lacedelli could not identify the site where the oxygen bottles were deposited – not at Camp 9, as planned, but in quite another place.

The report of Compagnoni and Lacedelli does not mention any exchange of voices after they first saw Bonatti and Mahdi climbing up the plateau at about 4.00 pm until 10.00 that night – an interval of about six hours (and even that first sighting is reported without any mention of an exchange of voices).

In part this lapse may be consistent with the testimony of the other protagonists, but this does little to make such events historically clear and understandable. Furthermore, this interval ended with the incomprehensible 'misunderstanding' which led to the terribly dangerous bivouac of Bonatti and Mahdi. As things turned out, that bivouac (which they could not avoid because it was then too late) offered the very real prospect of a fatality, and Compagnoni and Lacedelli realised what had happened only next morning when it was too late.

In fact, between the first sighting at 4.00 pm, the first vocal contact just before Abram turned back at about 8,000 metres at 6.00 pm and the final exchange of voices at 10.00 pm there was no communication at all. So the four protagonists did not share a single tent that night. This would have been possible, though quite uncomfortable and demanding many contortions, seeing that the following evening five of them spent the night in a tent only a little larger.

(b) Compagnoni and Lacedelli carrying the empty 19 kilogram bottles of oxygen to the summit

A final hotly debated question of great significance concerns the alleged transport to the summit by Compagnoni and Lacedelli of the very heavy load of the trestles of oxygen bottles despite the oxygen being exhausted – a very significant hindrance to their progress at that height. According to their story, they climbed 216 metres in about two hours.

As noted above, this question is anticipated by Compagnoni and Lacedelli themselves in their report, and they advance four reasons. They say:

It would have been impossible to take off the trestles without a difficult manoeuvre on the steep slope.
They were convinced that the summit was quite close.
They realised it was getting late and didn't want to lose a minute.
They wanted to leave on the summit substantial, solid evidence of their climb.

We must stress yet again the methods we were compelled to use in reaching conclusions in harmony with historic criticism.

If the completely useless transport of the oxygen is correlated with the time and altitude of its presumed exhaustion (that is, at 4.00 pm and 8,400 metres as Compagnoni and Lacedelli insist) it becomes completely unacceptable, for reasons discussed above. In fact it would be a sort of 'miracle' in the final phase of the climb. But apart from this it is clearly contradicted by the discussion above concerning the timetable, the times of their climb and the ten-hour supply of the oxygen.

If it happened a very small distance from the summit at 8,600 metres, as theorised above, it becomes acceptable in some aspects, but in other ways is still contradicted by the documentation. The photographs clearly show the two climbers with the trestles on the snow near Compagnoni, either wearing the mask or having just taken it off. This gives the lie to the story of the cessation of oxygen flow unless one makes further conjectures unacceptable per se (see above). Even though not completely impossible, such a conjecture seems anyway to demand ad hoc adjustments with no documentary support, i.e. the unorthodox use of the mask and the even less credible taking it off and putting it on again.

Alternatively, if the transport of the trestles is regarded as involving continuous oxygen flow, then the whole thing becomes simple. The story unfolds in a coherent manner, completely consistent with the photographic evidence and the technical provisos relating to the use of the equipment, as well as with the experience of other climbers.

We observe that:

First: Compagnoni and Lacedelli's second and third motives are acceptable only if, as theorised above, they found themselves on that part of the summit ridge which was flattening out near the peak – with the prospect of reaching the top in minutes rather than hours.

Second: the 'difficulty' described as their first motive would not induce many mountaineers to carry up a useless burden of 19 kilograms at that altitude, in a situation of extreme, total fatigue. Besides, according to normal alpine experience, discarding such a weight in such an uncomfortable situation, even on steep terrain, can be made easier by deep snow. Such a procedure does not seem so insidious and so fearsome as to produce a 'miraculous' ability to cover such a distance in such a short time.

Third: their fourth motive can be justified only if one believes the problem of reaching the summit had already been resolved. If they were still in the midst of the adventure, with the great uncertainty of reaching the summit at all, such an intention cannot be recognised as a priority. Quite apart from its weight, a load like that would itself prejudice their chances of reaching the summit.

Because of all these critical considerations we believe the most reasonable historic version is that which recognises the use of bottled oxygen by Compagnoni and Lacedelli either to the summit of K2 or to its immediate vicinity, as theorised and discussed above.

But notwithstanding these options, the latter possibility is difficult to accept in a critical historic manner because it demands so much ad hoc integration – it seems of rather slim probability, though no firm conclusion can be reached on the basis of the available photographic documentation available.

CONCLUSIONS

Our task and duty was to report in detail and to analyse the controversial questions relevant to a precise critical re-thinking of the first ascent of K2 on the 31st of July 1954 by the expedition led by Ardito Desio and organised by the CAI. We have set out our findings in four sections, in which we examine and analyse several crucial issues.

As the promoter of ceaseless cultural research, the CAI must preserve the historic memoirs of any such mountaineering achievement, as well as its own history, the history of the mountains and the adventures of the men who climb them. The Society should face its duty of total impartiality and look on Ardito Desio's account merely as the historic version elaborated by the head of the expedition. It should not regard that story as a unique 'official account' and even less as a certified 'key version' in terms of critical historic analysis.

We believe the CAI must make it quite clear that there is now a collection of testimony and documentation that has been maturing for many years which contradicts Desio's account, which has many historic inaccuracies and for which only Desio himself can be responsible. The official account indeed carries the warning that Chapter 8, The Assault on the Summit, was written by Compagnoni and Lacedelli. There has also been a succession of technical reviews, comparisons with other experiences of climbing the same route on K2, and now a quite appropriate criticism from many voices (promoted in part by the CAI itself). These writers demand that the CAI accept their criticism and prepare a new official version profoundly different from that of Desio – at least so far as it concerns the aspects discussed above. They insist that on such points Desio's version is either gravely deficient or unacceptable.

The 'narrative' form is indispensable for the formation of an historic saga which can give rise to tradition and popularisation. However, we do not believe it is our responsibility to transform our historic criticism into an 'account' of that sort, which must be fully documented and rigorously checked using methodical criteria. On that score we merely point out those past contributors of great importance in the preparation of such an 'historic account'. For example:

Sylvia Metzeltin and Alessandro Giorgetta
Walter Bonatti – Un protagonista al suo posto (A Protagonist at his Post), CAI Review, May/June 1994.

Roberto Mantovani and Kurt Diemberger
K2 – Una sfida ai confine del cielo, White Star, Vercelli 1995 (published in English as *K2 – Challenging the Sky*).

Reinhold Messner
K2 – Chogori, Corbaccio Press, 2004.

However, we believe that such narrative elaborations do not form part of our brief.

Finally, we set down below two short final conclusions which seem important, above all because of the approaching 50th anniversary of the first ascent of K2.

First: we must stress that the transport of oxygen by Bonatti and Gallotti from a little above Camp 7 to Camp 8, and by Bonatti and Mahdi – with the partial help of Abram – from Camp 8 to a height of about 8,100 metres, was fundamental to reaching the summit of K2.

Indeed, in the final climb to the summit, it is clear there was a double conquest of K2. One was the work of Compagnoni and Lacedelli: the other the efforts of Bonatti, who conquered his own K2 by the extraordinary feat of going down from Camp 8 to a little above Camp 7, then climbing from there up to 8,100 metres in the course of a single day, to bring Compagnoni and Lacedelli the oxygen without which they could not have reached the summit.

One would not seek to diminish in any way the extraordinary feat of Compagnoni and Lacedelli and others who, like Gallotti and Abram, were protagonists in the final phase of the expedition, nor to lessen the merit of the entire team and the expedition leader Ardito Desio. We wish merely to make it quite clear that, without the extraordinary, crucial and decisive achievement of Bonatti, the summit of K2 would not have been reached on 31 July 1954. He descended 227 metres, then climbed 700 metres at that very high altitude – carrying 19 kilograms, climbing without oxygen and with the worry of reaching Compagnoni and Lacedelli as night fell.

The unravelling of the facts reconstructed here makes it clear that Compagnoni and Lacedelli made use of the oxygen resources for some ten hours, till they reached the summit of K2 or its immediate vicinity. This is however merely a hypothesis, perhaps possible, but constructed with ad hoc conjectural artifice and historically really impossible to decide with absolute certainty.

The question of the oxygen is therefore one of the crucial and decisive points concerning which the official version must be considered unacceptable from the historic-critical point of view. As we have already pointed out, the feat of Compagnoni and Lacedelli was already of itself extraordinary, even in a new historic-critical version. It would really be belittled if it were made 'heroic' by arbitrary imaginative stories. Among other things, it would inject an unacceptable version of the expedition into the international alpine culture for which the CAI has responsibility as one of its important authorities. It would be most inappropriate to confirm, or allow people to believe, versions implying in a more or less ambiguous manner that the summit of K2 was reached without oxygen, while this has been demonstrated above to be completely unacceptable from the critical-historic point of view.

The process of making someone a 'hero' has never been a well-mannered business. But to our way of thinking, in the light of history, the decisive event in the first ascent of K2 was Bonatti and Mahdi's climb, achieved in part with Gallotti and with the help of Abram. The team performance was also admirable for the most part, but Bonatti and Mahdi's climb with the bottles of oxygen to 8,100 metres, not to mention their bivouac that night in the open and in a storm on the summit eve, was outstanding.

The agreement concerning the planned site of Camp 9 was not observed, and the camp was displaced to another site. Visual communication and the exchange of calls happened in an inadequate manner, and this rendered Bonatti and Mahdi's dedication in completing their task so effectively even more epic and worthy of highlighting for history – their actions were decisive in the reaching of the summit of K2.

Second: we are bound to stress a fact that unfortunately is easy to overlook because of the increasing disputes that have arisen over the years. These disputes make some of the protagonists stand out, and we tend to lose sight of something else. We refer to the wonderful 'team spirit' that from the very start led this expedition, sponsored by the CAI, to refer not to individuals but to all of them together as 'the team'. It seems to us that this is made more than ever clear by the critical-historic consideration of the events of final push for the summit.

From this point of view we must stress it becomes clearer than ever that the decision of Bonatti to descend and recover the bottles of oxygen, then climb back up to the place where Compagnoni and Lacedelli had placed Camp 9 (with the partial help of Mahdi, Gallotti and Abram) was, above all, an act of dedication to the success of the expedition inspired by the most profound 'team spirit'. This conclusion emerges from the direct testimony of the participants and the accounts of their actions.

There can be no doubt at all that the accusations against Bonatti were completely unjustified. In any case it could not possibly have escaped the notice of a mountaineer like Bonatti that the effort he was undertaking would have made it very difficult for him to take any further part in the climb to the summit next day. In any event, the protagonists had come to an agreement about that on the evening of 29 July.

It is also clear that on the 29th good weather was predicted for the next few days. This demanded the immediate implementation of a daring and very adventurous attempt to recover the oxygen, which was essential for the summit attempt.

The resolution, efficiency and timeliness with which this happened, and the contribution of all the participants in the final phase, constitutes the most conspicuous, significant evidence of admirable 'team spirit'. This seems to us to be an historic event of great importance that honours the whole expedition, patronised by the CAI and planned and carried out by Ardito Desio with great success.

Florence – Rome – Milan   **28.4.2004**